THE LANG
THE LANDSCAPE

In *The Language of the Landscape* Angus Winchester invites us to join him on a journey through a part of the Lake District he has known and loved since childhood. Along the way we discover how clues to the evolution, history and culture of the Lakeland landscape may be found in the names given to its farms, becks, villages, fields and boundaries and how they 'speak' to us through layers of memory and meaning, built up across the centuries.

This book is a personal journey in search of the essential spirit of a much-loved place. More than that, it teaches us how to look at landscape afresh and through a deeper understanding of its history appreciate it all the more.

Angus J L Winchester is Emeritus Professor of Local & Landscape History at Lancaster University. After studying at Durham University, he taught for several years in the extra-mural department of Liverpool University before joining Lancaster in 1990. His previous books include *Landscape & Society in Medieval Cumbria* (John Donald, 1987); *The Harvest of the Hills: rural life in Northern England & the Scottish Borders 1400-1700* (Edinburgh University Press, 2000); *The North West* (with Alan Crosby, in the 'England's Landscape' series, 2006) and *Dry Stone Walls: History & Heritage* (Amberley, 2016).

THE LANGUAGE
OF THE LANDSCAPE
A Journey into Lake District History

Angus J L Winchester

H
HANDSTAND PRESS

H

HANDSTAND PRESS

Published by Handstand Press.
13 Braddyll Terr, Ulverston, Cumbria LA12 0HD

www.handstandpress.net

First Published in 2019
Reprinted with minor corrections 2020

Designed and set by Russell Holden – Pixel Tweaks, Ulverston.
www.pixeltweakspublications.com
Printed in Poland for Latitude Press Limited.

Cover Photograph
Looking up Crummock Water, late November
by Val Winchester

ISBN: 978-0-9576609-7-7

For all those on whom this valley smiles more than any other and with special love to my sons, daughters-in-law, and grandchildren.

CONTENTS

ILLUSTRATIONS

Photographs

Maps

Plates

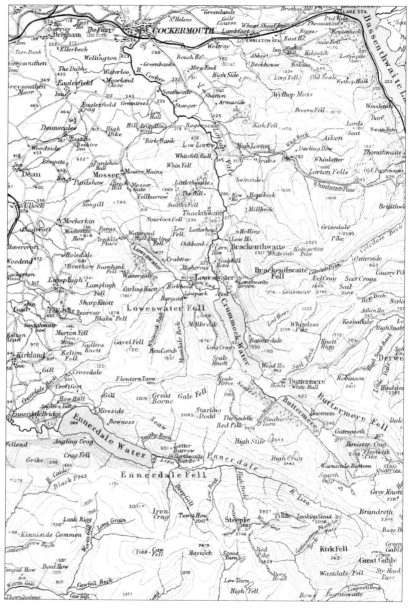

The Buttermere Valley
(From a map in Ward Lock's guide, The English Lake District, 17th edition revised, c.1916).

PREFACE

This is the story of a particular place, somewhere I have known and loved almost all my life, which has got under my skin and keeps drawing me back. It is the valley in the English Lake District where I grew up, my home in those formative years between the ages of five and seventeen which inspired my interest in the past and set me off on an academic career in landscape history. It started me thinking about what makes places special and how it is that through layers of association and history, they come to have meaning in our lives. For me, the names of places have an enduring fascination, not only in their power to evoke a sense of place but also, being coined long ago, as carriers of messages from the past. Through place-names the landscape can 'speak' to us of its history, as it can through its tangible features and through the accumulation of memory and meaning across the centuries. In the following pages my aim is to explore the Lake District landscape on all these fronts by delving into the history of this one Lakeland valley – the Lorton, Loweswater and Buttermere valley, from its foot in the town of Cockermouth to its source high in the fells above Buttermere.

Childhood is the once-in-a-lifetime chance to claim places, making them one's own in a way which slips away in later years. Anyone writing a book about the places of their youth brings their own perspective; in my case, the history of the area is coloured by the particularities of family history. It was during my schooldays that I developed a passion for the past that was rooted in the landscape around me and one key influence was family connection with the local area. Cockermouth had been the home of my maternal grandfather, Alfred Hall, a civil engineer who had spent most of his life far from Cumbria. He retired back to his native Cumberland when I was eight and listening to his memories of childhood in the 1880s and 1890s peopled the local landscape in my young mind with long-dead friends and relations. I became aware of an almost tangible fourth dimension of time-depth and historical meaning in the local places I knew so well. As my grandfather and his forebears were from the tight-knit world of old Quaker families in the area, the older generation of family friends who formed part of my childhood and who passed on memories from their youth were drawn disproportionately from the Quaker section of the community.

There were other early influences as well. My father, whose posting to Cockermouth as District Officer for the Forestry Commission brought us to the area, had an abiding interest in history and quietly encouraged my nascent fascination with the local past. It was through him that I met John Clark of Mossergate, who, like many farmers, had a keen interest in the history of his farm and of farming in general. I spent most Saturdays one winter helping him on the farm and, in our conversations, he passed on his practical knowledge and farming lore from older generations, which brought the historical record alive for me in a way that book-learning alone never could. These were the well-springs from which my fascination for local history flowed, sowing the seeds of an academic interest which led to a university career. As a student I soon moved on to take a wider view, delving further back in time to the earliest centuries of the written record to focus on the farming communities and landscapes of the Middle Ages.

I moved away and haven't lived in the valley for over forty years, so my perspective is now from outside. Yet the places of childhood become almost part of us, so I have carried this valley with me even when living elsewhere. Perhaps claiming a place as one's own is all the more important when one is only partly an insider. So, this is a personal approach to the history of the Lake District. It draws on several layers of memory: it's thus part memoir; part local history; part pen portrait – a celebration of what is to me a special place, seeking to use the history behind the landscape as a route into capturing something of the spirit of a place in a corner of the world which is charged with meaning for so many people.

Angus Winchester
Chapel-le-Dale, North Yorkshire, 2019

Buttermere and Crummock from the head of the valley.

CHAPTER 1

INTRODUCTION

A Lakeland Valley

Ille terrarum mihi praeter omnes angulus ridet.
(Horace, Odes, Book II, Ode VI)
This corner of the world smiles for me more than any other.

It was a perfect evening in early May, the end of a cloudless day when the first strong sun of the year burnt and taughtened the skin on faces and arms grown pale over the long winter. The village hall at Loweswater was packed for a meeting of a community project which brought together local people and academics to grapple with an environmental problem of algal bloom on the lake. By the time the meeting ended, the sun had dropped behind the hills but it still lit the craggy faces of Whiteside, Grasmoor and the Buttermere fells across the valley, flushing them an ethereal pink, so that they seemed to fade away into the distance as dusk fell. It was a moment of breathtaking beauty, where the landscape seemed to reach out to enfold us. For me it was the embodiment of a sense that this valley is the 'corner of the world which smiles for me more than any other'. And I was not alone: as we dispersed, I overheard one of the local farmers, looking up towards Buttermere, say to a young researcher, 'When you get to paradise, this is what it'll look like'.

To many of us in the hall the beauty of that evening enhanced what was to us already a special place, a landscape known over many years and laden with memory and associations. What made it so special? What gave it its unique character, the elusive quality often termed 'sense of place' or 'spirit of place'? These are two sides of the same coin, shorthand for the way that humans experience places as uniquely different from one another. 'Sense of place' focuses on the observer, involving the ways in which the landscape 'speaks' to us through the whole gamut of the senses. To me, 'sense of place' in the Lake District includes not only the magic of the view that May evening or the shape-shifting play of light and shade on the crags on a breezy autumn morning, but also the sound of tumbling water and the croak of a raven; the smell of bracken and sheep and of acid soil under oak trees; the feel of beck water, splashed cold on the face, and of legs scratched by the stems of bilberry and heather. 'Spirit of place', on the other hand, is a product of culture and imagination. It means endowing places with abstract qualities which are then experienced as being reflected back to the observer. We might say that a place breathes an air of mystery or loss, or that it is sacred, or its essence lies in an association with an individual or past event, preserving the memory of people now gone. Being a product of human culture, spirit of place often emanates from the past, so that history is never far from discussions of what makes places unique.

Places are often said to be 'inscribed' with memory and meaning; indeed, meaning and association are what convert a space (a mere tract of the earth's surface) into a place. We live life locally, experiencing daily life in specific places – after all, even in this digital age, we can only physically be in one place at a time. Our experience of place is primarily that of the human being: we see at eye level; walk at ground level;

hear at ear level, as it were. Familiarity with our surroundings – observing the annual rhythm of nature; noting the minutiae in our daily round (wisps of wool still sticking to a gate post; a worn flagstone repeatedly collecting a puddle) – can create what Rob Cowen has termed a 'tangible, emotional intertwining' between person and landscape. 'When people talk of "knowing" or "belonging" somewhere, this is what they mean', he writes. 'Familiarity comes with the overlaying of our experiences, memories and stories ... Time spent in one place deepens this interaction, creating a melding and meshing that can feel a bit like love'. Familiar places are freighted with memory, so that, on returning to them after being away, the landscape brings back memories from the past. What is more, shared experience of place lies at the heart of a community. People who have lived in one place for many years are, to quote Jonathan Bate, 'attuned to collective memory, to old association'; as Thomas Hardy put it, they have 'an almost exhaustive biographical and historical acquaintance with every object, animate and inanimate, within the observer's horizon'. To share memories of a locality in all its detail, recalling the names of places and people, forges a link between people, binding them together at a deep level and reinforcing a sense of shared identity. Local landscapes become what Paul Readman has called 'storied ground', places which gain their meaning not only from their physical qualities but also from the 'associational value' coming from the 'felt presence of the past'.

W. G. Hoskins, the founding father of landscape history, was convinced that 'One cannot understand the English landscape and enjoy it to the full ... without going back to the history that lies behind it'. This book follows his maxim by exploring the history of a place that has enthralled me since my youth, that valley in the north-west corner of the Lake

District, running from Buttermere through Loweswater and the Vale of Lorton to Cockermouth. In seeking its essence, I am delving into its past. 'History' here is not just tracing the evolution of features in the landscape (farms and villages, roads, fields and so on); it also encompasses how people have responded to landscape and the meanings they have bestowed upon it, through myth and story and through identifying specific places as being somehow special. Drilling down into the history of this one valley forms much of the foreground of the book, but the valley can also be a point of departure from which to tap into wider themes in the history of the landscape, both in the Lake District and on a broader canvas.

Landscapes can speak to us as a 'rich historical record', as W. G. Hoskins famously said. If we can learn its language it has much to tell us, through its place-names, through its tangible features and through the accumulation of memory and meaning in particular places. In the most direct way perhaps, the language of the landscape is all around us in the place-names inscribed on maps ancient and modern. These include a wealth of minor names, some now obsolete and almost lost, which identified every farmstead, lake and stream, hill, wood, field and track. All names hold meaning, even if it is obscured by age and the loss of the languages in which they were coined; as such they are a point of contact with numberless generations who, across the centuries, have lived in and experienced this same corner of the world. The names peppering the modern map can continue to transmit memory. In this place-based journey into the past, place-names provide the starting point for an exploration of how men and women have claimed, tamed and changed a landscape, and how particular places have wormed their way into human consciousness and culture. Interpreting the meaning of place-names is a specialist task, requiring deep linguistic knowledge and expertise, so a book such as this must stand on the shoulders of those giants of place-name study who have elucidated the roots and meanings of Lake District place-names.

***

Much has been written over the years attempting to capture the essence of the Lakeland landscape and distil it into words. When the Lake District National Park Partnership proposed the Lake District for inscription as a UNESCO World Heritage Site in 2016, it needed to pin down the key elements of the region's 'outstanding universal value'. Those drafting the proposal identified the root of its value as lying in a fusion between the 'extraordinary beauty and harmony' of the landscape and its role since the eighteenth century in spawning new ideas about the environment and the need to protect it. The proposers saw the Lake District as, at heart, a farming landscape, its beauty and harmony having been created and maintained by deep-seated and continuing 'agro-pastoral traditions'. Its physical manifestations – 'stone-walled fields and rugged farm buildings' – are the product of a distinctive local economy, in which 'relatively independent farmers' have reared local breeds of sheep, notably the Herdwick, in a farming system where the use of common fell-grazing remains a key part. Continuity of farming tradition over several centuries has created a local environment which has had a profound impact on western culture.

The Lake District is an historic landscape in harmony with the physical environment, which has evolved since the medieval period. True, it contains elements inherited from a much deeper past (the stone circles, cairnfields and settlement sites left by prehistoric peoples, for example) but most of what we see – the placing of dwellings, the parcelling of ground into plots and fields, the lines taken by roads and tracks – are the product of the last millennium or so. Much of the fabric of today's landscape – the buildings, hedges and dry stone walls, the tarmac or metalled roads and tracks – is comparatively recent; most buildings and field boundaries are little more than three or four hundred years old. But if the fabric is comparatively young, the positioning of features and the lines taken by lanes or field boundaries are often much older, determined by patterns of use and ownership inherited from medieval times. This is a landscape largely created by farming, in a society dominated by independent yeomen rather than powerful, large landed estates. As farmers renewed the infrastructure of their farms, they had an inherent tendency to respect the lines and positioning of the past: their power was restricted to their own land, so if they were replacing a boundary between their field and a neighbour's with a new fence or wall, the pattern of rights in land dictated that it continued to follow the pre-existing line dividing the two properties.

But continuity can be overstated. Large parts of rural Britain have been 'rewritten' across the past two and a half centuries, sweeping away the older landscape in the cause of 'improvement', land reform or 'landscaping', so that, in some areas, most features are comparatively recent. Oliver Rackham drew a distinction between what he termed 'planned' and 'ancient' countryside, the former being the landscapes rewritten, often on a drawing board, since around 1750; the latter those which have evolved, retaining older features inherited from a medieval past. In the Lake District, the farms and fields of the valley floors and lower slopes of the fells are largely a product of slow evolution over many centuries, yet even 'ancient' countryside like this contains planned elements. The grids of enclosure walls dividing the fells, most of which date from the nineteenth century, and the lakeside villas, pleasure grounds and plantations which were a product of the 'discovery' of the Lakes in the eighteenth century, were inserted into an older farming landscape, obliterating parts of it. The Buttermere valley has fewer of the villas and designed landscapes than other parts of the Lakes; most of its features have been created by farming. Like Cumbria as a whole, it is mostly 'ancient countryside', where 'rewriting' in the nineteenth and twentieth centuries has been limited, preserving older patterns from the earlier worlds of the medieval and early modern centuries. Much of the Buttermere valley is an old landscape in an old country.

* * *

Wordsworth famously introduced his guide to the Lake District by asking his readers to imagine the view from a cloud 'hanging midway' between Great Gable and Sca Fell, looking down on the valleys radiating from the central fells beneath them 'like spokes from the nave of a wheel'. Enumerating the dales and lakes clockwise from the south, he came to the valley which forms the focus of this book:

> The vale of Buttermere, with the lake and village of that name, and Crummock-water beyond, next present themselves. We will follow the main stream, the Cocker, through the fertile and beautiful vale of Lorton, till it is lost in the Derwent below the noble ruins of Cockermouth Castle.

In this book the view is reversed, as the journey moves upstream from the low country around Cockermouth to the backdrop of fells to the south, and winds into the hills up the Vale of Lorton and deep into the Lake District proper, where craggy and scree-strewn mountainsides fall steeply to the shores of Crummock Water and Buttermere. The tract of territory explored here coincides closely with 'The Buttermere Valley' as defined when the Lake District was proposed for inscription as a World Heritage Site in 2016 and with the 'Melbreak Communities', the four modern parishes of Blindbothel, Buttermere, Lorton and Loweswater which collaborate over community matters. To residents and outsiders alike, it possesses a unity, underpinned by geography.

It is also a place of great beauty, despite not being as well-known as some other Lake District valleys. W. G. Collingwood wrote, 'I always think of this valley as made by Heaven for summer evenings and summer mornings; green floor and purple heights, with the sound of waters under the sunset, or lit with the low north-eastern sun into pure colour above, and the greyness of the dew upon the grass'. For the Lakeland artist W. Heaton Cooper and his wife Ophelia, the sculptor, Loweswater was the place 'nearer our hearts than any other in the world'; while the doyen of fellwalkers Alfred Wainwright, who is remembered in a memorial window in Buttermere church, so loved the valley that he asked for his ashes to be scattered on Haystacks. As one section of an iconic landscape, the Buttermere valley now attracts thousands of visitors every year and is taken back in memory to every corner of the world.

My journey into Lake District history begins behind the narrow yards and industrial buildings in the old heart of the town of Cockermouth, where the River Cocker is 'lost in the Derwent'. Most places named from their position at the mouth of a river are, not surprisingly, to be found on the coast where fresh water disperses into the open salt sea. But Cockermouth lies eight miles inland. In its final moments, the Cocker's waters bisect the town, hemmed in by stone walls and crossed by a low-arched bridge, before curving like a slip road to join the wider River Derwent by a tapered grassy point carrying a park bench. The two rivers seem gentle on a lazy summer afternoon but they have given

Cockermouth its recent unhappy fame when, in November 2009 and again in December 2015, storms caused them to burst their banks and rage through the town, flooding shops and houses. Both Cocker and Derwent carry water from becks deep in the Lake District fells and the Cocker, especially, rises swiftly. Though Cockermouth's newer houses now spread uphill to the safety of higher ground, the core of the old town lies below the walls of the medieval castle, close to the rivers. Flooding has been a perennial threat across the town's history – a litany of flood years runs back across time: 1966, 1938, 1932, 1918, 1874, 1852, 1764, 1761 ... The misery of sodden furnishings and the financial losses incurred by flooded warehouses have been all too real to successive generations.

Cockermouth has been the focal point for communities living in the catchment of the River Cocker for more than eight centuries. Much of the land in the valley was held from the lords of the medieval honour of Cockermouth, the estate headquarters in the Castle being the destination of rents paid; the town's weekly market and its cattle fairs in the summer months – and Mitchell's livestock auction since Victorian times – were the points of exchange for farm produce; cloth woven from local wool was finished in the town's fulling mill; hides from slaughtered cattle went to its tanneries; tallow to the tallow chandlers. Schoolchildren from farms and villages upstream, deep in the fells, went to secondary school in the town; the town's doctors and its cottage hospital served the sick.

The tract of land which forms the focus of this book coincides with the Cocker's catchment area. Its outer boundary follows the watershed, that invisible line so graphically described in the old northern English phrase 'as heaven water deals' (in Latin, *ut aquæ coeli descendit*, 'as the water of heaven falls'). It is a piece of land roughly twelve miles from the river's source to its foot and no more than five miles wide, embracing a range of terrain, from the rocky peaks of the high fells to fertile farming country around Cockermouth which turns its back on the hills. Along the length of its course, the valley runs through three distinct landscapes. From the amphitheatre of Warnscale Bottom at the head of Buttermere, it is a true Lake District valley with the twin lakes of the valley floor lying in a narrow trench hemmed in by rugged fells (Plate 1). The crag-bound gables of Grasmoor and Melbreak, flanking Crummock Water, form the entrance to this upper section. At the foot of Crummock Water the landscape changes; the valley opens out into a broad undulating vale a mile across, joined by the shallow bowl of the Loweswater valley (Plate 2). As the river steps down between the wooded knolls of Brackenthwaite Hows and Redhow, the enclosing fells become gentler, the green hills of Low Fell and its neighbours on the west side separating the valley from the low country beyond. Having gathered water from the Whinlatter hills down the side valley of Whit Beck, the wide Vale of Lorton leaves the Lake District behind where the slopes of Whin Fell and Harrot form an abrupt edge to the fell country (Plate 8). This marks the sharp transition to the final section of the Cocker's course, as the river flows through lowland countryside for a couple of miles before its final descent through wooded banks to Cockermouth. Here the catchment is at its widest, where the farmland between Embleton and Eaglesfield is drained by two of the river's longer tributaries, Tom Rudd Beck and Sandy Beck.

For much of its course, the line of the watershed is obvious, a sharp, natural rim running along the crest of the hills; only in the low country behind Cockermouth, where small streams emerge from patches of mossland, is it difficult to locate. The watershed across the fells is not only a feature of the physical environment, it is also part of the cultural landscape, as is shown on the modern Ordnance Survey map by the lines of dots along the fell tops, indicating the boundaries of the civil parishes which form the lowest rung in the hierarchy of local government. In much of rural England, these invisible lines are among the oldest features in the human landscape, the modern parishes being the latest incarnation of administrative territories which can be traced back deep into the medieval centuries.

In Cumbria, most civil parishes are the descendants of 'townships' or 'vills', the basic units of civil administration (for peace-keeping and tax collecting) in medieval England. These were typically economic units as well (in much of lowland England, a village and its fields, for example). As townships frequently also had an identity as a unit of landownership – as a separate estate or manor – they were the primary building blocks of rural society. The stability of this territorial framework meant that when lawyers and administrators wished to locate an individual place (a hamlet, a farm, a lane or a wood) they usually did so in relation to the township in which it lay, using the same names across the centuries, until modern times.

Leaving the town of Cockermouth to one side, eight rural townships have embraced the totality of the Cocker valley and its tributaries since the Middle Ages: Buttermere, Brackenthwaite, Loweswater, Lorton, Embleton, Whinfell, Blindbothel and Mosser. All are recorded as territorial entities before 1300; half of them before 1200. Those eight townships (which were rationalised in 1934 into five modern civil parishes: Buttermere, Loweswater, Lorton, Embleton, and Blindbothel) are the core places with which this book is concerned. Their names form the scaffolding of local history – the enduring place-names used to pin places into the administrative landscape.

Each township has its own distinctive character, determined primarily by the physical landscape. Buttermere and Brackenthwaite are true upland communities, where small areas of farmland cling to the lake shores, surrounded by towering fellsides. Loweswater and Lorton are also valley communities, backed by the fells, but they centre on wider vales of cultivated land. Mosser, Whinfell and Embleton flank the outer edges of the lower hills on the fringes of the Lake District, looking out over the Cumberland plain. Blindbothel is lowland farming country with the fells in the distance.

The early tourist guidebooks to the Lake District used a succession of viewpoints (or 'stations') to show visitors the best scenes. In this journey upstream to explore the history of the valley from Cockermouth up to Buttermere, I'll be pausing to consider the history of different features in the local landscape, using a series of 'stations' as points of departure to delve into different themes. I'll look in turn both at tangible elements in the landscape (farmsteads and fields, boundaries, hills, watercourses, woodland and minerals) and at how people have responded to the landscape (through myth and story, religion, and the magnet-like attraction of the hills). Just as the waters flowing down the becks in the Cocker's catchment combine to create the whole river, my aim is to bring the historical views from each chapter together to present a rounded picture of this landscape, capturing something of its unique sense of place. The story starts with the place-names.

Townships in the Buttermere valley, the forerunners of civil parishes

Loweswater signpost.

CHAPTER 2

PLACE-NAMES
Bitter Beck

Not far upstream from the River Cocker's curving confluence with the Derwent, Bitter Beck spews into the river from a culvert just above Cocker Bridge. It is a small stream, barely three miles in length, draining the low hills to the east of Cockermouth. After cutting a steep-sided gill down through fields to the eastern edge of the town, it runs past the houses, hemmed in by deep walls at the end of the yards and gardens along St Helen's Street, before being confined underground for its final few hundred yards. Unusually, the modern name of the beck is comparatively young. 'Bitter Beck' is a nineteenth-century euphemism, replacing with an inoffensive word an older name which bluntly described the character of the beck as it flowed behind the houses in Cockermouth. Not surprisingly, it was used as a sewer as well as a drain for a tannery. Its earlier name was 'Skitter Beck', literally 'shit beck', a down-to-earth label for a filthy, polluted stream.

Customary usage such as this lies at the heart of place-naming. Some names may have been imposed from above; names in Old French associated with the Norman Conquest, such as Bewley (*beau lieu*, 'the beautiful place') and Egremont (*aigre mont*, 'the sharp-pointed mound'), are likely candidates here. But most minor names have grown organically from the grassroots. They were in origin utilitarian labels, making it possible to identify specific places in the landscape in order to communicate with others and help to prevent misunderstanding. Once coined and fixed, this function did not change, even when the memory of how a name originated had gone – and, with it, an understanding of the reason behind it. Over centuries, the meaning of the words in a name might fade, so that the label became the unique and accepted identifier of a particular spot of ground, the name becoming fused with the place.

Setmurthy is the name of an arc of settled land at the foot of Bassenthwaite Lake, at the eastern end of the ridge of hill where Bitter Beck has its source. The name has been meaningless – in the sense that what it described would not have been understood – for many hundreds of years, as the two words from which it is derived were probably unfamiliar even by 1300, leaving it and other similar place-names marooned and incomprehensible. The name probably dates from the eleventh century when Gaelic speakers from the Western Isles or Ireland interacted with Norse-speaking communities in Cumberland. They called the place *saetr Muiredach*, which can be roughly translated as 'Murdoch's summer pasture'. Most major place-names (the names of rivers, regions, towns and villages and administrative territories such as Setmurthy) date from before the Norman Conquest and many of the names of farms and hamlets originated in the medieval centuries. They were created largely from languages such as Old English, Old Norse and Middle English, which died out or changed beyond recognition, so that the meanings of many major names are at best only hazily understood today. But the very local, minor names (of woods, lanes, small streams, hillsides and fields, for example) continued to evolve into the modern period and to incorporate idioms of local speech, here the rich vernacular tongue of Cumberland. Today, these names are to most people almost as meaningless as those from the Middle Ages, as the local dialect which thrived well into the twentieth century has ebbed away.

***

The act of giving names to features in the landscape is a fundamental part of turning the spaces around us into places; they are claimed and given meaning by being named. Then the passing of a name down the centuries through communal memory fuses place and name to create a cultural entity which gathers associations through time. In the words of the geographer Christopher Tilley, place-names 'transform the sheerly physical and geographical into something that is historically and socially experienced. ... In a fundamental way names create landscapes. An unnamed place on a map is quite literally a blank space.' The place-names which run as a theme through this book – many of them the very local names given to minor features – are windows onto how successive generations have lived in and used the landscape and how they have imbued places with meaning. In one sense, I am exploring in the context of the Lake District a topic which has been highlighted in the Gaelic-speaking territories on the far western seaboards of Britain and Ireland, where the language which gave the names – and the culture of the crofting communities from which they sprang – survived until within living memory. In the 1980s Alasdair Maclean, recapturing the dying embers of crofting life in the Ardnamurchan peninsula of western Scotland, and Tim Robinson, recording in detail the names of the Aran Islands and Connemara in western Ireland, lamented the loss of the wealth of minor place-names, many unrecorded on maps, as the Gaelic languages declined. Calling this 'one of the most vital yet least considered areas of cultural erosion', Alasdair

Maclean tells of a rock on the way home from a peat moss which once had a name recording its use as a resting place by generations burdened with creels of peat. With the loss of its name, 'you may say that the rock itself has been obliterated for it is no longer significantly there. ... Deprived of its human attachment it has become one more rock in an anonymously rocky landscape'.

Minor place-names are the fruits of deep familiarity with the land, gained at walking pace and through physical labour across the centuries, when every sinew of the surface was felt under foot, every bushy place and boggy corner was known and remembered for the way they affected the task in hand across the working year. Tim Robinson talks of how 'countless previous acts of attention [are] enshrined in place names' and elsewhere makes the point that names not only denote a place, but 'most of them also have a connotation; they make a condensed or elliptic remark about the place, a description, a claim of ownership, a historical anecdote, even a joke or a curse on it.' In short, place-names carry messages from the past. As the Scottish place-name scholar Simon Taylor has put it, 'Messages are therefore encoded in a name, messages which bear invaluable information about the name-givers and their world.'

Place-names fix memory to place, recording it in a name which is then passed down the generations, transmitted orally and in writing, so that an echo of the response to place survives long after the initial memory has been lost. But the chain of memory is fragile, as Alasdair Maclean noted. The rapid pace of social and cultural change since the middle of the twentieth century has often broken the link, cutting modern inhabitants adrift from the local past. The scale of the re-peopling of Lake District communities as newcomers replaced natives, combined with the helter-skelter of modernity, has broken the thread of tradition and distanced today's generation from the lives of those who lived and worked in the landscape before them. A sense of connection with the much-loved landscape of the Lake District is now genuinely global – yet, even among those who live there, very few now have that direct knowledge of the land that comes from making a livelihood from it and getting one's hands dirty. This is the paradox at the heart of the Lake District, a disconnect illustrated vividly in the success of James Rebanks' autobiographical account of life as a hill farmer. The international appetite for his book and his online blogs suggests that there is a real desire for even a second-hand connection with the land. Social and technological change, the loss of familial continuity and loss of the rich dialect in which many place-names were coined now separate us from the world which made the places discussed in this book.

* * *

'Embleton bottom', to the east of Cockermouth, is the setting for a collection of stories in Cumberland dialect, which illustrate well the vernacular speech of the area. *Betty Wilson's Cummerland Teáls* were written in the 1870s by Thomas Farrall, an Aspatria schoolmaster who haled from Embleton. They were part of the flowering of dialect writing in the Victorian era, appearing originally as weekly 'sketches' in the local newspaper. Set at some unspecified time in the early decades of the nineteenth century, many of the stories hinge on encounters between drink-loving natives and visiting holiday makers. Homely and humorous, they were also nostalgic attempts to capture the spirit and sounds of the brisk vernacular of west Cumberland. The ring of the dialect can be caught in snatches of dialogue from Betty Wilson's tales, such as the rollicking yarn called '*A Loweswater Herb-*

Pudding', in which a visiting botanist, coming to Loweswater, 'leets ov a laal lad stannin' beside a yat'. The botanist orders him to open the gate but gets short shrift: 'Oppen't the-sel, thoo láazy beggar!' Not surprisingly, the botanist 'wasn't suitet' and, 'thinkin' ta flay [frighten] t' bit lad' tries to pull rank. But the youngster fires back, 'Thoo'll nut cum up ta Loweswatter ta flay me, mind that noo. Just oppen't yat thesel, and be varra thankful Ah'll let the!'

Dialect had been recorded in writing and preserved as an important aspect of regional heritage for almost a century by the time Thomas Farrall was writing. A seminal compendium of the Cumberland dialect had been compiled by William Dickinson from Lamplugh in his *Glossary of the Words and Phrases of Cumberland*, first published in 1859. The study of dialect flowered, becoming a popular lecture topic in the decades before the First World War. The local historian of Cockermouth, John Bolton, lecturing in the town in 1909, celebrated the wealth of homely similes in which Cumbrian dialect was rich: 'as whist as yer shaddah' (as silent as your shadow); 'as snod as a mowdiwarp' (as snug as a mole); 'as daft as a yat as'll oppen bëath ways' (as silly as a gate that'll open at both ends); 'hingen a lip like a mudderless fwoal' (a graphic evocation of sadness needing no translation). The ancient penchant for riddles in the vernacular, shared with local societies across Britain, yielded this Cumbrian variant of the well-known conundrum: 'fower stiddy standers; fower dilly-danders; two lookers, two crookers, two flip-flaps and a fling-by'. The answer to which, of course, is 'a cow'.

Such was the language of rural west Cumberland. It had been on the wane for many decades, if not centuries, by the time Thomas Farrall was writing. The dialect of the Lake Counties had been recognised as distinct and archaic by antiquaries from the seventeenth century and members of even the most remote rural community would have been aware of another, more formal, English through attending church and school. From the sixteenth century, exposure to the language of the Bible and, especially, the *Book of Common Prayer* would have chipped away at the vernacular, pushing it to the social margins. The rage for publishing dialect tales and verse in the nineteenth century suggests that, even then, there were plenty of people who wished to recapture the language of their forebears and their youth, creating a market for dialect books. Although much of the canon consisted of humorous self-parody, it helped to foster a sense of local pride in place.

Despite the depredations of schooling, a trans-Atlantic popular culture and the widening of horizons as a result of two world wars, broad dialect survived on the farms and on market day in Cockermouth in the 1950s and 60s and, in those days before universal ownership of television sets, it lay not far beneath the surface in the primary school playground. It wasn't part of my life at home. In fact, when I started in the infants' class at Fairfield School, a soft-faced arrival from the south, I'm told that I came home and declared, 'They don't speak English here!' But even at home, echoes of Cumberland dialect formed part of family lore. My grandfather, who had had his Cumbrian accent drummed out of him when he was sent away to school, owned a copy of *Betty Wilson's Cummerland Teáls* and passed on to us snatches of dialect that his father had recalled from his childhood on a farm near Wigton in mid-Victorian times.

Cumberland dialect has now largely fallen out of everyday use, part of the gradual erosion of traditional rural culture across Britain which gathered speed across the later twentieth century. In the 1960s, the older generation on farms and in villages still spoke with a dialect-rich vocabulary, even though the technological revolution then sweeping through farming increasingly made many traditional rural terms redundant and gradually impoverished the language. Take the cowshed or byre, a feature of every farmstead, where a handful of milk cows were tethered over winter. Now dry, dusty and decaying (if it survives at all), the byre has lost not only its dark warmth and the sweet, intimate smell of beast and hay, but the language of its component parts: the 'booses' (pronounced 'bëusses') of wood or slabs of slate, separating the stalls; the 'rood-stëak' to which the cow was tethered; the 'foddergang' into which hay was forked from the loft above.

As the working language of the Cumbrian countryside, heard in farm kitchens, lanes and fields, at mill and smithy, the dialect was the language which populated the landscape with names. It flowed from two distinct well-springs. It possessed a strong injection of Old Norse vocabulary as a result of Scandinavian colonisation in the Viking Age, but its roots lay in the same Northumbrian Old English as that from which Scots evolved. The Scandinavian dialect legacy is well known; it shows itself not only in the surviving use of 'fell' and 'beck', but produced much of the distinctive richness of vocabulary captured by the dialect writers: 'laik' (to play), 'loup' (leap), 'flay' (scare), 'bray' (beat); 'slape' (slippery), 'brant' (steep); 'stee' (ladder), 'stegg' (gander), for example. Scandinavian influence also gave English words a harder edge: 'birk', 'kirk', 'sec' (for 'birch', 'church' and 'such'); 'lig' and 'brigg' (for 'lie' and 'bridge'). Behind the Old Norse overlay, Cumbrian folk speech was part of a wider northern variant of Old English. It shared with lowland Scotland and north-east England not only elements of a common vocabulary ('byre' and 'bairn', for example) but also the northern vowel sounds. 'Stone' and 'bone' become 'stane' and 'bane', 'cow' and 'ground' become 'coo' and 'groond' north of a line roughly from Morecambe Bay to the Humber and variants of those 'ai' and 'oo' pronunciations are found throughout the areas into which Northumbrian Old English spread, through to northern Scotland. In Cumberland 'ai' was pronounced as a diphthong ('he-am' and 'e-ak' for 'hame' and 'aik' – 'home' and 'oak' – for example), with the accent on the second part, so that those words become 'yam' (or 'yem') and 'yak'.

As a result of this northern heritage, the lexicon of landscape terms in Cumbria is quite different from modern standard English – and from the regional vocabularies of southern counties. It is part of that rich regional 'word-hoard' evoked so vividly by Robert Macfarlane in *Landmarks*. While 'fell' and 'beck' continue in widespread use as alternatives for 'hill' and 'stream', a richer vein of differentiation is found in place-names. Not only was there 'how(e)', a generic term for a smaller hill or mound, the dialect also distinguished between different types of hill: 'dodd' (a rounded hill, sometimes the shoulder of a higher peak: the Ordnance Survey noted that Dodd 'frequently applied to barren eminences in Cumberland'), 'knott' (a compact hill or a craggy outcrop), 'tongue' (a bank of hillside between two streams), for example. A similarly rich texture of differences was applied to watercourses: 'sike' (a small stream, often slow-moving); 'gill' (a steeply falling stream in a narrow valley); 'dub' (a deep pool); 'grain' (a place where streams fork); 'force' (a waterfall); 'spout' (a smaller waterfall or the place where water issues from a spring). The common species of native tree each had its dialect name – 'aik' (oak), 'birk' (birch), 'eller' (alder), 'hollin' (holly), 'burtree' (elder) – as did other common forms of vegetation: 'whin' (gorse), 'ling' (heather), 'seave' (rush), 'bleaberry' (bilberry) and 'gale' (bog myrtle). Leaves gathered for culinary use included 'sour dockin' (sorrel) and 'Easter mergiants' (bistort, the key ingredient in Cumberland herb pudding). Wildlife likewise had northern names – 'brock' (badger), 'todd' (fox), 'mowdiwarp' (mole), 'hagworm' (adder), 'paddock' (toad), 'brandling' (salmon parr), 'pyat' (magpie) and 'tewit' (peewit) – while, as one of the livestock-rearing regions of northern and western Britain, dialect terms identified farm animals precisely by age and gender: 'stott' (bullock), 'why' (heifer), 'segg' (a gelded bull); 'tip' (ram), 'gimmer' (young female sheep), 'wedder' (castrated male sheep), 'hogg' (a sheep in its first winter), 'twinter' (a sheep in its second winter). And man-made features also had their Cumbrian vocabulary: 'yat' (gate), 'lonnin' (lane), 'dike' (usually a bank or stone wall, rather than a ditch), and 'kirk' (church).

From this rich language sprang place-names with a range of meanings. Many are topographical, a description of a place by reference to some distinguishing characteristic in the local landscape: Aikbank and Birkbank (banks of oak and birch respectively), Miresyke (a boggy stream), Spout House (a dwelling near a spring), for example. Others record how the landscape was used in the past, identifying a place by reference to an activity. Millbeck, a stream captured to turn a wheel; Watching Crag, a look-out post; Pottergill, a stream-side where a potter once lived or dug clay, are local examples. The name Lambfoot Rake, the lane rising steeply from Lambfoot in Embleton, leading up the hillside to the former common around the headwaters of Bitter Beck, records centuries of movement through a populated landscape, of physical work and mundane tasks. What was distinctive about this lane was that it was the 'rake', the route up which Lambfoot's sheep and cattle were driven to the common grazings. The name claimed it for Lambfoot as well as recording the cyclical seasonal trudge of farmworkers, prodding reluctant cattle on the path to the fell. When Embleton common was enclosed in

1824, centuries of such driving ceased but the name survived.

* * *

Place-names on today's maps are essentially those recorded
by the Ordnance Survey when it undertook the definitive
large-scale mapping of Britain in the middle decades of the
nineteenth century. The Survey had to decide which names
to include on the map and how they should be spelt, so names
were collected and entered into 'Name Books' to record the
source of the name and any variant spellings. These books
survive from the first large-scale survey in England for only
the four northern counties and Hampshire – the rest were
destroyed when Southampton was bombed during the Second
World War. In the early days of the Ordnance Survey not
only was there a separate series of maps and plans for each
county but separate sets of 'Twenty-five Inch' (1:2,500) plans
were published for each parish. In early printings, a 38-inch
by 25-inch sheet might contain only the corner of a parish;
beyond the parish boundary was nothing but pristine paper.
So, the Name Books were arranged parish by parish. For
most of the Buttermere valley this meant the ancient parish
of Brigham; Loweswater, as a distant outlier of the ancient
parish of St Bees, was covered by the book for that parish. On
each page were entered the name as written on the map; the
'various modes of spelling' the name; the authority for those
spellings; where the name was to be placed on the map (Bitter
Beck was to be written '45 Chains West of Greenlands'); and
'Descriptive Remarks, or other General Observations which
may be considered of Interest'.

As they checked and collected names, sheet by sheet, the
surveyors needed three authorities to confirm the form and
spelling of each name, whether that of a town or village, an
isolated cottage, or a small wood, stream or crag – all were
treated with the same care. If a name appeared on earlier

maps this would be noted, but for most names a triumvirate of local men – ideally landowners, clergymen, estate agents, postmasters or schoolmasters – was consulted to determine 'local usage and custom' and the spelling 'which is considered to be most generally useful and acceptable in the locality concerned'. For most of Embleton the authorities were two farmers, Thomas Fearon of Beck House and Isaac Mandell of Howe End, together with John Robinson, the parish clerk. Three yeomen confirmed the names in Lorton; two farmers and the clergyman in Buttermere. They were chosen not only for their status but also for the length of their memory – clergy and professionals excepted, most were members of old-established families with deep roots in the locality.

In ascertaining and recording the names in use in the early 1860s, the Ordnance Survey was not only fixing place-names but was also selecting which to include. The surveyors weeded out minor names which they felt lay outside their remit, including the most minor names of all, those by which individual fields were known. Field-names represent the finest grain in the naming of places, often capturing topography and the use of the land in its most intimate detail. Luckily, the names of individual fields the length of the Buttermere valley had been recorded a couple of decades earlier, on the tithe plans of the early 1840s. By giving each field a number by which it could in future be identified, the Ordnance Survey sounded the death knell for field-names, which are now largely lost unless recorded on a tithe plan or other early map.

Once set in stone on the definitive First Edition maps, most names have survived to the present day and continue to appear on the modern map. However, in parallel with the formal names on the map, other names – unmapped and thereby informal – have survived in common usage. For example, despite a century and a half of being recorded as 'Hopegill

Head' on Ordnance Survey maps, the saddle-backed peak dominating the Vale of Lorton continues to be known locally as 'Hobcarton' (Plate 3); the sunny arc of pebbly beach near the foot of Crummock Water, nameless on the map, retains its local name 'Sandy Yatts' (or 'Sand Yatt'); the ruined house on Whinfell, named as Crosshill by the Ordnance Survey, has long been known locally as 'Drythrapple Hall' ('dry throat hall') – a mocking name for an isolated cottage in a boggy field, perhaps alluding to some now long-forgotten incident in the past. 'Lavender Gardens', the name current in Cockermouth in the 1960s for the town's sewage works, is self-evidently ironic. Informal names such as these span a spectrum, from those in wide currency, despite not being named on the map, to other, more ephemeral names used by small groups of individuals. In the latter category are a couple of names of points on the skyline of the fells around Loweswater. The inhabitants of Lowpark and Highpark told time from a crag on the north end of Melbreak which they called 'Noon Point', as the sun stood directly above it at midday; early in the twentieth century my grandfather's family and friends knew the nick in the skyline of Watching Crag (next to Low Fell) as 'Cut Cheese', because of its shape.

Other names which failed to make the 'official' record created by the Ordnance Survey survived for a time before fading from use. When I spent the autumn of 1974 as a research student, living in Beth Alexander's cottage at Lowpark, Loweswater, Beth, who had come to Lowpark in 1936, passed on to me names which she had been told in the 1930s. She recalled her neighbour, the then elderly Will Tyson, telling her a clutch of old local names, not recorded on the Ordnance Survey maps. The twin peaks which overlook Loweswater on the north were, he said, known as 'Dick Roger' (the summit named Darling Fell on the map) and

'Dick Knave' (the unnamed southern point of Low Fell), while the peak of Brackenthwaite Hows was 'Dick Robin'. Nearby, Scalehill Bridge was formerly called 'Deepa Bridge'. Two of these names seem to have have been in use until not long before the Ordnance Survey arrived, as they are recorded in the eighteenth century: 'Dick Knave' is so named on a map published in the *Gentleman's Magazine* in 1751, and 'Deepa Bridge' appears in the lists of county bridges and on an estate plan of 1782.

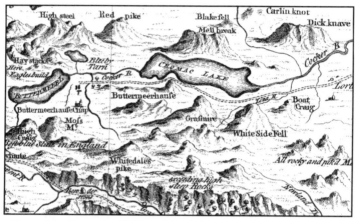

Extract from George Smith's 'Map of the Black Lead Mines &c in Cumberland', published in *The Gentleman's Magazine* in 1751.

Minor place-names might remain fluid until fixed immutably on the engravers' plates from which the first Ordnance Survey maps were printed. The name Bitter Beck had changed comparatively recently to accommodate Victorian sensibilities and another product of recent change was Palacehow, an old farmstead tucked under Brackenthwaite Hows near the foot of Crummock Water (Plate 4). Until around 1800 it bore a completely different name, 'Withebeckraine' (sometimes rendered 'Withmoorcrane'). This older name continued to be used in the parish register until 1806 but the new name, Palacehow, appears on Peter Crosthwaite's map of the valley published in 1794, suggesting that there was a period of overlap until the more elegant name, which echoes the names of its neighbours, Pickett Howe, Cornhow and Turnerhow, won through.

Changes such as these make it impossible to give a short answer to the simple question 'How old are these minor names?' At the most local of levels, there was a shifting kaleidoscope of names across time, as some dropped out of use and new names were coined. As we go back in time, fewer names find their way into the written record. Most of the minor names on Ordnance Survey maps were first recorded only from around 1550, when an explosion in written English (in mundane records such as parish registers, title deeds, lawsuit papers, wills and probate inventories, for example) saw the names of farms, fields, woods, streams and lanes being written down for the first time. A few such names can be traced back before 1300, but most surviving medieval records were concerned with the more important place-names, those of administration: the parish, the manor, and the township. However, even within the constraints of the surviving documents, it is possible to glimpse lost names from the medieval centuries. One such was 'Ureby', a lost settlement somewhere immediately east of Cockermouth, near land now occupied by the Windmill Lane housing estate. It was recorded from 1260 in the minor name 'Ouerbyfeld' or 'Ureby Field', which referred to an open field lying across the ridge south of Bitter Beck. Its second element is the Scandinavian word for 'settlement or village' and its first is probably 'over' in the sense of 'higher or upper'. It was probably the precursor to the town of Cockermouth, which was founded in the half century before 1200. Other shadowy medieval places hinted at in early charters included 'Oustwic', somewhere near Embleton, and 'Ingilberdhop', probably now represented by the farms at Hope and Hopebeck, near Lorton. But the loss of settlement names was the exception; the majority can be traced back as far as the written record will go. In Cumberland, that means back to around 1125 at the earliest: lying outside William the Conqueror's kingdom, almost all of the county is absent from Domesday Book, that great survey carried out in 1086 which provides the earliest record for many place-names elsewhere in England. But whether recorded in Domesday Book or later, most township and parish names would have been old when they were first written down. The oldest names on the modern map thus long predate the written record.

The names of the eight townships within the Cocker's catchment shed light on the chronology of settlement upstream from Cockermouth. The lower grounds around the margins of the Lake District proper were old-settled places with histories reaching deep into the centuries before the Norman Conquest; they were territories which were old even in the Middle Ages. By contrast, the valleys reaching into the heart of Lakeland were a frontier of settlement, a zone where colonisation took place later. The names of the eight townships within the Cocker's watershed reflect this.

The three townships immediately upstream from Cockermouth – Blindbothel, Embleton and Lorton – all bear names referring to human settlement and tell of peopled places. Their names contain Old English elements which almost certainly date them to the time, between c.650 and c.850 AD, when Cumbria fell under the sway of the Anglian kingdom of Northumbria. They take us back to an era before the Scandinavian settlement in the tenth and eleventh centuries. The name Blindbothel (which refers to a territory rather than to any place within it; there is no village bearing the name) is something of a mystery. Its second element, 'bothel', is an Old English word (*boðl*) meaning 'house, building', which seems to have been used especially of important, high-status buildings (perhaps 'lord's hall' is a useful shorthand), but the significance of 'Blind-' (which is written 'Blende-' in the earliest records) is unclear. Whatever the name's precise connotation, it tells of Anglo-Saxon occupation of the low land beside the Cocker at the foot of the fells. Embleton and Lorton are examples of the commonest form of English place-name, where the second element is the Old English word *tūn*, meaning 'farmstead, estate or village'. Lorton's first element has baffled place-name scholars; one suggestion is that it is a lost river name, *Hlóra* ('roaring'), describing Whit Beck as it pours off Whinlatter. In Embleton, the first element is probably the Old English personal name *Ēanbald*, presumably that of an early owner of the estate perhaps twelve hundred years ago, providing an isolated shaft of light in an otherwise unilluminated landscape.

Lorton and Embleton lie in the lower stretches of the valley, where the Cocker emerges from the edge of the hills. Looking at the Lake District as a whole, the distribution of place-names containing the word '-ton' is striking. With few exceptions, they form a ring around the foothills of the fells, hardly penetrating into the valleys. Along the eastern margins are several Huttons, Barton, Helton and Bampton; across the south more Huttons, Patton, Broughton East, Colton and Broughton in Furness; up the west, Irton, Kelton and Murton. Only Coniston lies in the heart of the fells. Even the Scandinavian settlement names originating between around 900 and 1100 tend to be in the lowlands or on the edges of higher ground. Names containing the element '-by' (the Scandinavian equivalent of *tūn*) – such as Ireby, Castle

Sowerby and Ponsonby – are peripheral to the fells. Reaching back before the start of the written record, these names are, in Simon Taylor's words, 'messages from a world which is otherwise extremely scantily recorded'.

By contrast, the names of township territories deep in the fells are quite different, usually taking their names from the local landscape. Some refer simply to topographical features, the valley itself (Borrowdale, Eskdale, Langdale, Wasdale) or a lake (Buttermere, Grasmere, Loweswater) or hill (Whinfell – 'the gorse-covered hill'). Others are a reminder that the uplands were a zone of colonisation in the medieval centuries and refer to clearings in woodland (as in the 'thwaite' names like Brackenthwaite ('the brackeny clearing'), from the Old Norse *þveit*, 'a clearing') or to the use of the hills as grazing grounds (as with Mosser, 'the summer pasture by the mossland').

It is popularly held that it was the Vikings who colonised the Lake District but, in reality, the carving out of new farms took place over a much longer period than the 'Viking Age' of the tenth and eleventh centuries. Across Europe new settlements were founded on previously empty land in the four centuries of land hunger between 900 and 1300, pushing back the frontiers and claiming ever more marginal land. Much of the peopling of the Lake District valleys and the creation of the bones of the landscape we have inherited can probably be dated to that time. The final stages of this great wave of colonisation, when some, perhaps many, of the Lake District's farms and hamlets were established, took place in the century or so before 1300. Many township communities in the upper reaches of valleys deep in the fells were probably several centuries younger than those in the old-settled lowlands on the fringes of the Lake District.

Even older than settlement names, in many cases, are the names of rivers and hills, the stable landmarks which shaped the lives of inhabitants across the centuries. A few of the high fells bear ancient names. Helvellyn, for example, may be derived from Brittonic, the Celtic language spoken by the native Britons, the *Cymry*, who inhabited Cumbria before Anglian and Scandinavian settlers brought the Old English and Old Norse languages and whose presence is recorded in the name Cumberland. However, perhaps surprisingly, the names of several of the fells embracing the Buttermere valley are comparatively young: Red Pike, Grasmoor, Whiteside, Haystacks and Low Fell all remain intelligible to us today. Some are older, like Whinlatter, which contains the Gaelic word *lettir* ('slope'), and Melbreak, which may be the Gaelic *Meall breac* ('dappled hill'), suggesting that they date from the tenth or eleventh century when Gaelic speakers formed part of Cumberland's ethnic mix. Perhaps the oldest local survival is Penn, not a separate hill but one of the spurs on the north-west flank of Whiteside, which is probably the Brittonic word *penn*, meaning 'head' or 'end'.

Notwithstanding the name change from 'Skitter Beck' to 'Bitter Beck', it is the names of watercourses, particularly rivers, which are often the most ancient. As permanent features of the landscape which flow from the territory of one community to another, they tend to carry names of enduring antiquity. Rivers were major dividing lines in the landscape, omnipresent features which presented real obstacles to movement in early times. Here, as elsewhere in the country, river names are inherited from the pre-Anglo-Saxon, Celtic past: Derwent ('river with oak trees') is based on the British word for 'oak'; Cocker and the lake name Crummock both seem to stem from British words meaning 'crooked'.

When we use the names Crummock and Cocker today, we are unconsciously linking with people who walked in this same landscape and saw the same lake and river glinting through the trees many centuries earlier. These names have been passed down from parent to child for perhaps sixty generations and were recorded in writing for the first time perhaps twenty-five generations ago. But even they are comparative newcomers, dating from no earlier than the arrival of the Celtic languages in the first millennium BC. Even at that date, this was an old country.

On a shelf of green hill near Elva Plain farm, right at the head of the sykes and ditches which combine to form Bitter Beck, are the remains of a Neolithic stone circle, built probably five thousand years ago. Only perhaps half of the stones remain, a broken ring of low recumbent granite boulders in a windswept field behind a steading on land which had been open common grazing until the 1820s. From there, a panorama sweeps from Skiddaw in the east, across the Wythop valley with the Hobcarton range rising behind it to the south, to the silver sliver of sea to the west. Elva Plain was a place of importance to the people who knew this hill five millennia ago and had endowed it with meaning sufficient to cause them to arrange a ring of stones as a focus for ritual or ceremonial acts. They would have seen Skiddaw's bulk over which the sun rose and the glinting sea over which it set; they would have known the small rocky outcrop on the crest of the hill behind and would have chosen the site for their stones. The languages spoken by the stone circle builders and their near contemporaries, the communities who quarried stone axes in the Langdale fells, are lost to us but they, too, would have pointed out by name the hills and becks among which they lived. Their place-names have gone – the names by which we now know these places may be ancient to us but they were coined millennia after the stones were arranged. The only tangible legacy is their circle of stones on the hill close to the watershed of Bitter Beck. Long after it was built the stones had acquired a supernatural aura, haunted perhaps. The rocky knoll below which they stood came to be known as the 'elf hill' and called 'elf-howe'. Centuries later, the Ordnance Survey recorded the name as it was then spoken – Elva. This short word encapsulates the huge time depth involved in the claiming of space and the naming of places in the British landscape.

Group at a clipping in Lorton, taken by Frances Mary Peile on 10 July 1888. Her husband, William Allason Peile, of old yeoman stock from Mosser, is on the left of the back row. Next to him is Mrs Clementson of White Ash, High Lorton, and, kneeling bottom right, Willie Bragg, the coachman at Lorton Park.
(identifications by Clara Wigham of Kirkfell House, Lorton, in 1974)

CHAPTER 3

PEOPLE

Tom Rudd Beck

Personal names link people to localities. Surnames exhibited strongly regional and local patterns until the nineteenth century and even forenames, which, being actively chosen, reflect cultural associations, had a regional dimension. Both surnames and forenames link those to whom they belong to particular parts of the world, even when they have moved away from the place of origin of their name. My own name made me an outsider in Cockermouth, despite having Cumbrian forebears. A surname which had been Scottish for centuries (despite originating in southern England) and a quintessentially Scottish forename set me apart from those carrying local names. When a gaggle of us from the two secondary schools in Cockermouth were chatting on the pavement after school one day, a girl I didn't know overheard one of my friends calling me by name. Pricking up her ears, she asked my name and, when told it, exclaimed disparagingly, 'What a nëam ta gah ta bed wid!' Unless we decide to change them, we take our names to bed with us all our lives, so that the person and the name fuse, much in the same way that a place and its name become inseparable.

The personal names of pre-modern Cumberland shared common characteristics with other parts of northern England. Northern surnames were characterised by a large number of patronymics (father's names), such as Robinson, Pearson and Jackson, probably the result of Scandinavian influence. They became hereditary only in the later Middle Ages. There were also very local 'locative' (place-name) surnames, such as Mirehouse, Westray and Birkett, which can often be pinpointed precisely in minor place-names on the ground. Forenames were less local but strong regional patterns persisted. Lancelot (often shortened to 'Lanty' in Cumberland) was more common across the four northern counties than elsewhere in England but it also exhibited more local concentrations: it was frequent in eastern Cumbria but much less common in west Cumberland, for example. Miles was a common forename in southern Cumbria but less frequent further north, while Thurstan was a Lancashire name, rather than a Cumbrian one. Personal names gave local colour to communities, acting, like place-names, as tokens of local identity and signifiers of home.

***

On the outskirts of Cockermouth a stream bearing a personal name joins the River Cocker. Tom Rudd Beck falls into the river down a series of waterfalls over stone steps in a narrow gorge just upstream from Jubilee Bridge. It drains much of the neighbouring parish of Embleton, running westwards towards Cockermouth, crossed and re-crossed by the line of the disused railway, to enter the town behind the cemetery, its deepening course flanked by housing and allotment gardens. Its lower reaches wind through a valley, which was one of the town's industrial quarters until the later twentieth century. The beck's water powered Little Mill, the town's fulling mill in the Middle Ages (it had become a corn mill by 1578), and, in the mid-eighteenth century, the valley below the mill contained a tannery, a skinner's yard and a former dye works. The final reaches of the beck were no doubt stinking and polluted. The tanneries proliferated in the nineteenth century and a large textile mill – the Tweed Mill – (which was short-lived, the premises becoming a cycle-car factory on the eve of the First World War) was built on the south bank of the beck in the 1870s. By the 1960s the tanneries and the tweed mill had gone and this was what the poets Paul Farley and Michael Symmons Roberts would call an 'edgeland', a maze of corrugated iron workshops, scrubland and odd waste places along the tired and tarnished beckside which still bore the stains and scars of its industrial past.

Who was Tom Rudd? It is an unusual name for a stream and the informality of 'Tom' gives it a homely ring. We know that the beck's name is comparatively young, having replaced an older one within the last three hundred years. It can be traced back in the written record more than two centuries to a title deed of 1778, which identified the stream bounding one end of a property as 'Ureby Beck otherwise Tom Rudd Beck'. The lawyer drafting the deed appears to have captured a moment of transition where the modern name was beginning to supplant an older one. As we saw in the previous chapter, 'Ureby' referred to a lost settlement on the edge of Cockermouth, the name of which survived in minor names recorded from the thirteenth century.

Since 'Tom Rudd Beck' seems to have been replacing the older name in the eighteenth century, we should probably be looking to find an individual of that name living in the Cockermouth or Embleton area before 1750. Rudd is not an uncommon surname in Cumberland and there had been Rudds in the Cockermouth area for hundreds of years – a Thomas Rudde held a burgage in the town in the thirteenth century. There are several contenders for the man named in the beck and no certainty is possible, but one candidate who stands out is the Thomas Rudd who married Lucy

France in Cockermouth in 1655. He became a member of the Congregational church in the town in 1668 but was excommunicated in 1674 after some inhabitants of Embleton accused him of 'unrighteousnese, oppression, & crualty', a charge he vigorously denied. He was reinstated four years later but in 1704 he was excommunicated again, for 'unjust dealeing, malice, & crualty to others'. His links with Embleton and, we may imagine, his notoriety perhaps make him a plausible candidate to be the man remembered in the name of the beck.

But who linked his name to the stream of water flowing into Cockermouth from Embleton, and why? Was it his neighbours or perhaps his adversaries? And when and how did a description ('the beck associated with old Tom Rudd') become a place-name (Tom Rudd Beck)? The answers to these questions – which could be asked of any place-name – are lost but, as the memory of the man himself faded, the association of his name with that particular beck was strong enough to survive and be passed down in common usage among members of the local community.

The names of people lie all around in local place-names, from the unknowable Anglo-Saxon and Scandinavian landowners recorded in the names of villages across England, to identifiable individuals of later centuries, like Tom Rudd. Other names refer to anonymous individuals, hinting at connections between specific people and places. We know nothing of the old woman (Old Norse *kerling*) commemorated in Carling Knott, overlooking Loweswater, nor of the youth or servant (Old English *cnafa*) recorded in the lost hill name 'Dick Knave' directly across the valley. Not all place-names recording individuals are of long standing. Peggy's Bridge, for example, at the head of Buttermere, commemorates the life of Peggy Webb-Jones, who died in 1990. All of these are markers, denoting the changing composition of the local communities who lived in, worked and engaged with the landscape.

The very earliest personal names preserved in the place-names of the Cocker valley are pinpricks of light in the darkness of the age before written records. Perhaps the earliest is *Ēanbald*, a man bearing an Old English name, who is recorded in the name Embleton (*'Ēanbald's* settlement or estate'). When he lived is unknown. He was almost certainly a pre-Conquest owner of the estate but whether he lived early or late in the Northumbrian age is impossible to say. He may have been named after one of his namesakes who were archbishops of York in the 780s and 790s. We can be slightly more confident about the chronology of two men bearing Gaelic names, who probably arrived (or were descended from settlers who arrived) during the Viking age of the tenth and eleventh centuries, when people of mixed Scandinavian and Gaelic culture (and probably blood) settled in Cumbria from north-west Britain. The two named individuals are *Muiredach* (or Murdoch, to use the Anglicised version), the man whose name is preserved in Setmurthy ('Muiredach's summer pasture') and *Cartán*, who is recorded in Hobcarton (*'Cartán's* valley'). Their contemporaries, men bearing Scandinavian names, are perhaps surprisingly few and far between. A handful of place-names may contain Norse personal names, but place-name scholars are not fully convinced by any of them: Honister might contain the Scandinavian name *Húni*; Armaside may record someone with the Old Norse name Hermundr (but it could be the Anglo-Saxon, Old English name *Heremund*); Ullscarth (the former name of Hatteringill Head) might contain the Scandinavian name *Ulfr* (but it could simply be 'owl'). These names, arguably recording people who lived before the Norman

Conquest, give a flavour of the cultural and probable genetic mix of the local population – or at least of the upper levels of local society, since it is likely that the men whose names are recorded were landowners.

It is not until the thirteenth century that written records preserve the names of members of the wider local community. A key document is a survey of the half of the honour of Cockermouth belonging to the de Fortibus family, probably drawn up in 1270 after the death of the male heir. The parchment roll, preserved in The National Archives at Kew, contains detailed rentals of each of the family's manors, including Cockermouth itself, Whinfell, part of Buttermere, and communities over the watershed in the Newlands valley, an area of late colonisation, as its name makes clear. Though dating from two centuries after the Norman Conquest of England and from a time when the names of most men and women were drawn from the normal lexicon of personal names in medieval England (John, Robert, William, Richard; Agnes, Joan, Alice, Emme, for example), a few older names survived as indicators of the ethnic or cultural heritage of the local community in the thirteenth century. At Cockermouth, 14 of the 161 burgesses bore older names or were the children of parents who had done so. Some of the names were Norse, as is to be expected in an area where there had been a strong layer of Scandinavian settlement. These included Lyolf the weaver and Lyolf the cobbler and three men whose fathers bore Norse names: Thomas and Adam the sons of Gamall and Richard son of Asketill. But there were others with Old English names ('Bruning' and women called 'Godyth'), two with British Celtic names ('Mungou' and 'Trute') and one whose father may have borne a Gaelic name (Henry son of 'Feril' – perhaps the Irish *Fearghal*). As late as the thirteenth century the mixed heritage of communities in west Cumberland was still evident.

Even in the heart of the fells, where Viking colonisation is often assumed to have opened the land to settlement, the surviving older names were by no means exclusively Norse. Although two women in the Newlands valley had Scandinavian names ('Sygerida the weaver' – from the Old Norse name *Sigrídr* – and a widow, 'Engerith', Old Norse *Ingiríðr*), another, 'Aldith daughter of Godwyn', bore a purely Old English name – both her name and her father's were common in Anglo-Saxon England. Over in Buttermere, one man was called 'Lewynns', again derived from an Old English name, *Leofwyne*. The heritage of those living deep in Derwentfells was far from purely Viking; this part of the Lake District was a society of mixed blood with strong Anglo-Saxon roots.

The rentals of 1270 also provide a flavour of the character of communities at that time. Whinfell had many of the attributes of established agricultural settlements in medieval northern England. As well as 48 acres of demesne land (land farmed directly by the lord of the manor), which by 1270 had been let to Thomas of Rogerscale and William Rothery, a further fourteen people held smaller acreages of land for which they paid money rents and, in a few cases, oat flour. They also owed labour services on the lord's demesnes (in most cases a day's ploughing, a day's harrowing and a day reaping in harvest) which had been commuted to money payments by that date. Whinfell also contained a further nine houses or cottages without land, the tenants of which paid a small money rent and a day's reaping. Up in the Newlands valley in Derwentfells there were also farming communities, like 'Rogersate' (the earlier name for Little Town), where four men each held a house and 10 acres of land; another held 4 acres and a water mill; and a further five tenants held a house and a small plot. They did not owe labour services, probably because (in contrast to Whinfell) theirs was new land, only recently taken in from the hills.

Farming was not the only mainstay of the local economy in the Middle Ages; there were also substantial numbers making a living in other ways. On the lower slopes of the fellsides at Buttermere, there were ten tenants, most of them holding a house and a tiny patch of land (an acre or less). Two men had the by-name *piscator* ('fisher'), hinting at the economic value of the lakes, rivers and becks. Across the fells in Newlands, a handful of tenants held houses with small acreages of land at 'Goderikescale' (now Gutherscale) but they were outnumbered by eleven landless cottagers. The by-names again suggest a community scraping a living from the resources of this valley: two named 'le turnur' presumably worked with wood, as did Adam *carpentarius*; there were also two *piscatores* as well as workers in textiles: a woman *textrix* (weaver) and a 'walkere' (a fuller of cloth).

From the time of the 1270 rental until the middle decades of the sixteenth century, details of the people who lived in the valley are few and far between. The intervening three centuries saw massive change. Population was cut back hard in the fourteenth century by famine, cattle plagues and the Black Death of 1348-50 – exactly how hard in the local area it is impossible to say. Economic conditions across the north of England remained depressed in the first half of the fifteenth century but revived later in the century. The population of the Lake District valleys probably began to grow again before 1500, so that the detailed rentals and surveys of the mid-sixteenth century come from another period of expanding numbers.

How much continuity there was between the communities in the valley in 1270 and those living there in the decades around 1550 is hard to say. The composition of communities had changed: the cottagers who were such a striking feature of the thirteenth-century had largely gone; most of those who paid rent to the lords in the sixteenth century were farmers. Surnames became hereditary across the late-medieval centuries but almost the only link between the by-names of the 1270 rental and the Tudor surnames are the people called Fisher in the Newlands valley who may perhaps have been descended from the men termed *piscator* in 1270. The Black Death and later outbreaks of plague would have created a genetic bottleneck, as population nationally is thought to have been cut from possibly 6 million in 1300 to around 2.5 million by 1400. The Tudor communities were descended from those who survived or from others who moved in to take over land left vacant by those who did not.

The Tudor surveys show that the Lake District valleys were densely settled, with evidence of holdings being divided to enable more families to make a living from the land, sometimes combining farming with other work, especially textiles, tanning and woodland industries. In that era of population pressure, Lakeland townships, like rural communities across the country, also contained mobile, landless people, seeking employment and often on the verge of outright poverty.

In many places the farms recorded in the sixteenth century can be tracked through to the eighteenth and nineteenth centuries, to the time when outsiders used the term 'statesman' to describe a typical Lakeland farmer. The statesmen (the term is a clipped form of 'estatesman') were, to quote Wordsworth, 'small independent proprietors of land ... men of respectable education who daily labour on their own little properties ... which have descended to them from their ancestors'. Their independence stemmed from the security provided by 'customary tenantright', a tenure tantamount to freehold but subject to the periodic payment of 'entry fines' and other dues, which characterised most of the Lake Counties. Though technically tenants holding their farms from the manor, they were small landowners in all but name. The term 'statesman' seems to have emerged to describe such men only in the later eighteenth century; before that, and to themselves, they were 'yeomen' or 'husbandmen'. The new term was a product of the 'discovery' of the Lake District; it reflected what J. D. Marshall called 'the image of the simple, virtuous rustic of Gilpin, Gray and West'.

Wordsworth famously described the statesman society of the Lake District valleys as a 'pure commonwealth', a 'perfect Republic of Shepherds and Agriculturalists', a relic of a golden age, shut up in the hills. In the myth he created, it was 'an ideal society ... whose constitution had been imposed and regulated by the mountains which protected it'. He picked out two features which, he claimed, distinguished these communities. First, they were gentry-free: 'Neither high-born nobleman, knight, nor esquire was here'. There was some truth in this. The Lake District valleys had been retained in the Middle Ages, notionally as hunting forests, by the feudal overlords, such as the barons of Egremont and the lords of the honour of Cockermouth. Most of the land continued to be held directly from these estates, administered from the old baronial castles outside the Lake District proper and mostly in the hands of absentee aristocrats. There were very few resident gentry: whole valleys – Langdale, Dunnerdale, Wasdale, Borrowdale, Newlands, Buttermere and Loweswater – had no gentleman's house. In the seventeenth century only two major landowning families had seats in the heart of the fells, the Radcliffes on Derwent Water and the Flemings at Rydal and, of these, only the Flemings were regular residents.

Wordsworth stressed the stability of communities in his 'pure Commonwealth': many of the statesmen ('these humble sons of the hills') were, he claimed, proudly aware that their farms 'had for more than five hundred years been possessed by men of their name and blood'. Wordsworth's description was, of course, a caricature, and work by modern historians has shown that such long-term continuity of landholding was the exception rather than the rule. It was by no means an unchanging, timeless society – Lakeland farming communities evolved, with a turnover of people much greater than Wordsworth had implied. Old families died out, new families arrived; land was bought and sold, let and sublet, so that by 1800 the number and size of farms and the structure of communities were very different from what had been there in, say, 1550. In general, land was held in fewer, larger holdings and there was greater social stratification: there were yeoman owner-occupiers, tenant farmers and an increasing non-landholding element (labourers, industrial workers, craftsmen and so on).

Wordsworth made it clear that he was writing especially about the upper reaches of the Lakeland valleys but the farming communities the length of the Cocker valley also exhibited key characteristics of his 'pure Commonwealth'. Most were gentry-free communities, certainly by the later Middle Ages. Although they lay on the outer edges of the Lake District, the townships of Mosser, Blindbothel, Loweswater and Whinfell were classic statesman country, the tenants of Mosser having the ultimate freedom of freehold tenure since their farms had been enfranchised to them in the early seventeenth century. It was quintessentially an area of independent family farms. Some were run by 'respectable and well educated yeomen' who lived on their own estates, a group whom William Green, writing in 1819, identified as worthy of note at Loweswater. But that did not mean that the society of these townships was homogeneous. In his description of the community at Loweswater in the 1790s John Housman drew a distinction that would have been equally true of the neighbouring townships. There were, he said, two distinct groups in Loweswater, the 'people of property', on the one hand, who 'have received a tolerable education, and have been somewhat from home' and, on the other, the stay-at-homes, who see 'no people but their neighbours, and no country but their vales and surrounding mountains' and whose 'ideas are simple, and their notions confined to narrow rules of nature'.

Compared to some other Lake District townships, Loweswater, Mosser and Whinfell appear to have been particularly stable communities. Between one quarter and one third of the holdings remained in the same family from the first half of the seventeenth century to the late eighteenth, a span of at least four or five generations. What is more, in the majority of cases, these holdings were farms which remained owner-occupied. Their owners, Housman's 'people of property', were resident, overseeing the farming of their land (if not holding the plough and clipping the sheep themselves) and forming a stable backbone of independent yeomen who ran the affairs of the township.

Surnames persisted. The earliest lists of inhabitants to survive from the Tudor period are the muster rolls of 1535, listing those men who possessed the gear necessary to undertake military service to defend the Border – whether they could appear on horseback armed with bows, or on foot armed with bills; and whether they possessed armour (a leather or chainmail 'jake' or tunic and a 'sallet' or headpiece). Only the more substantial inhabitants – those who could afford such equipment – were listed, but the musters provide surnames of at least part of the community which can be compared with a more detailed listing a century later contained in the Protestation Returns, completed in early spring 1642, which name all men over eighteen. The two lists reveal a high degree of surname stability: more than 80 percent of the surnames recorded in Loweswater in 1535 were still present in 1642; the comparable figures were 70 percent or more in Lorton and Mosser. Although many names were part of the wider pool of names found across that part of Cumberland, some were concentrated in particular townships and continued to be associated with them across the years: in Loweswater 13 households were headed by people with the surname Iredale and 5 by members of the Burnyeat family in 1662, and both names were long-lived there. Other enduring surnames included Stubb and Rudd in Brackenthwaite; Peile, Winder and Bell in Lorton; and Allason in both Mosser and Whinfell.

Some families remained attached to specific farms for several hundred years: the Fawcett family were at Mossergate by 1625 (and probably long before, since Thomas Fausyd appears on the Mosser muster roll in 1535) and remained there until the nineteenth century. Though the family moved to farm in Hampshire in the 1880s, John Fawcett still owned Mossergate in 1910. Elsewhere, farms remained in the family but passed down the distaff side. Lanefoot in Whinfell, for example, held by Richard Wilson in 1560, remained with his descendants for 250 years, passing twice through the female line, until it was sold by Jonathan Stainton in 1808. A succession of yeoman dynasties stretched across the seventeenth and eighteenth centuries: Allason of Cragg End; Wilson (then Thwaite, then Stainton) of Lanefoot; Head of Brandlingill; Dixon of Toddell; Robinson (then Allason) of Beech Hill; Rogers (then Harris, then Fletcher) of Underwood; Fawcett of Mossergate; Mirehouse of Miresyke (Plate 5). It is tempting to over-stress this continuity: each death and marriage resulted in subtle shifts, re-arranging the building blocks of the community, while changing family fortune and individual personalities ensured continuing flux. But strings of descent such as these would have given a cohesion and sense of solid stability to these communities.

Where a family retained a farm across several generations, their name became associated with the particular plot of ground on which they lived. As this was a world of scattered farms, dotted along the valleys, in which each holding tended to have a consolidated core of land around the farmstead, the link between land and family was particularly evident. It stood in marked contrast to village society, in which neighbours lived cheek by jowl and most of the land of each holding was scattered in strips across open fields and meadows. Coming to a village, a visitor was entering a shared space, where their arrival would have attracted attention, the news passing rapidly by lowered voice and nod of the head at the doorcheek, to be recounted by firesides at nightfall. In much of the Lake District, where farms lay dispersed across the fields, a visitor would have to make a deliberate journey down a lane, across a field or over a corner of the common to reach the house of a particular family. They would, of course, be seen by people working in the fields or driving cattle, so that their coming would be known and noted across the neighbourhood but, in seeking out the Fawcetts' place or the Allasons' ground, they were entering a family's private domain.

The idea of a family's farm constituting a separate piece of land, of a distinct place belonging to that family, is hinted at in early descriptions of Lakeland communities. In medieval estate surveys from northern England, farms in villages were usually described in terms of the traditional units of service and assessment, the bovate (or 'oxgang' to use the vernacular term) or the 'husbandland', terms which were synonymous with shared rights and responsibilities. In a survey of Greystoke barony from 1472, for example, holdings in the villages of Greystoke and Stainton were described as 'husbandlands'. In contrast, the holdings of tenants scattered across the broken ground of Matterdale, Berrier and Watermillock on the edge of the fells north of Ullswater, were each described in Latin as a *placea*, a term which is perhaps best translated 'plot' or 'site' and suggests individuality and an absence of communal farming. A century later, when Crown surveyors recorded the forfeited Cumbrian estates of the earl of Northumberland in 1570, they wrote of the tenants in the western dales of the Lake District that their 'habitacions are most in the valleys and dales where every man hath a small porcion of ground, which albeyt the soyle be hard of nature yet by continuall travell [i.e. travail, labour] ys made fertyle to there great releyf and comfort'. Again, each 'small portion of ground' linked a tenant to his own particular place in the landscape.

The link between family and place in the Lake District is seen most clearly in the names of farms which combine a surname with the element 'ground' or 'place'. They are frequently found in batches, distinguishing neighbouring farms by reference to their owners, as in Stainton Ground, Carter Ground, Jackson Ground and Stephenson Ground at the head of the Lickle valley near Broughton-in-Furness, or Roger Ground, Walker Ground, Keen Ground and Sawrey Ground, around Hawkshead. At the head of Loweswater lie Hudson Place, Jenkinson Place and Iredale Place and there was formerly a Johnson Place there as well. But some valleys contain only one or two: Middlefell Place at the head of Langdale; Fisherground and Dawsonground in Eskdale; Fisher Place by Thirlmere. In all, there are more than forty such names in the Lake District.

The families whose names are preserved in 'place' and 'ground' names are often found to have owned the farms for several generations in the period 1550-1750. To take the four 'Place' farms at Waterend at the head of Loweswater as examples, the Iredales, Jenkinsons and Johnsons were all in occupation by 1614. The documentary record doesn't allow us to establish how much earlier they had been there but a Jenkinson and an Iredale were members of the earliest recorded manor court jury for Loweswater, in 1474. The Johnsons and the Iredales had gone by 1700 but the Jenkinsons continued to own Jenkinson Place into the nineteenth century. Hudson Place was an exception. The Hudsons only took over in 1776; before that the farm had been known as Woodville or Woodall Place after the family who had held it from at least 1528 (when John Woodhall of 'Watterend' served on the manor court jury) until they sold it in 1758. Sometimes the opposite happened: a family recorded fleetingly at an early date departed, yet the name survived. In Eskdale, for example, Dawsonground may be linked to members of the Dawson family, who held land in the valley in 1521, and a Fisher held Fisherground in 1578; but neither surname appears in the records of ownership thereafter. So, enduring family possession of a holding does not provide a complete explanation of these names: for one thing, by no means all farms which were passed down a single family over many decades carry names of this type. In many cases, linking a surname to a farmstead was probably a means of distinguishing between farms within a part of a township which otherwise bore only a rather general name ('Waterend', in the case of the examples from Loweswater).

* * *

The farming families who exhibited such continuity and

attachment to particular dwelling places need to be seen in context. Lake District communities were subject to migration and turnover of population, as were rural communities across the country. Even where a stable core of yeoman owner-occupiers can be identified, a majority of farms did not remain in the same family over many generations, and by the eighteenth century at the latest a substantial proportion of farms were not occupied by their owners; tenants on short leases would come and go. Then there were the non-farming sections of the community (the shoemakers and blacksmiths; tailors and publicans), not to mention the live-in servants, both maid servants and farm servants - young men and women hired at the six-monthly hiring fairs, who might stay for one term or for several. Finally, there were the poor, often less visible in the surviving records: the aged and the disabled; widows left penniless; unmarried mothers; temporary lodgers in search of work.

There were also differences in the trajectory of population change at a local level, even between the eight townships in the catchment of the Cocker. Broadly, the communities where farming predominated to the exclusion of other livelihoods tended to remain fairly stable from the seventeenth century to the early nineteenth, while townships with a wider range of occupations grew. A list of households paying the newly introduced Hearth Tax in 1662 suggests that the smaller townships each contained 20 or so households: the numbers of taxpayers were 16 in Blindbothel, 17 in Brackenthwaite, 22 in Buttermere and 23 each in Mosser and Whinfell. To these should be added an unknown but probably small number of households which were not listed as they were exempt from paying on the grounds of poverty. The total population of each of these townships in the mid-seventeenth century probably lay in the region of 80 to 100. By 1831 the number of families in each of these townships had changed little, at around 20-25 families, and the total population of each was then only slightly higher, in the range 90 to 130. The breakdown of occupations included in the 1831 census shows that, with one exception, the smaller townships were overwhelmingly farming communities: the exception was Buttermere, where there were twice as many non-farming as farming families, reflecting the arrival of quarrying and tourism. Of the larger communities, Loweswater, which remained predominantly agricultural (60 families employed in farming in 1831, as against 10 in 'Trade, Manufactures and Handicraft' and 20 others) appears to have remained fairly stable, its population standing at around the 400 level from the mid-seventeenth century, apart from a short-lived peak of 454 in 1831, boosted by lead mining. In contrast, Lorton, which had a wider range of non-farming households, continued to grow until the 1860s as a result of the water-powered industries in High Lorton.

Meanwhile, the 'discovery' of the Lake District by writers and travellers and the growing aesthetic attraction of the lakes and fellsides drew newcomers to the valley, at least in the summer months. Buttermere and the Cocker valley did not experience the rash of villa-building and hotels seen in the Keswick and Windermere areas in the nineteenth century, but they did share in its outer ripples. A lakeside villa on the shore of Buttermere at Hassness had been built by 1803 – one of the early generation of Lakeland villas – but further villa-building was effectively restricted by John Marshall, the Leeds industrialist who purchased much of the land fronting the lakeshores of Buttermere, Crummock and Loweswater in the early nineteenth century. The only other new house with a lake view was Mire Close (later renamed Loweswater Hall), overlooking the head of Loweswater, a 'compact residence' built in the early 1860s. Further down the valley, a handful of small villas – private houses for moneyed Victorian families – were set in the fields around Lorton. The newcomers were small in number during the nineteenth century but the families and their servants formed pools of a different class and culture, socially distanced to a greater or lesser extent from the rest of the local population. At some periods the new villas were occupied only seasonally, a skeleton staff of servants remaining when the family were absent.

The social character of the communities in the valley moved along increasingly divergent paths during Victoria's reign. Up at the head of the valley, Buttermere became an established part of the Lakes tour. By 1891 there were three hotels there (the Victoria, the Fish and the Buttermere Hotel, a temperance establishment). The villa at Hassness had become home from the 1870s to a retired solicitor, Frederic Reed, and his family, swelled by a full retinue of servants: cook, housemaid, parlour maid, kitchen maid, coachman and gardener. By the later decades of the nineteenth century Loweswater and Lorton also contained a good number of middle-class people of independent means, attracted by the scenery. In contrast, the townships of Mosser and Whinfell, behind Low Fell and lacking the views of lake and mountain, remained farming communities.

The arrival of newcomers, however, did not stem an overall downward trend in population. Maximum population figures were recorded in the first half of the nineteenth century, except in Lorton where a short-lived burst of industrial activity made 1861 the peak census year. After those peaks a downward drift continued well into the twentieth century. The population of the eight townships in 2015 stood at 1,038, a drop of one quarter since 1801. Much of this is the story of rural communities across the country: a drift of people from the countryside to towns. The throwing together of farms into fewer, larger units; a shrinking agricultural workforce; the loss of rural crafts and industries and the depletion of rural services have all contributed. Until the later decades of the twentieth century, town life exerted a pull and moving away was seen as the only way to get ahead.

The past half century has seen perhaps the most wholesale social revolution in the valley since the Middle Ages. The decline in the number of farms has gathered pace. Fifty years ago, in 1969, there were 22 farms in the three townships of Buttermere, Brackenthwaite and Lorton (that is, down the main Cocker valley from Gatesgarth to Shatton); today there are 12. While most of the farms in Buttermere survive, only two of the ten in Brackenthwaite remain. It is a similar story in neighbouring communities, as, indeed, in hill farming areas across northern England. The land is still farmed (sold or let to holdings which survive) but is divorced from the farmstead which once formed its heart. As a result, the farming families, which had been the backbone of these communities, have dwindled to a minority.

The downward drift of population, however, has slowed – indeed, it has been reversed in Loweswater and Lorton, which saw their lowest census figures in 1961 and 1971 respectively. In the past, farm amalgamation led to the desertion and dereliction of former dwellings or their conversion into farm buildings, but recent decades have seen an abrupt reversal. Farmhouses have been sold separately from the land as sought-after properties; redundant barns and outbuildings have been converted into new dwellings. The make-up of communities has been transformed as farmhouses, cottages and barn-conversions have been bought up by new arrivals, many of them commuters or retired professional people from afar, who sometimes use their Lake District property as a second home or let it out to holidaymakers. It has been estimated that 16 per cent of the dwellings in the four parishes making up the 'Melbreak Communities' are second homes or holiday accommodation, not occupied permanently. The new settlers, sometimes coming only for the summer season, have no need to scrape a living from the resources of wood and water as the cottagers of the Middle Ages did, but rely on wealth generated elsewhere. However, in most cases, the homes they have acquired have a history stretching deep into the past and it is to that which we now turn.

Toddell in 2019.

CHAPTER 4

DWELLING PLACES
Toddell

The How, the Hill and Brandlingill;
Toddell, the Wood and Aikbank Mill.

So ran a childhood ditty, recalled from her youth at the end of Victoria's reign by an old family friend, Lil Hawkins (née Peile), who was born in 1880 at Rogerscale, in the quiet farming countryside on the northern flank of the Mosser fells. It was chanted by rote to learn the order, clockwise, of the farmsteads along a half-mile stretch of Sandy Beck, the first three on the northern bank in Blindbothel township; the second trio on the southern bank in Mosser and Whinfell townships. Why such a ditty was needed, I don't know. Perhaps it was a bit of fun, learnt at a grandparent's knee.

The farms in the ditty lie in the valley of Sandy Beck, a stream which moves slowly across the low land at the foot of Whinfell to join the Cocker a couple of miles above Cockermouth, not far upstream from the bridging point at Southwaite. Its headwaters are a series of small streams rising on the Mosser fells, which form steep-sided, wooded gills as they cut through the boulder clay of the lower slopes, before combining at the foot of the hill. The farms and hamlets beside Sandy Beck and its headwaters look away from the main Cocker valley, separated from it by the low ridge of hills containing the peaks of Fellbarrow and Low Fell. Two roads lead west from the main Cocker valley to this unfrequented countryside. The high road across Whinfell is a product of enclosure in 1826. A narrow metalled strip between wide, straight verges, long deemed 'Unfit for Motors', it rises steeply through old farmland onto the former open fell, cutting across the lie of the land between large rectangular fields laid out at enclosure. Flanked by outgrown thorn hedges, it is a windy walk with wide views across Cumberland to the Solway, with Criffell and the Galloway hills beyond. The low road is older and lazier, winding its way from farm to farm, past Rogerscale, around the foot of the fellside. After crossing Sandy Beck it turns through fields, becoming 'Mirk Lonning' ('dark lane'), which merges at its western end with the network of lanes running up the hillside to Mosser.

The scatter of farms and hamlets around Sandy Beck formed three separate townships for the purposes of local administration: Mosser, Blindbothel and Whinfell, none of which contained a village or even a significant cluster of dwellings. For centuries this quiet country, hidden away on the edge of the fells and looking away from the Lake District, was a world of small yeoman farms, some of them descending through the same family for many generations. It was an independent-minded area, a stronghold of Quakerism for the two centuries following George Fox's missionary journey into Cumberland in 1653. As late as the end of the eighteenth century, when rural Quakerism was on the decline in Cumbria, roughly one-third of the families in Mosser and a quarter of those in Whinfell were Quakers.

One such family were the Dixons of Toddell, one of the old yeoman houses which formed part of the backdrop of family memory for my grandfather and his siblings in Cockermouth. Those family connections meant that it was

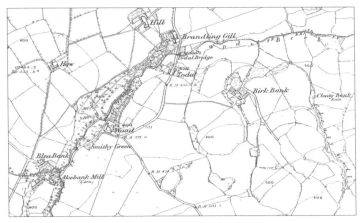

Toddell and neighbourhood
(Ordnance Survey Six-Inch Map, Cumberland Sheet 54, 1st edition, surveyed 1864).

one of the places for paying a visit during the summer holidays of my childhood. In the 1960s Toddell was a place where time seemed to have stood still. An unpretentious building, right on the road side, its front bore a small Victorian porch, which was rarely used and has since gone. Instead, the entrance was by a stable door straight into the kitchen from the lane. There, Kathleen Dixon (1891-1971), the last of the family to live at Toddell, an elderly spinster with capable hands, wearing a broad apron fresh from baking, would welcome us. With the exception of the Rayburn stove, the kitchen had probably changed little since the nineteenth century. It was the working heart of the house, with old wooden forms and a built-in bread cupboard adorned with pewter mugs and platters, which bore the initials 'A W', said to be those of Ann Wilkinson, one of the seventeenth-century owners of Toddell. Beyond the kitchen was the dining room, formal and wood-panelled, its walls carrying portraits of Kathleen's forebears (not the Dixons, but her Irish mother's family); and beyond the dining room lay the parlour, a small chintzy room,

Victorian in its furnishings, where we would be given tea. Kathleen pointed out the marks in the plaster of the ceiling left after the removal of the cupboard bed across the end of the room, in which her grandfather William Walker Dixon (known as Walker Dixon) had been born in 1817. Toddell then was a farmhouse where history could be touched, both in the fabric and furnishings of the house and in family lore. Kathleen's grandfather had lived to a great age, dying when she was in her late teens. She remembered his stories from his childhood in the 1820s and 1830s. He recalled the cloud burst on Mosser Fell one morning in March 1828, when flash flooding swept away the bridge at Aikbank Mill. The beck behind Toddell rose to flood halfway up the orchard. To be told such stories at only second hand almost 140 years after the event gave an almost dizzying connection with the past, collapsing time through the voices of an old bearded yeoman patriarch who died in 1910 and a rather shy elderly lady in the 1960s. And in our conversation, that five-generation link to the past was being forged in the very same room where the young Walker Dixon had been born. I felt that I was glimpsing the dying embers of a vanished world.

To reach behind living memory requires a written record and Toddell was the link to the remarkable richness of archives preserved by the old Quaker yeomen families of Mosser and Whinfell. Kathleen Dixon's cousin, Gorton Brooker, was an engineer in India who had a passion for local and family history and had collected a wealth of material in the 1920s and 1930s, printing numerous family trees on a hand printing press in Calcutta. Towards the end of his life, when he was almost blind, learning of my fascination for local history, he shared some of his knowledge, passing on a set of Six-Inch maps of the area which had originally belonged to his brother-in-law, my great uncle, Dick Hall. To me, they were pure gold – I pored over them, drinking in the detail as only a teenager can. They formed the starting point; I soon started reading surviving letters and family papers, the records of the Quaker meeting at Pardshaw Hall, and the staple fare of local historians (tithe plans, wills and probate inventories, manorial records, title deeds and so on) and began to people the farmsteads along the Sandy Beck valley with the families who had lived there in the seventeenth and eighteenth centuries.

It was from Gorton Brooker that I first learnt of the existence of the diary of Isaac Fletcher, one of the Quaker yeomen of Mosser in the eighteenth century. For a quarter of a century, from 1756 until a month before his death in 1781, except when prevented by illness, Isaac Fletcher kept a brief record of his daily activities in a series of printed pocket diaries, now preserved in Carlisle Library. The entries are often laconic (some days he simply wrote 'Nothing remarkable') but taken together they paint a vivid picture of life in Mosser at a time when the great changes of the industrial revolution were beginning to gather pace. Farming underpinned the life of the community, the annual rhythm of ploughing and sowing, lambing and clipping, haytime and harvest structuring the lives of the yeomen and their families. Most of the farms were small – around 50 acres apiece – and were worked by the family and a live-in farm servant, helped at busy times by day labourers like 'old Adam' (Adam Thompson) who lived latterly in a cottage at Mossergate. Oats and smaller quantities of barley, wheat and rye were grown, and each farm maintained a small breeding herd of cattle and a flock of sheep on the common. The town of Cockermouth bound the farming communities of its hinterland together, the weekly market and fortnightly cattle fairs in spring and autumn and the twice-yearly hiring fairs at Whitsuntide and Martinmas (11

November) being key markers of the passing of the seasons. In their home community, the yeoman farmers acted together to manage the communal affairs of Mosser township. Each year, one would serve as constable, another as overseer of the poor, a third as surveyor of highways. In the absence of a church building, informal 'vestry' meetings were held in farmhouse kitchens to confirm the accounts of each officer, consider disputes with other parishes over the settlement of paupers, or decide on matters to be reported at the manorial court at Egremont to which Mosser sent a 'turnsman'.

For Fletcher and some of his yeoman neighbours, however, farming formed the background to a much wider world. Isaac Fletcher was a local leader in the Quaker community, his position as clerk (a role which combined being chairman and secretary) giving him considerable influence. He also provided legal services, as a sort of 'barefoot lawyer'. Formal legal training was closed to him as a Quaker but he devoted much time and energy to drafting deeds, writing wills and having them proved, acting as an arbitrator in civil disputes, surveying and valuing land and directing the enclosure of commons. In this, he played a distinctive and influential role in the community. One area of activity which he shared with many of his fellow yeomen was an involvement in trade and commerce. Proximity to Whitehaven, a busy west coast port in the eighteenth century, drew yeomen from the countryside of western Cumberland into trade across the Irish Sea and the Atlantic. Fletcher was a partner in business activities as varied as establishing a brewery in Whitehaven, importing Irish yarn, running a stocking factory in Cockermouth, importing graphite ('black lead') from America, and mining lead in Galloway and in northern Ireland. In each of these projects he acted in partnership with fellow Quakers, both Whitehaven merchants and other yeoman, often connected to him by marriage.

The tentacles of trade reached into many of the yeoman farmhouses of the area in the eighteenth century. Some, like Jane Burnyeat of Mosser Mains, held shares in ships; others became partners in ventures across the Atlantic which saw family members emigrate, sometimes in an attempt to gather in debts. Four members of the Gill family of Eaglesfield and six of the Wilson family of Greysouthen, a branch of the Wilsons of Graythwaite in Mosser, had emigrated to North America by the 1770s. When Jonathan Dixon of Toddell remarried in 1766 against the wishes of his sons, Jonah and Jonathan, young men in their twenties, both of them went to Philadelphia. Isaac Fletcher, the youngsters' uncle, acted as go-between in the strained relations between father and sons. One November day in 1767 he went to Toddell with another mediator and found the old man 'guttering in a field'. Standing in that wet field on a cold late-autumn day, they talked money, but Jonathan would not budge on forwarding funds to his son until a conciliatory letter from young Jonathan, which brought tears to the old man's eyes, changed his mind. 'I observed the tears run down his cheeks and he could scarce speak to me for some considerable time after', wrote Isaac. In the end, both Jonah and young Jonathan came back to Cumberland five years before their father died, Jonah taking over Toddell and Jonathan the family's other farm at Waterend, Loweswater.

* * *

The farming landscape in which Isaac Fletcher and his contemporaries lived was typical of many parts of the Lake District. Farmsteads lay scattered singly or in very small groups across the fields, linked by a network of lanes. The old yeoman steadings were the latest rebuilding of dwellings on sites which, in almost all cases, had been occupied for many centuries. There are grounds for thinking that much of the scattered settlement pattern had been in place since the great wave of medieval colonisation of the uplands in the two centuries before the Black Death. By 1300 the countryside had filled up and most of the farms and hamlets on the modern map had been established. As is generally the case in Cumbria, the names of many farms, probably dating from the Middle Ages, record their position or the character of the landscape. Some are self-explanatory – Crag End, Lanefoot, Wood, Beech Hill, Fellside – others almost so: Aikbank, Toddell (contracted from 'todd-hole', fox hole), Whinnah ('whin how', gorse hill). A couple of names take us back to perhaps the twelfth century, when the area was used as summer grazing for surrounding settlements: Mosser itself, 'the summer grazing ground by the moss', and Rogerscale, 'Roger's shieling hut'.

Some, at least, of the names of hamlets and farmsteads can be traced back to the era of colonisation before the Black Death. For example, the rental of Whinfell in 1270 identified some of the tenants by reference to their farms. They included Thomas de Rogerscalles (Rogerscale); Robert de Cragge (probably Crag End), Gilbert *de banco* ('of the bank', presumably High Bank or Low Bank); Adam del Hou (How), and 'the tenants of Todholes' (Toddell). The sites chosen as dwelling places, which remained the sites of hearth and home for many centuries, had been established by then. What we see today represents successive waves of rebuilding and remodelling, the earliest standing buildings usually dating from no earlier than the seventeenth century.

However, the farmsteads whose names appear on the modern map are the survivors of a more populous landscape of settlement, in which dwelling places have fallen out of use in the intervening centuries. Within half a mile of Toddell were the sites of two dwellings which had gone by Victorian times. One of them, Cleaty Bank, deserted by 1841, survived to be marked as a ruin by the Ordnance Survey in 1863. 'Cleaty Bank was once a farmhouse', they wrote, 'but none of the buildings remain except part of the walls of a stable'. The other lost dwelling had probably gone long before then: only a memory survived in the 1840s in the field-name 'High Toft', a 'toft' meaning the site of a house.

Loweswater, where the farmsteads similarly lie scattered across the farmland of the valley sides, is also a place of lost and deserted dwellings. A scramble part way up the steep north end of Melbreak gives a view across the low, wide valley with the lake of Loweswater in the distance on the left (Plate 6). Dwellings – a few of them working farms; the majority now private houses on former farmsteads – lie spread out across the fields. Samuel Taylor Coleridge, passing Loweswater in 1799, described it as 'a sweet country … Somersetshire hills and many a neat scattered house with trees around of the Estates Men'. Roughly in the centre, where roads and trackways converge, stands the church, picked out only by its bellcote, and the long white range of the adjacent Kirkstile Inn. By Lake District standards this is a broad vale of cultivable land and it is not surprising that it formed an early core of settlement; a chapel, doubtless on the site of its bellcoted successor, existed by around 1160, to serve the community here between the lakes.

A few ruins are still named on the map (Mill Hill, Peel and Pottergill) but these represent only the late phases of desertion at Loweswater. A seventeenth-century observer standing on the northern flank of Melbreak would have seen smoke rising from at least five further homesteads within a mile of where he was standing: Bargate, immediately below him where the lane from the church opened onto the fell; Steel Bank, close to Mill Hill in the fields towards the lake

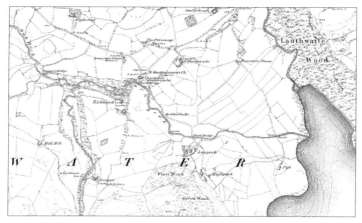

Loweswater in the 1860s
(Ordnance Survey Six-Inch Map, Cumberland Sheet 63, 1st edition, surveyed 1861-3).

of Loweswater; High Iredale and Stockbridge, near the foot of the lake, below High Nook; and Rigbank, on the opposite side of the valley near Foulsyke. Once a dwelling ceased to be inhabited and became a roofless ruin, its name, like its fabric, would slowly crumble and fade from view.

The lost farmsteads of Loweswater were part of a long process, stretching back to the seventeenth century. Loss was rarely sudden – an exception was the destruction of Bargate by fire around 1910. The trees surrounding the farmstead survive but the house and buildings are no more than grassed-over mounds of rubble, a line of ash and sycamore trees a cart's width away from a field wall the only sign of the track down to the burnt-out ruins. In most cases the loss was part of a general trend towards the accumulation of land into larger holdings and the consequent desertion of farmsteads belonging to holdings which ceased to be farmed separately.

Bargate survived long enough to be recorded in early photographs – a figure leans against the door jamb of the porch not many years before it burnt to the ground – but most of the lost farms at Loweswater have left no visual record. Across the beck from Bargate stood Steel Bank, a holding which continued to be inhabited until the later eighteenth century. The last entry in the parish register to mention it is the burial of Joshua Topping in 1763, a lodger there, 'who was both Dumb and Deaf all his life'. Two buildings were shown there on a map of around 1780 but only a barn is marked on the tithe plan of 1839. By the 1860s, when the Ordnance Survey was pinning down names, it was described as 'formerly a farmhouse but now used as an outhouse'. Today, only the footings of walls survive around the spreading sycamore which marks the site.

Across the valley, a ruined and roofless stone shed on the roadside near Foulsyke is the location of Rigbank, another dwelling which had gone by Victorian times. Rigbank had come into the hands of the lord of the manor in 1668 and remained part of the manorial estate in the nineteenth century. John Marshall, the Leeds industrialist who bought the manor in 1814, combined its land with that of Pottergill, a holding higher up the fellside (itself now a ruin), to create one farm, sounding the death knell for Rigbank as a separate dwelling. Sir Wilfrid Lawson, the lord of Loweswater in the seventeenth century, provides us with a detailed description of Rigbank in 1670, soon after he acquired the property. The buildings then consisted of a 'fire House & Bire ajoyneing'; a separate 'Chamber with a Chimney'; two barns ('Leathes'), one for hay and one for corn; and another byre 'with a Chamber at the End of it'. It was clearly a complex of buildings with more than a single dwelling: the separate 'chambers' may have housed farm servants or lodgers. Beside the buildings were two orchards (one an 'Aple Garth', the other a 'Plume Garth'), a 'wood garth' and 26 acres of inbye land (equating to around 42 statute acres, assuming that these were acres of the customary measure used in Cumberland). It appears to have been a typical Lakeland farm of the later seventeenth century – and a far cry from the single-storey shed on the site today.

Some of the earliest lost settlement sites in Loweswater cannot now be pinpointed easily on the ground. The Burnyeat family, who were substantial landowners, holding Crabtreebeck, Thrushbank and High Nook in the eighteenth century, took their name from a lost farm in Loweswater called 'Burnyate', mentioned in the manor court roll for 1521; but precisely where 'Burnyate' was is not known (it may have been an earlier name for High Nook). Nearby stood another lost farmstead called 'High Iredale', which also gave its name to several local families, one of whom, in turn, gave their name to Iredale Place at the head of the valley. An echo of the name 'Iredale' survived into the twentieth century. Beth Alexander of Lowpark had heard in the 1930s that a field on the right of the lane between High Nook and Watergate, formerly covered with daffodils in springtime, was known as 'Ardale Green'. As a place-name (meaning 'the valley of the Irish'), it probably recalls settlement by Gaelic speakers during the Viking period and, as it seemingly refers to a whole valley, perhaps it originally applied to a wider area than a single farmstead.

In spite of all these lost dwelling places across the valley floor at Loweswater, the winnowing out of farmsteads here was much less than in some other Lake District valleys. On marginal land where holdings were small, the shake-out could be much greater. Take, for example, Wasdale Head, pinned between the high fells at the head of Wastwater. In the sixteenth century there were no fewer than eighteen holdings crammed onto the narrow tongue of farmland at the head of the lake. The number fell rapidly as land was thrown together into larger farms. By 1750 there were just ten holdings and only five a century later.

∗∗∗

In the evolving landscape of farmland on the valley floors, the hamlets and farmsteads stood as anchor points. The dwelling places which remain have undergone repeated renewal since medieval times, altering in detail the layout of the steadings. Taking the Cocker valley as a whole, several phases of renewal can be identified in the fabric of houses and cottages. The first is the classic vernacular tradition associated with the 'Great Rebuilding' in the period between around 1660 and 1720. In this part of Cumbria, buildings of that date were typically long and low, with the house and barn under one roof. Houses were rubble-built (often hidden behind a protective layer of roughcasting) with the jambs, lintels and sills of doors and windows made of 'freestone', the easily-worked sandstone of the Cumberland plain, which varies from a soft pink to a hard white. Their defining characteristic is the stone-mullioned window, wider than it is high, divided into two or more frames by vertical stone mullions, neatly shaped and chamfered in the seventeenth century; often flat-faced after around 1700. The windows are sometimes surmounted by a drip course, a line of projecting stones to shed the water. Few facades from this period survive unchanged, mullions having been removed or windows replaced by larger openings to let in more light. Even where the layout and windows have been modernised, internal fittings, particularly the highly polished oak spice cupboards beside the inglenook fireplace or, as at Toddell, a prized built-in court cupboard (or 'bread cupboard'), sometimes survive.

A later phase of building, particularly widespread in western Cumberland during the area's rising wealth in the middle decades of the eighteenth century, saw elements of 'polite' architecture brought into farmhouse construction. From this period date the solid farmhouses framed by projecting, V-jointed quoins with a symmetrical façade of vertical sash windows around a central porch. They speak of the comfortable circumstances of the Georgian yeoman farmers: roomy and light, fashionable without being showy. In Loweswater several of these handsome houses were built adjoining the older, mullion-windowed house which then became an annexe, downgraded to dower house, servants' quarters or scullery. Godferhead and both the steadings at Lowpark take this form, the proud Georgian façade set at right angles to the lower seventeenth-century building (Plate 7).

As new notions of husbandry spread in the nineteenth century, major investment was often made in farm buildings. A large barn, sometimes dwarfing the farmhouse, would be built in the yard, providing stalls for cattle, stabling and a cart shed on the ground floor and storage for hay and corn above. Many of the Lake District's 'bank barns', built into the slope with direct access to the upper floor from the ground on the uphill side, date from this period. The shape of the farmstead often changed, the simple linear plan of older steadings evolving into a loose courtyard as farm buildings were built at right angles to the house.

When major rebuilding or remodelling was undertaken, it became the practice here, as elsewhere across the northern counties, to include a permanent marker of the event by incorporating a stone bearing the date, often over a doorway. As was the norm across the region, the initial of the surname appears at the top of the panel, with the initials of husband and wife below and date to one side or underneath. Until around 1720 the initials and date were in wide lettering, standing proud of the background, which had been cut away by the mason. These chunky inscriptions gave way across the early eighteenth century to fine, flowing lettering incised into the face of the stone. The contrasting styles survive in stones around the door of one of the Quaker yeoman farmhouses in the area, Whinfell Hall. When a new doorway was made in the eighteenth century, it was surmounted by a plain panel incised 'W / J S 1734', recording the names of John and Sarah Wilson and the year of their marriage. But an older stone was preserved and re-set in two sections either side of the door. It read 'A / I E' and '1694', the wide, plain letters set in a neatly cut-back rectangle recording Japheth and Elizabeth Allason, members of the family from whom the Wilsons inherited the farm. In placing a new date stone and preserving the older one, the builders were expressing a sense of lineage and family memory.

Isaac Fletcher's home at Underwood tells a similar story. He inherited the farm from his mother, Margaret, who was the daughter of Thomas Allason. Preserved in the wall of an outbuilding at Underwood is a damaged date stone carrying Thomas Allason's initials and a date, which probably read '1666' before the top was broken off. It was presumably retained from an earlier building dating from Isaac's grandfather's time – perhaps the 'old house' at Underwood which housed labourers in the 1760s. Isaac Fletcher himself seems to have rebuilt the farmhouse at Underwood, giving it the not quite symmetrical, sash-windowed façade it has today. The back door carries a dated lintel of 1742, also damaged so that only the initial 'I' of his forename survives. That was the year before Isaac married his neighbour Susanna Harris and the date stone suggests that he carried out some possibly major building work before embarking on married life. Further rebuilding followed. In the autumn of 1756 he rebuilt the porch (presumably the stylish sandstone structure which survives) and undertook some re-roofing, while the following summer saw a major undertaking when he rebuilt the stable, barn and byre, creating a building 24 yards long. The work, he recorded, involved up to six wallers at any one time, and the timber raising, when the roof trusses were erected, took place on a hot, windless day in July. At some point he added a small semi-circular plaque of lead above the house porch, bearing his and Susanna's initials ('F / I S') in relief, but no date. We know from his diary that he had a personal interest in lead mining as he dug trial pits for lead on his land at Mosser in the later 1760s, as well as being a partner in lead mines in Galloway and northern Ireland in the 1770s. The plaque can be thought of as a memento of this episode in the history of Underwood, part of the story of a Georgian yeoman encapsulated in a tangible object preserved in the fabric of his farmhouse.

Even in the absence of such explicit marks of ownership, the buildings on a farmstead provide a mute record of periods of wealth and renewal from the world of the yeoman dynasties. As such, old farmhouses of the seventeenth and eighteenth centuries, many of them modernised by new owners, are now protected by the state as listed buildings. The social revolution in the countryside since the 1960s has frayed almost to breaking point the cord of connection and memory linking today's inhabitants with the yeoman society which created the working – and now treasured – landscape of the Lake District, but the dwellings survive.

Lorton from Fellbarrow.

CHAPTER 5

FARMLAND AND VILLAGE
The Vale of Lorton

'The Vale of Lorton' – the name suggests the rich, fertile
farming countryside of rural England, more Welsh Marches
perhaps than Lake District. Vales are best viewed from a
vantage point, spreading out into the distance, and the Vale of
Lorton is no exception. The road south from Cockermouth
rises to a crossroads at Round Close Hill, where the ground
drops away, opening up a panorama of the fells: Ladyside
Pike (shaped like a miniature volcano) to the left, then the
saddle of Hobcarton, the long bulk of Whiteside and the crags
of Grasmoor, with the Buttermere fells (High Stile and Red
Pike) behind. In front of the fells, bounded by lower, green
hills on either side, lies the Vale of Lorton, a widening of
the valley where Whit Beck, flowing down from Whinlatter,
joins the Cocker. Two streams, Blaze Beck and Aiken Beck,
falling through the forestry plantations and hill pastures on
Whinlatter, meet at Scawgill Bridge and become Whit Beck
('the white beck', presumably from its colour as it breaks over
the rocks), which then cuts through a narrow valley down
to the village of High Lorton, before running out across the
fields on the floor of the Vale. Following Whit Beck down
its course is to take a journey back in time, through the
history of the way land has been parcelled out and divided
into fields to create the patchwork of fences, walls, hedgerows
and lanes that are the essence of the English countryside.

It's the 'landscape plotted and pieced', one of the 'dappled things' for which Gerard Manley Hopkins gave God thanks in his poem 'Pied Beauty'.

The fields were places of physical toil in all seasons before the coming of modern farm machinery, producing the crops and rearing the livestock on which the local economy depended. The annual round of ploughing, seedtime and harvest on the ploughland; of mowing, turning and gathering hay in the meadows; of tending, feeding and moving livestock in the pastures, took men, women and children into the fields across the year in all weathers. Winter was the season for repairing field boundaries, clearing gutters, hedging and repairing walls, when biting winds and sleety-rain might sluice the valley. Spring would see, in the words of the Irish poet Patrick Kavanagh, 'The dragging step of a ploughman going home through the guttery / Headlands under an April-watery moon'. Summer brought haytime, when working in the fields was not all hard grind. A farmer at Thackthwaite in the early nineteenth century recalled the beauty of early mornings in the hay meadows. On hot summer days, when the heat could become 'almost unbearable in these mountain valleys with scarcely a breath of air', he would get up before sunrise to go to mow, his breakfast brought to him in the field – 'a can of warm coffee with two or three eggs in it, and a good slice or two of bread and cheese … a good kind of feed for the hot weather and hard work', he thought. 'It was pleasant to be in the meadows those early mornings. The whetting of the scythe, the dew on the grass, the singing of many birds, and the rising sun glinting over the eastern fells gave to the time a poetic attractiveness which only those who have experienced it can at all appreciate'. In autumn the corn fields would be thronged, as all hands were brought in to reap and bind, the stooks of oats and barley left standing in the fields to dry. It was an anxious wait in some years if the weather broke: on occasion, the stooks might not be brought in until a dry spell in November.

The land and its living things – flowers, bushes, trees, insects and reptiles, birds and mammals – were known in a way which only comes from repeated encounter and close observation. That tree in the corner of the field from which the owl always called at dusk on frosty evenings; wool hanging again from the thorn bush rubbed by sheep each year; the damp patch by the gutter near the gate where the yellow flag irises grew and the dragonflies darted in summer. Such details came to be used to identify particular spots and were incorporated into the names of fields. Each field had its name and those names communicated a distinctive aspect of each plot of ground – the quality of the soil, perhaps; how the field was used; who had owned it; or the plants or animals it contained. Field-names, springing from the intimacy which came with toil, offer a window into the history of how the landscape of fields developed over the centuries.

Following Whit Beck downstream, across the couple of miles from Whinlatter Pass to the floor of the Cocker valley at Lorton, is to pass through three distinct 'fieldscapes', where the land has been plotted and pieced in different patterns: first, up in the hills, dry stone walls running straight as a die up steep fellsides; then, small fields, some hedged, some walled, their curving, irregular outlines mirroring the hummocky ground on the lower valley sides; and finally, more straight-sided, rectangular fields, this time mostly bounded by thorn hedges or wire fences on the flat valley floor. Each pattern of fields tells a different story.

The Whinlatter road above High Lorton, curving round the flank of Kirk Fell, runs just above what had been the limit of enclosure until the nineteenth century. A narrow

Lorton, showing the contrasting field patterns from the enclosed fells to the valley floor *(Ordnance Survey Six-Inch Map, Cumberland Sheet 55, 1st edition, surveyed 1863)*.

tongue of old enclosures ran up both sides of Whit Beck and ballooned to take in the few level fields around the site of the old inn at Scawgill. Above them, on either side of the valley and beyond, lay open common land stretching up to the fell tops. It remained unenclosed until the tide of Parliamentary enclosure, which swept away around 2.3 million acres of common waste in England and Wales, reached Lorton in 1832, when the common grazings (3,867 acres of fellside) were divided up and enclosed. As in so many upland communities across northern England, a revolution took place in just a few years. The common ceased to exist, being divided into sections allotted to individuals. Lorton's enclosure came towards the end of a frenzy of enclosure in the years following the Napoleonic wars. The nearby commons on the lower fells on the edge of the Lake District had been enclosed since 1815: Embleton and Setmurthy in 1824, Whinfell in 1826, Wythop in 1830. Most of the higher fells upstream from Lorton, however, remained unenclosed and survive as common land today, though the commons at Loweswater and Mosser were divided in the 1860s.

The process of enclosure saw rectangular allotments, some consisting of huge slabs of fellside, others of smaller plots on the lower slopes, being assigned to those with a legal interest in the common – the lord of the manor who owned it and the commoners who had common rights over it. The new landscape, drawn out in a draftsman's office, laid an artificially straight-lined arrangement of new fields across the curves and clefts of the hillsides. From the northern bank of Aiken Beck a series of long, thin allotments radiated out, running straight up to the skyline between Lord's Seat and Graystones. The wild mountainous fellsides on either side of Hobcarton Gill were overlain by a grid of straight-edged blocks. Here, as across the northern uplands, the miles of new walls required in a short space of time created work for teams of professional wallers, paid by the rood. Their new walls were built of quarried stone: thin sharp-edged wedges and slabs of dark grey slate.

New fields required new names and the tithe plans of around 1840 (within a decade of enclosure at Lorton) capture something of the process of naming. Although many enclosure allotments retained the bald label 'Common', others were more specific. Some carried the pre-existing name of the bank of fellside they covered: 'Tooth Howe', 'Kirk

Fell', 'Aiken', for example. A few seem to have preserved an earlier name for part of the common which went unrecorded on the Ordnance Survey plans: 'Whinrigg' on the hillside above Gillbrae in Lorton, and 'Knott Hill Common' behind Whinfell Hall are examples. A handful show more active naming, by referring to ownership, such as 'Priest Field' (belonging to Revd William Armistead, the curate of Lorton) and 'Peter Field' (owned and farmed by Peter Robinson in 1840).

Most of the new enclosures did no more than create new parcels of landed property; the piece of fell land within them remained unimproved rough grazing, now used privately rather than communally. A few fields on the lower slopes of the former common were reclaimed and improved. Sown grass stands out fresh green from the surrounding rough pastures, the tell-tale narrow ridge and furrow of nineteenth-century ploughing showing that the allotment had been subject to back-breaking paring and burning of the sods, followed by ploughing, probably for a couple of crops of oats, before being put down to grass. Where the former common was improvable, new farmsteads were sometimes established in the early nineteenth century, like the significantly-named Waterloo and Wellington farms on former moorland near Cockermouth, enclosed in 1815, the year of the battle of Waterloo. But the low fells on the edge of the Lake District were at best marginal land and thus on the limit of new farmland where new farmsteads were needed. One was built on a lower part of Lorton common, at Darling How, while across the vale a farm was established at a height of 300m at Hatteringill after Whin Fell was enclosed in 1826. It proved to be a short-lived venture. Immense labour would have been involved in bringing the grassy hilltop at Hatteringill into cultivation: the surface would have been pared and probably burnt; stones – thousands of them – were cleared (some piled into heaps which survive on the fell today). After ploughing, it was limed heavily: Walker Dixon of Toddell recalled as a youngster seeing hundreds of cartloads of lime being carted from Pardshaw Crag. He himself had helped to house oats from Hatteringill: 'It was very bad weather at the harvest season and, a fine Sunday occurring, the neighbours gathered and assisted John Moffat [the tenant at Hatteringill in the 1840s] to secure his crop'. The circular 'stack bottoms' on which the stooks of oats were placed to dry survive where the straight-walled occupation road enters Hatteringill land (Plate 9). But farming high on Whin Fell proved to be an uphill battle: by 1851 Hatteringill was uninhabited and by 1861 it had ceased to be recorded as a dwelling on the census.

Back across the valley on Whinlatter, the major change in use of the former commons did not take place until the middle decades of the twentieth century. Having been converted to private property, the allotments laid out in the 1830s could be bought and sold and, from the 1920s, the Forestry Commission bought up much of what had been Lorton Fell to extend their existing holdings across the watershed in Thornthwaite. The lower sections of the allotments up Hobcarton Gill, around Darling How and up Aiken Beck were planted with conifers between the 1920s and the 1950s, and a couple of forest workers' cottages were built in a bleak and isolated location near Whinlatter. The new plantations accentuated the ruler-straight lines of the enclosures laid out by the enclosure commissioners. At the edge of Forestry Commission property the trees stop abruptly on one side of a wall running uphill to the skyline.

* * *

Below the edge of the former common lay what the Parliamentary enclosure commissioners termed 'ancient inclosures' – farmland already in private ownership and divided into fields long before the enclosure of the commons. In pre-enclosure days, the boundary between farmland and open common (the 'intake wall' or the 'fell dyke') was the fundamental division of the landscape. It was not only the boundary between enclosed, private space and the open, shared space of the commons but was also the dividing line between how the land was used – plough land, meadow and improved pasture on the farmland; rough grazing ground on the fells. In general, the boundary was the point at which thinning soils and increasing slope defeated attempts to make more productive use of the land. In Lorton the boundary line had remained fairly static for several centuries before the enclosure of the fell commons. The highest fields in the 'ancient enclosures' on the lower slopes of the fells above Scales and Highside were probably enclosed during late-medieval times, pushing the limits of enclosure up the lower fellsides in the fifteenth century. In the language of estate accounts, they were 'improvements', taken in from the edges of the common and tacked on to existing fields. In the vernacular they were 'intacks', a name by which one of them at Highside was still known in the nineteenth century.

The narrow valley through which Whit Beck runs from Scawgill down to High Lorton was another area of late-medieval intaking, creating the tongue of fields on either side of the beck, running up into the hills. Known as 'Stockdale' (a name which survived in the nineteenth century for the field furthest upstream on the north side of Whit Beck), the valley's intakes can be traced back to the fifteenth century. Stockdale was described as an 'improvement' in 1482 and a reference to a shieling there, which had fallen out of use by 1500, perhaps suggests that a summer pasture was being tamed and enclosed. The first element of the name 'Stockdale', of which there are several examples in the Lake District, means 'tree stumps' or 'logs', hinting at clearance of woodland.

These intakes were the outer, final ripples of medieval colonisation, the bulk of which took place earlier, in the centuries before the Black Death. Swinside, Scales, Highside, Gillbrea and Armaside, hamlets along the valley sides around the villages of Lorton, were in all likelihood established in the great sweep of medieval colonisation between 900 and 1300. The fields surrounding them, along the margin of the fells, are completely different in character and size from the vast rectangles of Parliamentary enclosure. Even today, this is a landscape of small, irregular fields with curving hedges or walls. The field-name 'Ruddings', which occurs several times in the vicinity of Gillbrea, records the origins of these fellside farms as medieval clearings in woodland – 'rudding' or 'ridding' meant 'cleared land', from the Middle English word *rydding* which refers to the action of clearing or removing. It survived in the Cumberland dialect 'rid', meaning to 'uproot trees and hedges'.

On one farm at Scales, it is possible to trace the patchwork of fields back to the sixteenth century. Cuthbert Bell's holding in 1578 was essentially the same as that held over two hundred and fifty years later, in 1840, by John Jennings. In 1578 it contained a little over 23 customary acres (around 37 statute acres) and consisted of six small fields scattered among those of neighbouring farms at Scales, together with a larger block of land divided into seven small closes. The names of the six small fields survived virtually unchanged in Victorian times, allowing them to be identified on the tithe plan of 1840: 'one Crofte of Ar[able] land' adjoining the farmstead (this was represented by 'Croft' and 'Little Croft' in 1840); a close of arable called 'Little Close' (the name survived unchanged in 1840); a close of meadow land called 'the Crofte Foote' ('Croft

Foot Meadow'); another meadow close called 'the broad mires' ('Broad Mire Meadow'); a close of arable and pasture called 'Soskyll Raynes' ('Sosgill Rains' and 'Little Sosgill Rains') and an arable close called 'the highe syke' ('Syke'). The names of these fields describe the use and quality of the land: 'croft' was the name commonly given to a fertile, fairly level field close to the farmstead; 'mire' referred to boggy ground and 'syke' to a small stream or gutter; 'rains' meant strips of land, especially the grassy balks between plough strips. Other field-names along the lower fellsides around Lorton are equally revealing. Patches of plough land are recorded in the names 'Meal Ark', near Gillbrea (referring to a chest in which oatmeal was kept and usually implying a notably fertile field); 'Rye Fold' near Highside (naming the crop grown there), and 'Twenty Riggs' nearby (describing the number of plough ridges the field contained), for example.

Most of these fields survive today, their boundaries formed by a mixture of hedge banks and dry stone walls. The walls here are quite unlike those created by Parliamentary enclosure on the former commons – they are built of rounded, water-worn stones cleared from the fields, a legacy of the painstaking hand labour of clearing stones from ploughland and meadows across the generations. The landscape of fields along the valley side is one which has evolved over many centuries. Around Scales (Plate 8), the lines of field boundaries, if not the hedges and walls themselves, were probably laid out in medieval times. Elsewhere, piecemeal change – throwing two fields together here or realigning an awkward kink in a boundary there – make this a dynamic landscape, as does the replacement and renewal of field boundaries. But it is in this zone, between the valley floor and the enclosure walls on the fellside, that the landscape predating the nineteenth century survives most intact.

Much of the field pattern in neighbouring townships was similar – a patchwork of irregular fields surrounding scattered farms and hamlets, which had been inherited from the medieval centuries. The field-names of Whinfell, Brackenthwaite and Loweswater townships are comparable to those around the fellside hamlets surrounding Lorton. A scatter of fields named 'Ruddings' or 'Riddings' show that these were landscapes of woodland clearance. Many fields are named 'Parrock', simply meaning a small enclosure, a name typical of long-enclosed farmland across Cumbria. Meadows are recorded in the frequent name 'Ing' (derived ultimately from the Old Norse *eng*, 'meadow') and patches of particularly fertile ploughland were alluded to in names such as 'Meal Ark' (of which there was another example at Cleaty Bank in Whinfell) and 'Honey Pot' (at Jenkinson Place in Loweswater).

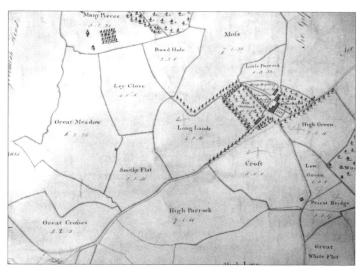

Field-names around Foulsyke, Loweswater, recorded on an estate plan of 1782 *(CAS, DWM/2/96).*

Back in Lorton, on the flat floor of Lorton Vale, the fields possess a different character again. They tend to be larger than those around Scales and the other valley-side hamlets and to be generally rectangular in shape. They cover the former open fields and meadows of the two villages of High and Low Lorton, a core of early (almost certainly pre-Norman) agricultural settlement on the fertile, wide and well-drained floor of the valley. It is as though the villages have been flung to the edges of the open fields, leaving only the church (and its Victorian schoolroom and vicarage) on the lane which divides the land between the two. Both villages are long, thin settlements, strung out along a road. High (or Over) Lorton runs along the break in slope where the land begins to rise as Whit Beck emerges from its side valley. Low (or Nether) Lorton clings, in places almost precariously, to the bank of the River Cocker. It's likely that the two villages represent the division of an earlier single settlement of 'Lorton', probably in the twelfth century, when High Lorton and its lands were granted to Carlisle priory.

The open fields in the Vale of Lorton were more extensive than many in the Lake District, but wherever there was a sufficiently large tract of fairly level, well-drained land on a valley floor it was likely to have been cultivated in strips, giving shares of the ploughland to each of the farms in an adjacent village or hamlet. There were open fields at Braithwaite and Buttermere, and at Coniston and Grasmere, for example. Estate surveys from the sixteenth and seventeenth centuries help to reconstruct the open fields of the two villages at Lorton. The core lay on the flat land stretching north from Whit Beck to Casshow Wood. 'Crossegate loane', the lane running the length of this area, past the church, divided the valley floor between the open fields belonging to each village. Parts, at least, of Low Lorton's fields remained open in 1578. Descriptions of farms in the village in the great survey undertaken for the earl of Northumberland in that year show that they held plough land in various named furlongs 'in Lorton field'. Again, those names can be identified on the tithe plan of 1840. By then, the open fields had been long since enclosed (probably in the seventeenth century – certainly High Lorton's farms held all their land in the former open fields as 'closes' in 1649). As so often in Cumbria, enclosure of open fields, probably taking place in piecemeal fashion over several decades, resulted in the outlines of the open field strips being preserved in the boundaries of the new enclosures. The result, in Lorton as elsewhere, was a landscape of thin, strip-like fields grouped into blocks which followed the alignment of the bundles of open-field strips they replaced, respecting the layout of the furlongs. Lorton's tithe plan of 1840 (based on a survey made around 1827) shows such a pattern across the valley floor between the two villages.

The field-names here were quite different from those of the irregular closes on the lower fellsides. Groups of strip fields often bear a common name, that of the furlong in the open field on which they lie. Low Avelands, High Avelands, Great Avelands and Wilkinson Avelands, for example, a group of fields just to the north of Whit Beck's confluence with the Cocker, represent the furlong in Lorton field named as 'Avenham' in 1578. Other furlongs in Low Lorton fields were 'Laythelds' ('Laithwaite' in 1840), 'Sandy Butts', 'Above the Dyke' and 'Ullwray' ('Alleray' in 1840). The pattern of field-names in High Lorton suggests a similar sequence of furlongs in a former open field, bearing the names 'Kirks', 'Flatts', 'Windings' and 'Brooms'. In the absence of earlier evidence, the names are a clue to the appearance of the medieval open-field landscape. Some refer to the physical structure of the open fields: a 'flatt' is a furlong, a section of the field in which

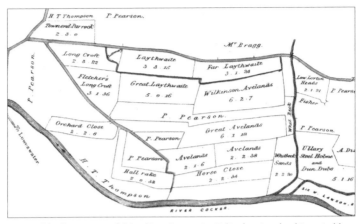

Part of the former open fields of Low Lorton in 1843, showing the thin strip-like fields created by enclosure of furlongs in the open fields *(CAS, DDIX/Box 4/20).*

all the strips run in the same direction; 'riggs' or 'lands' are the strips themselves; 'butts' are short strips, often at right angles to a larger block of longer strips. 'Above the Dyke', the name of the fields south of Low Lorton between the main road up the valley and the lane to Hopebeck, suggests the existence of a major boundary ('dyke' in the sense of a bank and ditch) within the fields, either between the village crofts and the rest of the open fields or perhaps followed by the line of the modern road. Closer to the River Cocker lay the shared meadows, recorded in the field-names 'holm' (meaning an 'island' and often referring to a patch of higher land by a river) and 'ing'. Sometimes the name of a group of strips sheds light on a feature in the long-lost landscape of the open fields: 'Ullwray' (now represented by Hullary Wood) means 'owl-haunted nook', for example. Other names can hint at the processes behind the development of the open field: 'Avenham' is from a Scandinavian word *af-nám*, meaning land taken in from the waste.

The strip-like fields and their evocative names survived until the mid-nineteenth century. Sometime in the 1840s or 1850s the landscape of the former open fields south of Low Lorton was completely rewritten. The old narrow fields were swept away and replaced by large rectangular fields which survive largely unchanged today. George Lucock Bragg, the owner of the Lorton Hall estate in the 1840s, was responsible for the destruction of the older landscape. He was a gentleman landowner, improving his estate, who rebuilt much of the Hall and also reorganised the layout of his farms.

***

The daily workings of the farming landscape depended on the ability to move from farmstead to field, between fields and from the fields out onto the fell commons. Roads and paths, like buildings, appear and disappear, though much of the network of lanes and tracks has a long pedigree as a well-established web of routeways. Some were public arteries making a way through the valley between private property on either side. Those leading to market had had the status of 'the king's highway' from medieval times; these were the 'beaten streets', to coin the phrase used by the seventeenth-century antiquary, John Denton, which were the ancestors of later main roads. They were the routes trodden repeatedly by the feet of men, women and livestock as animals were moved down from the breeding grounds in the fells. As late as the 1960s, flocks of sheep continued to be driven on foot down the Vale of Lorton to market at Cockermouth. Earlier times saw other reasons for the movement of livestock, such as the collection of tithes. The testimony of Jenat Birkett, an 80-year-old widow from Borrowdale, in 1602 recalls how she had helped her father-in-law, the local tithe collector, drive tithe lambs gathered from Lorton and neighbouring settlements home along the lanes and, when a young girl (presumably in the 1530s), had 'rydden on horseback ... and brought home in pannyers upon the horse she rood on both tythe hens, tyth geese, tythe chickens & tyth egges out of ... Lorton & Withope & other places'.

Other tracks and lanes ('lonnings' in the local dialect) were local routes to the church or chapel, or occupation roads giving access to fields. When looking at roads through the old enclosed farmland, linking farm to farm, questions present themselves. Did routes come first or did the position of hedges and walls determine the lines they took? Sometimes there are clues in the detail of the relationship between route and field pattern. If field boundaries seem to continue across a road from farmland on one side to the other, the road perhaps originated as a line across fields. Conversely, where a track swings and curves around the ends of fields, in extreme cases in a series of dog-legs, we can envisage that the route has been determined by the pattern of field boundaries or by the ends of plough strips in an open field.

Lanes in the valleys, the product of many centuries of trudging hooves and human feet, required constant maintenance if they were to remain passable. Throughout England, many roads were notorious for being 'verie troublesome in the winter halfe' in the sixteenth century. Responsibility for their upkeep had lain since 1555 with each parish (in Cumbria, each township), which was required by law to appoint a surveyor of highways each year to oversee the repair of roads within its bounds each summer. Labour was provided by the local community, each householder being required from 1562 to provide six man-days of labour annually. The system remained largely unchanged in the mid-eighteenth century when Isaac Fletcher recorded the yearly attempts to repair the highways in Mosser each June. On Tuesday 8 June 1773 he noted: 'Lads [i.e. his sons] all gone to the highways. Took two carts and two men to each, which will answer to two days' work'. He sent two carts and four hands the following Friday and Saturday, noting that this 'finishes the six days statute work for this year.' The following year his sons Isaac and Billy were repairing the road over Mosser Fell to Loweswater, carting stone from the crag at Askill Knott, just above the road. It was Fletcher's turn to serve as surveyor in 1776. He met those who had been sent to labour at Mosser Mains and set them to work on 'Kirby-gate lane', the road leading towards Pardshaw. Again, materials were got locally, this time stone from Pardshaw Crag. Each year a different section of the network of lanes was repaired by this communal, self-help effort, using unpaid labour.

It was an uphill battle. Before the nineteenth century most of the local roads were indeed 'verie troublesome' in winter. Walker Dixon, recalling his childhood in the second decade of the nineteenth century, remembered being told how narrow the lanes around Toddell were before they were widened around 1819: there was 'not room for two carts to pass & not room to walk opposite or alongside a cart'; in winter the ruts were 'axletree deep.' When walking, women wore pattens, wooden overshoes with an iron ring, to lift them a couple of inches off the ground in an attempt to keep their shoes out of the mud. Snow and ice made the lanes impassable. The narrow lanes could fill quickly with snow. In the harsh January of 1767 when there was heavy snow 'a yard deep', it blew into drifts and the lanes around Mosser were still full three weeks after the first heavy fall. In frost the lanes became an ice rink: 'the roads glaz'd; dangerous riding'; 'The roads all in a glaze with ice. Very dangerous traviling either on horseback or on foot' wrote Isaac Fletcher in January 1774.

Across the nineteenth century the state of the roads

improved greatly. Wheeled vehicles replaced packhorses as trade and tourism increased. The first concerted effort to improve the through routes had begun in the previous century with the introduction of tolls on turnpike roads to provide income for road repair. The Whinlatter route past Lorton to Cockermouth was turnpiked in 1762 as part of a scheme which included the central artery through the Lake District from Kendal to Keswick. A new road was built up the Whit Beck valley, bypassing the village of High Lorton. But this was the only turnpike in the area: all the other roads in the Cocker valley remained the responsibility of the townships.

* * *

High and Low Lorton are the only real villages between Cockermouth and Buttermere, where the houses have stood close together – in these cases along a roadside – since the Middle Ages. Across the rest of the valley and its tributaries the settlement pattern was one of scattered farms and cottages, spread out across the land or grouped into small clusters of farms as at Buttermere and Thackthwaite. The Lake District proper is not a region of villages. Many of its villages are products of the nineteenth century, when the attractions of mineral wealth and the aesthetics of scenery drew migrants to settle. Villages such as Eskdale Green and Boot, Chapel Stile and Glenridding developed at this time. But old-established villages, such as those at Lorton, also underwent radical change. High Lorton's history is typical of villages in northern England since the Industrial Revolution. Its buildings record successive phases of social change: a period of industrial activity, albeit on a small scale, in the nineteenth century, with a brewery and a thread mill and a clutch of workers' cottages; the arrival of an expanding middle class in a handful of comfortable Victorian houses set in their own grounds around the edges of the village; two pairs of identikit 1950s council houses at one end of the village, here capturing stunning views up the valley; and the conversion of almost every outbuilding and barn into dwellings for retired offcomers in the later twentieth century.

In 1649 High Lorton was a largely agricultural village consisting of a row of seven farmsteads strung out along the road between two lanes running up to the common (now Holemire Lane and the lane past Tenters). Each had a croft on the valley floor in front of it and a close 'above the house' ('abeun t'hoose' in the vernacular, giving the field-name 'Bunne house close') stretching up towards the common behind it. At the southern end of the village, across Whit Beck, was a further farmstead at Boonbeck ('abeun t'beck'). Even in the seventeenth century High Lorton had an enclave of cottages, presumably housing families who were not directly tied to the land. They stood in a row set back from the road, in what was later called Smithy Fold.

By the nineteenth century much of the land which had been attached to the High Lorton farms in 1649 had become separated and belonged to holdings outside the village. The village itself had been transformed into a community of largely non-farming families. Memories of High Lorton around 1810 tell of a village brimming with children and humming with activity. Smithy Fold contained the smithy and its attached public house (appropriately called The Horseshoe) and also a joiner's shop. In the village street were a bake house, a weaving shop, a dressmaker, a malt kiln, a dame school and a small shop selling tea, coffee, tobacco and snuff and (for the children) marbles and mint cake. Industries developed. The malt kiln at the south end of the village was the precursor of Jennings brewery, beside the beck at Boonbeck Bridge, which flourished from the 1840s until moving to Cockermouth in 1887. The knot of brewery buildings included a new malt house (now the village hall, the 'Yew Tree Hall') and a very short row of workers' cottages, with steep flights of sandstone steps climbing to first-floor entrances (Plate 10). Then there was the flax and thread mill beside Whit Beck, established in the 1830s on the site of an earlier fulling mill at Tenters, which continued in operation until around 1900. It employed over 30 workers in the 1860s and 70s, some of whom had come over from Ireland. High Lorton grew: it gained a school (built in 1809 and rebuilt twice, in 1859 and again in 1895) and a Wesleyan chapel (1840).

But industrial activity was only one aspect of the profound changes to village society and landscape during the nineteenth century. 'Lorton's green vale' drew the wealthy, who built comfortable houses with a view of the fells. In High Lorton, the house at Lorton Park was physically set apart, divided from the village community by a high, dark-slate wall running down one side of the village street, which enclosed what in Scotland would be termed its 'policies'. It ran the length of the street opposite the houses, forming a hard stone screen, sprouting toad flax and ferns from its lime-mortared face. Behind the wall lay a private world, rarely seen by village people. Lorton Park was one of three villas built in Lorton by an interconnected group of wealthy middle-class families in the nineteenth century. It was built on the site of the northernmost farmstead on the village street, which was set on the opposite side of the road from the others. The property had been bought in 1809 by the Dodgson family of Embleton. Around 1830 John Dodgson rebuilt the house as a Regency villa, probably funding it from his mercantile interests in Liverpool. Like so many houses built for the middle classes in Cumbria in the first half of the nineteenth century, Lorton Park was a product of Lancashire money. The new house, set in gardens containing a fishpond and exotic trees – cedar and weeping birch – faced up the valley and Dodgson's successors, his sister Mary Hutchinson and niece Eleanor Harbord (both of whom had married Liverpool businessmen), gradually bought up the village fields in front of the house between 1837 and 1866, giving them control of all the land opposite the village houses. This they converted into parkland, studded with clumps of trees and enclosed by the mortared, dark-slate wall to provide privacy. Most of the old field boundaries were swept away. At first it was the country retreat for the Liverpool-based family but from the 1880s it became home to three of the Harbord sisters. The leisured world of Lorton Park was epitomised by a royal visit in 1863 (by Prince Arthur of Connaught), an event still talked about in the village a century later. The working life of the village was among the cottages and houses on the other side of the road.

Outside the village a ring of gentlemen's houses was built in the second half of the nineteenth century. These middle-class Victorian villas would have been at home on the fringes of county towns across England: compact detached houses, often with stables and a coach house adjoining, set in an acre or two of gardens and grounds. Families connected to the Harbords built the two houses on the valley floor north of High Lorton. Oakhill was built in the 1850s by the Armistead siblings, the eldest of whom was the curate of Lorton; the youngest the wife of Eleanor Harbord's nephew, William Lancaster Alexander. By the late nineteenth century, W. L. Alexander had assumed the social standing of 'squire' of High Lorton. His sister Mary and her husband John Wilson, from a local family, built another villa, Fairfield, further out of the village, in about 1860. Up on the fellside above High Lorton, on an allotment of former common land was Kirkfell House, built 'in the Elizabethan style' around 1859 and home by the 1870s to Richard S. Whiteside, a retired wine merchant from Whitehaven. In the fields between the two villages were Broomlands (built before 1881), a villa with unimpeded panoramic view of the fells, and a vicarage (1892) two fields away from the church, a spacious house suitable for a Victorian country parson.

The story of Lorton, like that of many villages in the nineteenth century, was one of increasing social complexity and divergence. The growth of a non-farming element at both ends of the social spectrum – industrial workers and servants at one end; the middle classes in their villas at the other – created communities which were rural but no longer predominantly agricultural. Village society was a world apart from the yeoman farms in Whinfell, Mosser and Loweswater, only a couple of miles away.

Boundary stone on Sourfoot Fell, looking across the Loweswater valley. The stone, marked 'L' and 'M', was one of a series put up on the open common after the boundary between Loweswater and Mosser was finally determined in 1827.

CHAPTER 6

BOUNDARIES

Meregill

Where does one place end and another begin? Sometimes there can be no doubt: on reaching the summit of a mountain pass and peering down at a new valley dropping away below us, we leave one world and pass into another. Where, as is so often the case, a watershed marks an administrative boundary – whether between nation states, counties or parishes – we can stand with one foot on each side, aware that we are straddling the meeting point of two distinct places. At a local level, however, boundaries between places – some of them dividing lines of great antiquity – may be invisible, running unmarked along field sides, streams and roads or across open ground.

When I was a teenager in Lorton the horizons within which I felt I knew every inch of the landscape were limited to the areas I explored on foot and by bicycle. As a fourteen-year-old, I cycled to Loweswater most spring and summer Saturday mornings to visit a girl. The cycle ride took me along the narrow back road from Lorton Bridge, past Whinfell Hall to Thackthwaite and beyond. I soon came to know every gradient and turn in the road as I pedalled my old, heavy, iron-framed bike, with its Sturmey-Archer three-speed gears that I could never quite adjust correctly, the few miles to her house. The going got tough when the road, after following the river from Lorton Bridge, turned sharply at Littlethwaite and began its twisting ascent to Thackthwaite. At that point I also became aware that I had left Lorton behind and was entering new territory. It was a strong impression and, although I was unaware of this at the time, it had a sound historical basis. Just beyond Littlethwaite, the road crosses Meregill Beck (Plate 11), a small, insignificant stream trickling along field boundaries, before passing under the road at an angle, unnoticed. I must have crossed it numerous times without even being aware that I was crossing a stream. Yet Meregill Beck marks a major dividing line, a line of cleavage in terms of the history of the valley, separating the lower from the upper reaches and preserving the memory of patterns of ownership back in the Middle Ages. This modest trickle is a major historical boundary, part of the jigsaw of territorial boundaries which forms the framework of the rural landscape.

Meregill Beck is still the boundary between modern civil parishes, the successors to the medieval townships of Whinfell and Loweswater. The two townships lay in different ancient parishes, Whinfell being part of Brigham parish, Loweswater being a distant chapelry of the parish of St Bees, on the coast south of Whitehaven. We know that Meregill Beck has been an ecclesiastical boundary since 1220. At that time, the low fells between Loweswater and Whinfell were disputed territory, particularly when it came to the lucrative rights to the tithes of the expanding crops and flocks of the local inhabitants. Matters came to a head in 1218 when the pope ordered three churchmen from York to decide on the matter of the tithes of Mosser, the community on the back of these hills, and Thackthwaite, the hamlet along from Meregill Beck. In 1220 they ruled that the rector of Brigham should relinquish his claim to the tithes of Thackthwaite, which were confirmed to St Bees, but could take tithes from Mosser on condition that he paid a pound of incense yearly to St Bees. What determined their ruling was feudal lordship: St Bees was the mother church of the barony of Egremont; Brigham that of the honour of Cockermouth. Mosser and Thackthwaite lay in a zone of colonisation along the boundary between the two lordships. Even though both were much closer to Cockermouth and Brigham than to Egremont and St Bees, they were part of Egremont barony, so their tithes belonged to St Bees. These arcane minutiae of local history illustrate the interconnectedness between different aspects of rights and administration over land. The secular townships were nested within larger ecclesiastical parishes, the boundaries of which in turn were determined by patterns of lordship and the boundaries of baronies and manors.

Meregill Beck marked the point at which the seigniorial configuration of the valley changed. Downstream from the point where it trickles into the river, the land on both banks of the Cocker fell within the medieval honour of Cockermouth (and, hence, parish of Brigham); upstream, the Cocker itself became a major medieval boundary, its north-eastern side (the townships of Brackenthwaite and Buttermere) belonging to the honour of Cockermouth; its south-western flank, including Loweswater, forming part of the barony of Egremont. Meregill Beck carries its significance in its name: 'mere', a term deriving ultimately from the Old English *gemaere*, means 'boundary', pointing to the primary cultural significance of this small stream since the thirteenth century, if not before.

Carving space into territories is fundamental to claiming land and creating boundaries between places. It is a process which must have begun millennia ago but which continued until boundaries, like place-names, were frozen on Ordnance

Survey maps in the nineteenth century. One of the Ordnance Survey's main tasks was to record and map administrative boundaries of all levels and to do so in great detail. Boundaries were checked by being drafted out as strip maps in 'Boundary Remark Books' in which local information was collected and inscriptions on boundary stones were recorded. The final large-scale maps laid down the boundaries in definitive detail, tracing each and recording its course: 'c.s.' (centre of stream); 'f.w.' (face of wall); 't.b.' (top of bank); 'r.h.' (root of hedge); 'und' (undefined sight line between two points) and so on. On the Cocker, just downstream from Meregill Beck where the river has changed its course, the surveyors' quest for precision led to a mouthful of abbreviation: 'C.Tk.O.C.S.' ('centre of track of old course of stream').

The maps were formalising and pinning down on paper boundaries which had, in many cases, been established for hundreds of years. Before the Ordnance maps, boundary lines were passed down by word of mouth, transmission across the generations being reinforced by boundary ridings or 'beating the bounds' and, not infrequently from the sixteenth century, by recording a description of the boundary in writing. Beating the bounds was carried out under the auspices of one of the levels of local authority, usually the parish or the manor. The ancient custom of tracing out the boundary of a parish on foot took place at Rogationtide, in late spring, in the week running up to Ascension Day. In areas like the Lake District, where parishes were vast, manorial boundary ridings were probably more common, if sporadic. Whether the parish or the manor was the territory being perambulated, these were communal occasions, reinforcing a sense of community through the process of publicly reciting boundaries. When the bounds of Loweswater manor were ridden in 1792, the tenants needed to locate the boundary line across the open terrain of the fell tops ('over those trackless & desert Mountains – Starling-Dod & Highsteal-Top', as it was put). They marked the boundary by digging 'many Holes … upon the Wastes, at different intervals'. Records of boundary ridings elsewhere tell that, to aid the passing down of communal memory, young lads would be given uncomfortable reminders at key points along the boundary – being held upside down, given 'chinese burns', having their ears pulled or their heads knocked against a boundary stone – particularly where disputes might arise with neighbouring communities.

When boundaries were recorded in writing, they often included a wealth of place-names, some of which are now lost, not having been recorded by the Ordnance Survey. Take, for example, the boundary of the manor of Loweswater as it was described by the manor court jury in 1614. It defined a territory bounded by Buttermere, Crummock and the Cocker, stretching from Meregill Beck at the north to the top of Brandreth at the south and running back to the watersheds around Loweswater. But listen to part of the boundary in detail as it was recorded by the manor court jury. It began:

> at the lower end of 'Mearegill' by 'Drygilbeckfoote' up 'Drygilbeck' to the lake called 'Hulskarth Tarn', beyond the summit and height of 'Threafell' and 'Smyddyfell' to the lake called 'Surfell Tarn', as 'even water' [i.e. 'heaven water'] deals to a stone heap, thus across to 'White Ridding Gill', down the stream called 'Grathwayt' to 'Dubbeck'.

That first section of the boundary tracks a winding course across the low fells from Meregill Beck to Waterend at the head of Loweswater. Some of the names are lost but their locations can nevertheless be identified. 'Drygilbeck' is the headwaters of Meregill Beck, the stream emerging from the dry valley running down the depression between Hatteringill Head and Fellbarrow. 'Hulskarth Tarn', a body of water now drained, lay in that cleft beside Hatteringill Head, the older name of which was 'Ullscarth fell'. The second element of the name is 'scarth', a pass, referring to the gap between Hatteringill and Fellbarrow. 'Threafell' is Fellbarrow on the modern map; its older name may conceivably have originated as 'Threap-fell', meaning 'disputed hill'. 'Smyddyfell' remains unchanged as Smithy Fell. The names of both 'Surfell Tarn', now represented by a boggy hollow near the summit of Sourfoot Fell, and 'White Ridding Gill', now Whittern Gill, have come down to the present in modified forms. This section of the boundary was of particular concern to the manorial authorities because of competing claims with the manor of Mosser which will be discussed later.

Most of the remainder of the boundary of Loweswater recorded in 1614 followed the boundary of the modern civil parish, though there were a couple of exceptions where the manor and the township did not coincide. The boundary excluded the hamlets of Mockerkin and Sosgill, across the watershed, looking over to Dean, which were not part of the manor, though they were part of the parish; the manor extended no further than the 'headgarth' of the two settlements which marked the limit of their farmland along the edge of the common. The boundary then coincided with the modern parish boundary, up another Meregill Beck (this time dividing Loweswater from Lamplugh), along the crest of the fells ('as heaven water deals') over Haystacks to Brandreth. That fell was given its full name, 'Threfooted brandreth', drawing a parallel with a three-legged gridiron over a hearth, probably an allusion to the fact that three manors (Loweswater, Ennerdale and Borrowdale) met at its summit. From there the boundary descended by 'Stroddelbeck' (now Warnscale

Beck) to Buttermere – thus including the fellsides between Haystacks and High Stile which fell outside Loweswater township but were part of the manor – and thence back down the main valley to Meregill Beck. Even a single manor's comparatively simple boundary, almost entirely following watercourses and watersheds, had a complex history, parts continuing to be disputed over many centuries.

In an area like the Lake District, where boundaries so often run along the fell top watershed or along river and lake in the valley floor, it is tempting to see them as somehow 'natural' but this misses the point; the parcelling out of space into territories involved a complex cultural edifice of rights and custom, law and lordship. Ancient boundaries follow the rivers Duddon, Esk, Cocker and Eamont but not the Derwent in Borrowdale or the Ehen in Ennerdale. At local level, a tiny streamlet like Meregill Beck was chosen as a territorial boundary, while much more significant watercourses in the Cocker valley, such as Park Beck and Whit Beck were not. Why? We need to step back in space and time, to think about the claiming of territory, in general terms to begin with.

A starting point is to visualise a landscape devoid of people and then to imagine it slowly becoming populated as groups of humans settled, built houses, tilled land and reared livestock. We might envisage islands of settlement, separated by empty, unclaimed spaces. If we do, it follows that boundaries between settlements would gradually crystallise as neighbouring communities appropriated land and eventually reduced the unclaimed space between them to nothing. The point where their lands met became the boundary between the two communities. Such a scenario may have applied deep in prehistory and can be seen in the final stages of defining territories in medieval – and even post-medieval – times. However, historians of settlement now see that individual farming communities were operating from the Bronze Age, if not before, not in a void of unclaimed space but within a framework of what may be termed, for want of a better word, 'tribal' territories, larger tracts of land appropriated to a higher level of social organisation. Some sort of territorial structure is implied even earlier, in the Neolithic period getting on for 5,000 years ago, when people were working stone high in the central fells at the axe factories in Langdale and around the Sca Fell massif. Even deep in prehistory and deep in the fells notions of territory – of space claimed, of one group's place ending and another group's beginning, of boundaries and boundary markers – are implied by the increasing evidence that this was a peopled landscape, where groups were seeking and exploiting resources five millennia ago.

More extensive evidence of organised space comes from the Bronze Age, three to four thousand years ago. Cairns and field systems strewn over the lower fells, particularly on the south-west and north-east flanks of the Lake District, tell of settled farming communities at that time. It is unlikely that any traces of their territorial arrangements persisted into historic times, since the survival of their cairns and tumbled walls shows that they were abandoned, probably as the goodness was leached out of the soil when the climate became colder and wetter several hundred years BC. Without continuity of occupation, boundaries are likely to have been forgotten. The same is true of the latest prehistoric settlements, the 'native' farmsteads of the Iron Age or Romano-British peoples, which are scattered across the Lakeland dales, though not in great numbers (one example is at the foot of Grasmoor near Lanthwaite Green). Once they were abandoned, the memories of how the land had been held, which fields belonged to whom, which settlements had had rights over which pastures, were lost.

By Anglo-Saxon times, a clearer picture of 'tribal' territories emerges. These created a framework of what has been called 'extensive lordship', whereby superior lords claimed rights over large tracts of land containing multiple settlements, carving the countryside up into blocks of territory each containing a range of environments to provide the resources needed to sustain life. In lowland England this might be a river valley bounded by its watershed, stretching from coastal marshes to hill grazings, for example; in north-western Britain it might be a tract of land between two arms of the sea, stretching from coast to mountain. Communities within this territory would be able to draw on resources at a distance – pasture for sheep on coastal marshes; fuel and grazing for pigs from wooded areas; summer grazing on upland pastures. In the later Anglo-Saxon and Norman periods such a system of extensive resource use was breaking down in the face of population growth and shifting patterns of power and authority. Increasing numbers of mouths to feed put pressure on the unsettled or lightly settled areas of woodland and waste which had provided distant grazing grounds for existing communities, forcing a more intensive use of resources. The boundaries between villages would have crystallised as settlements jostled with their neighbours, claiming patches of woodland on the margins of their land, for example, and dividing it between them as it was grubbed up, cultivated and settled.

Elements of a similar story can be picked out in the Lake District. The evolution of the local medieval territories in the valleys took place within a framework of boundaries which divided the fells between large overlordships. From Norman times these were baronial estates centred on a headquarters in the surrounding lowlands, each estate having a section of the core of the fells, so that their boundaries radiated out, mirroring Wordsworth's 'spokes of a wheel' and respecting geography by following rivers and watersheds. In the western valleys of the Lake District the seigniory of Millom covered all the land between the rivers Duddon and Esk; the barony of Egremont (or Copeland), the land between Esk and Cocker; the honour of Cockermouth, the land between Cocker and Derwent (known as Derwentfells); and the barony of Allerdale, a slice of the fells east of the Derwent, running up to Keswick and Thirlmere. In each of these cases the upland segment of the fells belonging to the estate had the legal status of 'forest' – not in the botanical sense of being largely woodland but as a 'free chase' which was technically a hunting reserve belonging to the overlord (though there is little evidence of hunting actually having taken place). The names of Copeland Forest and Skiddaw Forest, still on the modern map, preserve the memory of their medieval status. These upland 'forests' remained under the control of the feudal overlords, who might grant parts away either to lesser landowners (thus creating new manors) or to monastic houses but who retained large parts in hand, receiving rents and services from peasant colonists as the land was settled and farmed.

When it came to boundaries at local level, the process of fixing dividing lines between places went hand-in-hand with the settling of the Lake District valleys. Most valleys contained cores of early settled land in which boundaries had probably been defined well before the Norman Conquest, and peripheral areas of less immediately attractive land which lay on the frontier of medieval colonisation. At one level, as the township names imply, the whole of an upland area like the Lake District can be envisaged as a frontier zone but, within it, it is possible to identify specific areas of colonisation. These are often found on broken ground around earlier settlements, where boundaries came to be determined and agreed in the era of the written record. The numerous 'thwaite' place-names in the Lake District identify the location of areas of colonisation in these centuries. 'Thwaite' is the Old Norse *þveit*, 'a clearing; a piece of land cut off and separated'. Names including the term are often found in clusters, one of the largest being in the significantly named township of Woodland, near Broughton-in-Furness. In the Cocker valley four 'thwaites' – Littlethwaite, Thackthwaite, Brackenthwaite and Lanthwaite – lie athwart the valley, dividing Loweswater from Lorton. They are in an area of rocky knolls, the largest of which – Brackenthwaite Hows and Redhow – remain partly wooded today. Groups of names like these are shadows of wooded peripheries between cores of earlier settlement. The Scandinavian root of the word 'thwaite' has meant that place-names incorporating it have been interpreted as evidence of Viking colonisation of the valleys before the Norman Conquest. But there is plenty to suggest that some 'thwaite' names originated much later: the first element of Bassenthwaite is a post-Conquest personal name, for example, making it very unlikely that the name predates the Conquest; some 'thwaite' names are recorded as new clearings even in the late thirteenth century; and we know that the meaning of 'thwaite' was still known in Cumberland as late as 1600. Explaining the 'thwaite' place-names, the first historian of the county, John Denton, wrote that 'wee yett call a great plaine peece without bushes a thwaite of land, if it be severed by inclosure'. So 'thwaite' became part of the lexicon of the medieval Cumbrian landscape, probably being used to coin new place-names well into the Middle Ages.

Over these centuries of colonisation, uncertain edges between communities were firmed up and boundaries across them were finally defined. The boundary between Lorton and

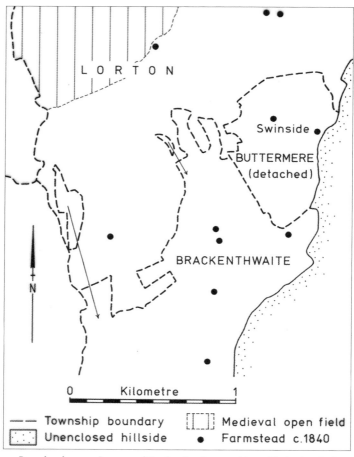

Boundary between Lorton and Brackenthwaite townships, with the detached portion of Buttermere township at Swinside.

Brackenthwaite townships is a case in point. The modern civil parish boundary still follows a crazy route along hedges and field walls, so that fingers of land in one township interlock with fingers of the other. It was even crazier before the 1880s when a block of fields by the Cocker and a single half-moon field on the lane to Hopebeck formed detached portions of

Brackenthwaite, surrounded by fields in Lorton. To confuse matters further, the farms of High and Low Swinside, up on the fellside immediately to the east of this erratic, interdigitated boundary, were neither part of Lorton nor of Brackenthwaite but a detached section of Buttermere township. Unlike boundaries following streams or hill tops, this boundary seems to make no sense. It appears to have been determined by events taking place during the period of colonisation in the twelfth and thirteenth centuries. Lorton was already an old-settled community by c.1170 when Alan son of Waldeof, the lord of Cockermouth, granted Brackenthwaite to Waldeof son of Dolfin. In the grant the limits of Brackenthwaite were stated to be 'from the cultivated land of Lorton as far as Rannerdale'. The 'cultivated land of Lorton' was presumably a fluid boundary, shifting as population growth there pushed the village's lands southwards up the valley. The complex, interlocking boundary with Brackenthwaite is probably the result of piecemeal appropriation of a buffer zone, probably partly wooded, between the two communities. Swinside's status as a detached part of Buttermere was also a legacy of the Middle Ages. Since the area lay within the forest of Derwentfells, any colonisation up the fellsides could be deemed to be encroachment onto the fringes of the private hunting preserve of the overlords of Cockermouth, rather than merely an expansion of the land of Brackenthwaite or Lorton. There were 'assarts' (land cleared for cultivation from woodland) at Swinside by 1259 and the rent for these was paid to the lord of the honour of Cockermouth and came to be collected by the manorial rent collector for Buttermere; hence Swinside's attachment to the township a couple of miles away at the head of the valley.

But some boundaries remained uncertain, particularly when they ran across unenclosed fells, where claims of ownership

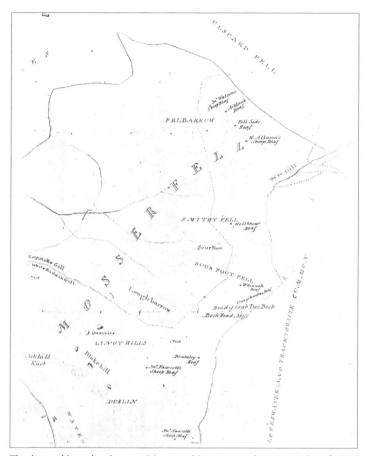

The disputed boundary between Mosser and Loweswater, shown on a plan of 1827. The line down the right-hand side is the boundary claimed by Mosser; the pecked line across the fell tops that claimed by Loweswater, which now forms the civil parish boundary. As the map shows, farmers in Mosser claimed sheep heafs on the disputed ground between the two lines *(CAS, DWM/1/106)*.

were inextricably tied to patterns of use. Contention over grazing rights on a forty-acre area of the common close to the boundary between Loweswater and Lamplugh surfaced in the 1520s, the lord of Lamplugh impounding livestock belonging to Loweswater men and fining them. Harrot, the hill on the boundary between Lorton and Embleton was still disputed in 1705: Lorton claimed the whole of the hill (which today lies wholly in Lorton parish) but the inhabitants of Embleton, it was claimed, 'hath had sheep going on the back side of Arrot for fortie years without disturbance'.

One section of Loweswater's boundary was settled only at a much later date. The smouldering dispute between Loweswater and Mosser over 'Waterendwood' is a striking example of a bank of fellside remaining in contention long after other parts of the boundary network had been settled. 'Waterendwood' was the hillside on the north shore of the lake at Loweswater, between two streams flowing down from Loftbarrow, Whittern Gill and Crabtree Beck (Plate 6). The modern parish boundary follows Whittern Gill, as did the manorial boundary claimed by Loweswater in 1614, but the township of Mosser continued to claim rights as far as Crabtree Beck until the nineteenth century. The roots of these conflicting claims lay in the grant of Mosser by Richard de Lucy, the feudal overlord of Egremont barony, to Adam of Mosser around 1203. The charter spelt out the boundaries of Mosser. What is striking is that Mosser appears to have been a pre-existing territorial unit, with known boundaries even by 1200: where the charter doesn't name a watercourse as the boundary, it uses the phrase 'the boundaries which are' between Mosser and its neighbouring communities, suggesting that these were already established. But the charter then went on to place limits on what Adam and his men of Mosser could do within those boundaries: they could till the land, build houses and clear the wood between 'Raysethwaytbec' (that is 'Graythwaite Beck', now Whittern Gill), Pardshaw and Cat Gill – the boundaries which survived until 1934 as those of the township and civil parish of Mosser

– but could only graze their livestock between Whittern Gill and Crabtree Beck, the area later known as 'Waterendwood'. Herein lay the seeds of contention. Within a century of the grant, the community at Loweswater had colonised part of the land between Whittern Gill and Crabtree Beck (around Grange, Askill and Miresyke), their new enclosures infringing the pasture rights claimed by Mosser. An agreement in 1290, forbidding further enclosure without the consent of the lord of Mosser and granting him 20 acres of land in compensation, aimed to settle the issue. It rumbled on, however, breaking out into lawsuits in the seventeenth century and again in 1827, when the farmers of Mosser wished to enclose their commons and were taken to court for trespass by the lord of the manor of Loweswater. A plan drawn up in connection with the case showed where the Mosser men claimed sheep heafs on the disputed ground.

Details such as these, charting the evolution of the dotted boundary lines on the modern map, illustrate the point that, at this local level, behind the boundaries between townships and manors lay a basic truth, namely that possession is nine-tenths of the law. Who used a particular plot, who profited from tilling it and taking the crop, grazing their livestock, digging peat, quarrying stone – these were the issues which were claimed and counterclaimed in the lawsuits. They were determined by patterns of rights and ownership and, ultimately, it was ownership that so often lay behind how space was divided between townships, manors and parishes. Payment of rent and tithes and the rights to exploit the resources of the land were the deciding factors, both dictating and dictated by the route of the boundary line. On the ground, these local boundaries are generally invisible. Pedalling my heavy bike up the lane and across Meregill Beck, there was nothing other than the name of the beck to tell me that I had moved from one parish to the next, no indication that I was crossing a line which had structured the lives of the valley's inhabitants for at least eight hundred years.

Fell grazings: looking south from the summit of Grasmoor.

CHAPTER 7

COMMON LAND
Brackenthwaite Fell

Grasmoor and Whiteside, steep gable ends overlooking the foot of Crummock Water, are the first of the high fells encountered on the journey up towards Buttermere. Their lower slopes are blanketed in bracken, which gives way upslope, as the soil thins out, to bilberry, shooting vivid green in springtime, and, higher still, among the crags, to heather, flat-brown until it bursts into purple in August. Grasmoor and Whiteside form the core of Brackenthwaite Fell, a block of stony, craggy, mountain ground cut into a number of separate steep fellsides by Gasgale Gill and Hope Gill. It remains common land today, part of the 16 per cent of Cumbria's land surface, most of it in the Lake District, which has that status. Unlike the fell commons of Lorton to the north and Loweswater, across the valley, Brackenthwaite Fell has never been divided as the result of an enclosure award. Covering over 3,000 acres, it makes up around three-quarters of the total land area of Brackenthwaite township, the farms and fields of which cling to the skirts of the fells from Rannerdale down towards Lorton and around the rocky knoll at the foot of Crummock Water, known as Brackenthwaite Hows. Today, Brackenthwaite Fell is part of a larger area of contiguous common grazing, covering over 10,000 acres and stretching up to Buttermere and over the watershed to include the fells surrounding the Newlands valley.

These are the surviving open commons of the medieval forest of Derwentfells, the 'land between Cocker and Derwent' which formed the private hunting forest of the lords of Cockermouth in the Middle Ages. The steep fellsides and long empty valleys running deep into the hills were valued as grazing grounds from an early date. Seasonal use as summer pastures, before permanent farms were established, is suggested by the place-names which include the element 'scale' (meaning a hut, specifically a shieling hut) and in 1270 the lords of Cockermouth used parts of Derwentfells as their own private pastures. They had flocks of 300 sheep in Coledale, the long valley running into the hills behind Braithwaite; a further 350 sheep and 60 goats in Hobcarton, the now-forested valley south of Whinlatter; and more sheep (400 wethers and 100 ewes) at Keskadale at the head of the Newlands valley. As settlements grew and in some cases (Wythop, Thornthwaite, Brackenthwaite) became separate manors, they increasingly claimed exclusive use of the fells adjacent to their farms. Although Derwentfells as a whole retained its identity as a unit of manorial administration into the sixteenth century and beyond, boundaries between townships came to be established, generally following the watersheds so that each community possessed its own section of fell grazings.

As elsewhere across upland areas of England and Wales, the fell commons provided other vital resources for local communities, yielding a range of products essential to the local economy. Vegetation such as bracken, heather and rushes was harvested for a variety of uses and peat was cut from the fell tops as fuel for the fire. The commons were complementary to the farmland of the valley floors. By the sixteenth century they possessed the legal status particular to most common land across the country – they were 'manorial waste', land which belonged to the lord of the manor but over which tenants who held land in the manor exercised use rights. As owner of the soil, the lord retained a number of monopolies (to timber, minerals and game, for example) but his use of the commons was restricted by the legal protection given to the rights of his tenants. The main common rights enjoyed by the farming community were the rights of pasture, which allowed them to graze their flocks and herds on the common; turbary, which gave them the right to dig peat and turf; and estovers, which allowed them to take vegetation of various sorts for necessary use around the farm. By the end of the Middle Ages, the fells were integral to the farming economy, walked over by generations of herdsmen and youths, known intimately in the day-to-day life of the community.

* * *

The greatest economic value of the fells lay in their use as grazing grounds, especially across the summer months. Managing grazing on the unenclosed slopes of the fell commons required cooperation between neighbours, smoothed by conventions designed to give fair and equitable access to the pastures and to foster neighbourly relations between the owners of livestock rubbing shoulders with each other on the open hillsides. The key institution here was the manor court, a local assembly held once or twice a year, usually in spring and autumn. Manor courts were held in the name of the lord of the manor and presided over by his steward, normally a trained lawyer. Decisions were taken by a jury of tenants of the manor – essentially drawn in this area from among the farmers. The courts were local institutions of some complexity, fulfilling a range of functions. They recorded changes of tenant; they adjudicated in disputes between tenants of the manor over matters such as debt;

they made and policed byelaws governing many aspects of local life, including the use and management of common land. In effect, they combined the roles of land registry, small claims court and local parliament. The touchstone of their deliberations was 'ancient custom', sometimes described as *lex loci* ('law of place'), a body of local rules which had evolved across the years. Maintaining harmony (or 'good neighbourhood' as it was often put) on common land was a key part of their role in Lake District manors from the later Middle Ages through to the seventeenth and eighteenth centuries.

The legal framework governing manorial waste required that use of the commons belonging to each community should be restricted to those who were entitled to it. Only animals belonging to those who had a common right could graze the manor's wastes, so manor courts put in place monitoring systems to apprehend 'foreign' livestock. This usually involved appointing men to impound animals which did not have a right to graze. In 1707, for example, Loweswater court appointed four men to drive the commons once a month and impound all livestock which did not belong to tenants of the manor. The manorial pound or pinfold, a small walled garth which still survives at Loweswater on the edge of the former common near Crabtreebeck, would hold the foreign livestock until they were released to their owners on payment of a fee known as 'pound loose'. Other relics of the traditional use of the fell commons lie scattered across the fells. Sheepfolds were built, where flocks were brought to be sorted at each gathering. Other folds, often close to the intake wall, are the remains of washfolds, built beside a deep pool or 'dub', into which sheep were plunged each summer to wash their fleeces before clipping. Short sections of dry stone wall, known as 'bields', were built on the fellsides to provide shelter for sheep in winter, like the group scattered across Swinside End (the windswept hillside at the north end of Brackenthwaite Fell).

The courts also sought to avoid overgrazing by controlling numbers on the common, the usual rule being that each commoner could put no more animals on the common in summer than he could keep over winter on the produce of his land. This limit (known technically as the 'rule of levancy and couchancy') was frequently breached in the Derwentfells area by the practice of wintering young sheep away in the lowlands and bringing them back to the fells in summer. In 1694 the court imposed penalties on three men from Lorton for 'carrying sheepe in winter time below Darwen [i.e. into the lowlands of Allerdale Below Derwent, north of Cockermouth] & for oppressing the lord's common in summer therewith'. A similar practice probably lay behind a case in 1703 when two men were charged with 'over-charging the common in joyning partnershipp with lowelands men for sheepe'.

Within the common belonging to each community, a further network of invisible boundaries divided the open fellsides into the heafs assigned to individual farms. Each heaf was the recognised grazing ground of a particular flock, the section of the common to which they gravitated and which included their 'lairing ground' where they settled at night. The flock's communal knowledge of the heaf and the defence of its boundaries were maintained by the mature wethers (castrated male sheep) which formed a significant proportion of most flocks until the twentieth century, and passed the knowledge down to each generation of lambs. From the Middle Ages, custom determined where the heaf of each flock lay and which route they were to follow up to the fell and, in cases of dispute, custom was moderated by the manor court. One of the earliest references to heafing was at Loweswater court in 1479, when a man was presented for 'wrongful *hefyng* in the mountains'.

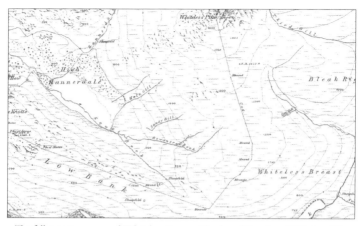

The fell commons around Whiteless Breast. The dotted line from Whiteless Pike to Low Bank is the boundary between Brackenthwaite and Buttermere townships *(Ordnance Survey Six-Inch Map, Cumberland Sheet 69, 1st edition, surveyed 1863).*

Records generated to settle disputes over heafs and gathering places preserve some of the many names by which places on the open fellsides were formerly known. Court orders from the 1670s and 1680s spelling out heafs and gathering places on the fells around Buttermere provide examples of this. Henry Peile's sheep were to lie between 'Ramps Gill' and 'Rontriegill' and he was to gather them to 'great Gate foote'; John Clark was to gather his 'oth back of Peatslacke'; John Norman was to gather some of his at 'Netley Gill'. With the exception of 'Ramps Gill' (a side stream deep in the fells, flowing into Sail Beck) and 'Rontriegill' (probably Rowantree Beck at the head of Rannerdale), these places cannot now be identified, illustrating the poverty of the place-names on the fells recorded by the Ordnance Survey. Occasionally, enough of these minor names can be located to reconstruct something of the lost geography of the heafs. For example, court orders of 1693 settled a dispute 'concerning the gathering and lyring of their sheep' which had arisen between Richard Allason of Buttermere and Robert Stubb, who had holdings down the valley at Beck House and Hollins in Brackenthwaite. Each man had two flocks grazing on the slopes of Whiteless Breast ('Whithills' or 'Whitels' in the manor court papers), the hill between Rannerdale and the Sail Beck valley which formed part of the unfenced boundary between Buttermere and Brackenthwaite commons. The names of the 'antient lyring places' of two of the flocks cannot now be located but the heafs of the other two flocks seem to have been side by side on Whiteless Breast. Allason's 'dray gill' flock (presumably named from Dry Gill, a stream on the eastern flanks of Whiteless Breast marked on the first edition of the Ordnance Survey map but unnamed on modern maps) was said variously to lair 'at the head of the bent under the pikeknots' (probably Whiteless Pike itself) or 'att Murke bottome above Lamb-fold' on the east side of Robert Stubb's heaf. Stubb was to gather his Hollins flock 'in a bottom in the bent on the west syde thereof nigh the Topp', presumably next to Allason's flock. The 'bent' implies a stretch of open grassland, probably identifying the heafs as being along the grassy watershed at the head of Rannerdale on the slopes of Whiteless Breast. The dispute flared up again in 1706 when Robert Stubb junior of Hollins drove his sheep 'contrarie to custom' off Whiteless and over to the wall enclosing Bleak Rigg in the Sail Beck valley, thus crossing the boundary into Buttermere's common. These detailed orders from over three centuries ago remind us that the fells were closely known and peppered with names. Today, only a few survive on the Ordnance Survey map; the rest have faded from memory, leaving many fellsides blank and nameless.

To a shepherd, the common was a patchwork of rights, invisible to outsiders but known and defended by those to whom they belonged. The boundaries between heafs might run up a beck or a gill, along a watershed, or as far as a particular rock outcrop or perhaps a tree. Sheep would keep to a general area but might not respect an unmarked line across an open fellside, so pragmatic understandings needed to be found. Evidence given in a dispute in 1847 by George Addison, a waller who had worked at Gatesgarth, suggests that there was an accepted flexibility in the boundaries of heafs: '170 yards on each side of a Boundary is the usual overlap in Sheep Heafs', he stated.

Each flock was distinguished by its sheep marks – both the red or black 'smit mark' on the fleece and the ear mark nicked into one or both ears – in order to reduce disputes. Further rules of 'good neighbourhood' governing the management of flocks on the sheep heafs were reiterated by the Derwentfells court in 1704: no one was to drive his sheep into another man's heaf to leave them to 'couch or lyar' there, nor to hound or drive other men's sheep from their heaf. Comparable rules were found in many manors across the Lake District to manage the ever-present potential for disputes and conflict over grazing rights on a common. A dialect poem from Westmorland, quoted by F. W. Garnett in his *Westmorland Agriculture* (1912) put it bluntly:

We've fratched and scaulded lang and sair, about our reights on't fell
The number of our sheep, and whaur the heaf was they sud dwell…
And oft we fratched and fret about, and throppled uddar sair,
Upon the whol' the fell hes meade mischief for iver mair.

Mischief on the fells and damage inflicted on sheep surface repeatedly in the records. Individuals were regularly hauled before the manor courts for 'baiting and slating' or 'hounding' the livestock of others on the common, or for 'staffhirding', turning animals back with a stick.

A remarkable instance from Mosser provides a vivid example of friction and unneighbourly behaviour. It is an undated account from somewhere around 1690, preserved in family papers, giving one side of the story of a long-running episode of animosity focusing on a sheep heaf on Fellbarrow. The writer, Peter Fawcett of Mossergate, detailed the abuse he claimed to have suffered at the hands of a neighbour. The Fawcetts had 'enjoyed a heaf of sheep for many years upon a mountaine or hill caled Threefell' (the earlier name for Fellbarrow). Since the death of Peter's father, several of their sheep 'hath been unmercifully almost torn in peeces of which I', wrote Peter, 'with sevrall others have been eyewittnesses, all which concluded it was always one man & one dog that did it because the sheep was all bit alike …'. Matters came to a head when Peter decided to spy on the dog and its master. He took his flock to the fell towards the end of May or beginning of June:

> I carried the sheep to the place whither I had used to carry them (I being Shepherd of them for 14 years last past) and I espied the suspected person with his Dog (& his brother). And I ran for getting out of his sight which I did, but he hastily comming up the mountain, got sight of me again. And he together with his brother came soone after to me and began most foolishly to speak & used much purulent, filthy, irksom matter to[o] tedious here to mention … following me as it were at heels, frumping and jeering taunting & mocking & continually me abuseing to the foot of the mountaine.

Seeing Peter Fawcett heading for home, his assailants went back up the fell 'for no good I had good cause to believe' and Peter later found three of his sheep injured. Since then, the assailant had continued to chase several of Fawcett's sheep and 'stoned them from place to place'. When confronted by Fawcett and others, he 'fell amocking after his awonted manner'. Peter Fawcett concluded his testimony by unveiling the name of his assailant: 'Now if thou ask who it was I shall tell thee it was Peter Robinson of Fellside in Mosser'. Whether this episode was a dispute over the boundaries of a heaf or ill-feeling and personal animosity from another cause boiling over on the fellside, we shall never know.

A perennial source of tension lay in balancing the grazing resources of common land with the numbers of livestock eating them. The temptation to put onto the fell more animals than a farmer had a right to, or to push numbers by seeing how many he could get away with, often led to overstocking. Overgrazing has a long history: manor court records from the seventeenth century frequently include people being fined for 'overcharging' the common grazings and 'oppressing' their neighbouring commoners. At Wasdale Head, on the wildest fellsides on the flanks of Sca Fell, overstocking became a problem by the nineteenth century when the number of cattle being grazed declined, to be replaced by sheep. In a dispute over grazing rights there in 1807, it was claimed that the recent shift away from cattle rearing had resulted in overgrazing. The fells at Wasdale Head were stinted, which meant that each farmer had a right to put a finite number of animals on the common. Stints were usually expressed in terms of 'cattlegates', the number of cattle a stintholder could graze, and conversion formulae were used to determine the equivalent numbers of other livestock. At Wasdale Head the ratio was 15 sheep to one horned beast (a bull, ox or cow), a high figure compared to other commons, where the figure was often 10 – or sometimes only 5 – sheep to one beast. When all the stints were exercised by sheep, the rate at Wasdale Head was found to be 'very unproportion'd and by far too great a Number for a Stint', leading to overgrazing. Reporting on

Eskdale and Wasdale in 1839, the tithe commissioner wrote: 'Far more sheep are kept in the district than the lands will keep in condition' and he predicted it would get worse, as 'the cupidity of each occupier to get as much benefit as he can off the common will lead to an increase in the numbers of the sheep of the district, & as the pastures are insufficient to maintain the present stock of sheep, such increase must necessarily deteriorate the quality & value of the flocks.' These were farmers commenting from an agricultural perspective, thinking about the quality of livestock and carcase, rather than any lasting damage being done to the fells themselves.

Across the nineteenth and twentieth centuries, the numbers of sheep grazing the fells remained high. In Loweswater parish, for example, the total number of sheep stood at around 6,500 to 7,500 in most years from the 1870s to the 1940s. Numbers grew slowly between 1950 and 1980 but then increased rapidly during the 1980s to more than 13,000 by 1988. This was the era of headage payments, which encouraged farmers to keep as many livestock as possible. By the 1990s, it was generally agreed that sheep numbers on the Lakeland hills were unsustainably high and were damaging the fabric of fells – the thin, vulnerable layer of soil and vegetation on which grazing depended. Voracious nibbling and mowing of the fellsides by sheep was seen as destructive of a richer ecology. The Lake District, in the phrase made famous by George Monbiot, had been 'sheep-wrecked'. The tide was turning and a series of agri-environmental schemes provided financial incentives to reduce grazing pressure on the fell commons, not only putting a brake on further growth but slashing the number of sheep in the interests of conservation. At the same time the number of commoners exercising their grazing rights was declining, here as on many other commons. Grazing rights for over 23,000 animals had been registered on Buttermere, Brackenthwaite and Above Derwent Common in the 1960s but, as the number of farms dropped, not all of these were actively used. By 1992 around 13,000 sheep were grazed on the common, a stocking rate of more than two ewes per hectare. There were by then 24 active graziers on Brackenthwaite Fell; by 2011 the number had dropped to 16. After the implementation of a Higher Level Stewardship scheme on the common, which brought the stocking rate down to 0.5 ewes per hectare, the number of sheep was reduced to less than a quarter of what it had been in 1992, a swingeing cut in the number of animals on the fells.

The face of the fells has changed since the 1990s as a result of a focus on nature conservation, which has become a driving imperative in hill farming policy. However, when numbers of sheep are so low, traditional heafing is hard to sustain – a flock will spread out, making it harder to manage. The heafing system which is such a deep-seated part of the cultural heritage of Lake District farming is under threat. The fells may appear greener but in places the lusher vegetation is the tussocky *Molinia* grass which represents a deterioration in the quality of pasture. Some cattle have returned to graze alongside the few remaining sheep but the depopulated common grazings can now feel strangely empty.

***

Competition for resources on the fells was long a feature of other common rights. The right of turbary allowed local communities to dig peat and turf for necessary uses, which included taking fuel for the hearth. Peat was the main fuel across wide areas of north-western Britain until the revolution in transport in the nineteenth century brought coal to even the most remote communities. In some upland areas, where deep peat beds blanketed the moors, it seemed to be an almost infinite resource, but in the fells of the northern Lake District amounts of peat were more limited. Waterlogged fell tops or wet valley bottoms with impeded drainage contained peat but much of the common land of the fells surrounding the Buttermere valley was steep and rocky or grassy and comparatively dry. Places where peat could be won are indicated by names containing the element 'moss': Wythop Moss lies in a hollow hemmed in by hills; Beckhead Moss and Whiteoak Moss are damp gathering grounds at the head of streams; Wandope Moss, not far from the summit of Grasmoor, and Buttermere Moss are wet saddles in the high fells; while Mosedale, as its name implies, is the perennially wet valley between Hen Comb and Melbreak.

Most of the regulations laid down by the local manor courts to govern turbary rights were concerned to limit access to what was a comparatively scarce resource and one which would dwindle year by year as long as peat-digging continued. Shallow and restricted peat beds were finite and non-renewable. In the later seventeenth century, the courts of Derwentfells and Loweswater both made similar regulations. In common with many other courts, they fixed May Day as the earliest date on which peat could be cut, presumably in an attempt to prevent some members of the community from getting in early. Loweswater court laid down in 1671 that no one was to 'grave' peats or turves before May Day and then six years later imposed tighter regulation on cottagers: no-one farming less than four acres was to cut peat before 6 May, 'nor then nor after any more peats then three day works yearly and one hundreth Turfes'. In 1682 Derwentfells court followed suit: no one in Lorton was to dig peat before May Day and cottagers were not to grave any turves before 3 May. As so often with records of this type, it is not completely clear what was going on.

Both farms and cottages would need peat for heating and if the number of landless households was increasing that would put extra pressure on resources. The limits placed on the quantity of peat a cottager could take imply a desire to preserve peat supplies but the delay in allowing cottagers to come to the peat banks hints at something else: perhaps the farming community (from whom the majority of the manor court juries would have come) were closing ranks against the landless, presumably in an attempt to preserve the best reserves of peat for themselves.

In many manors individuals were allocated their own area of peat – their 'peat pot' – from which to win fuel. The local manor court records are silent on this and a nineteenth-century memory from Loweswater, from the days before the fells there were enclosed, suggests that individuals did not have their own peat pots. The tradition, passed on to me by Beth Alexander of Lowpark, who had been told it by an elderly neighbour in the 1930s, recalled that once a year the farmers would gather on the summit of Melbreak to stake out their peat claims on the fell top for the following season. If this was the dying embers of a custom stretching back to the seventeenth century, it would help to explain the manor court orders. In the absence of allocated peat pots, communal self-regulation needed to be applied.

Peat-digging could conflict with other demands on the resources of the fells. One customary rule, found widely across northern England, was the requirement to 'bed' the peat pot by replacing the vegetated sod and digging in such a way as to draw water away, to prevent the dug surface from flooding. Failure to do this could lead to a penalty at the manor court, as in 1688 when Robert Pearson was presented at Loweswater court for 'keeping water' and digging peat in Mosedale Mosses in a manner which caused damage to his neighbours.

Turbary rights also allowed commoners to strip turf for purposes such as repairing roofs, which could likewise have a detrimental impact. In 1715 Derwentfells court sanctioned a group of men from Wythop Mill for digging turf for fuel, as stripping the turf had damaged the pasture of the sheep heafs and prevented others from obtaining vegetated sods ('flakes' or 'flaws') for use in repairing roofs. As with other common rights, the exercise of turbary rights required individuals to act in a way which fostered 'good neighbourhood', being aware of the impact their actions could have on the interests of others. The inherently destructive nature of peat-digging and turf-stripping brought these tensions to the fore.

***

In May fronds of bracken appear across the lower slopes of the fells. They show first as tender fists of pale lime green, dusted with golden down. Silently, the fists unfurl, first folding back to form a crook like a bishop's crosier, then opening fragile side fronds. At this stage, as the days grow warm, the young stems are easily snapped with a clean, sappy break, making them susceptible to trampling by cattle. By late summer, in the August heat, the bracken is a dense forest of hard, dark green stems, almost a man's height in sheltered places, buzzing with flies and acting as a reservoir of ticks, ready to brush onto passing legs. By autumn, it is brittle and blazing golden brown in the October sunshine. Wind and rain, snow and frost beat it down, the winter wetness darkening the dead fronds before they fade and crumble, bleached in the spring sunshine, and the cycle starts again.

Bracken is now regarded as a weed, blanketing everything, clogging pastures. In the twentieth century it seems to have spread, particularly as the horses and cattle which would have trampled and broken the tender shoots in spring have disappeared from the fellsides – the dainty hooves of sheep don't break it in the same way. But some of the spread of bracken may be the result of the end of traditional harvesting of the plant. Within living memory, dry bracken was cut in autumn and gathered in to provide bedding for livestock across the winter. Removing the dead fronds from the surface would have made the plant's rhizomes more susceptible to frost, helping to keep it in check; so the end of mowing it for bedding may also have encouraged its spread.

In earlier times, bracken was a sought-after resource in the Lake District, an integral part of the traditional farming system with multiple uses. It provided a readily-available alternative to straw, not only for livestock bedding but also as thatch for roofing, the hard, shiny stems of the plant being used as 'thack brackens' until slate began to replace them from the later seventeenth century. But the plant was also exploited commercially by burning it into potash, increasing the demand for bracken and leading to competition with its uses around the farm.

Bracken was the vegetation most fought-over under the umbrella right of 'common of estovers', the common right which allowed tenants in a manor to take vegetation for necessary use on their holdings. Its importance in the domestic economy of the Lake District is reflected in the rules laid down by manor courts as they attempted to reconcile its different uses. Specific areas of bracken-covered fellside were accepted by custom as being the 'bracken room' or bracken 'dalt' (dole or share) belonging to each farm; sometimes the courts would assign a 'dalt' to a holding, specifying its boundaries in detail. Taking bracken from the bracken dalt belonging to someone else would incur sanctions through the manor court. In many Lakeland manors bracken harvesting was forbidden before a specified date. Sometimes a distinction was drawn between cutting or pulling the stems for thatch and wholesale mowing for bedding or burning. The former was allowed from late August or early September, while mowing was not allowed until later – Michaelmas day (29 September) or the day after often being specified. Competition for bracken was fierce. In 1690 Derwentfells court ordered that no one in the manor of Braithwaite was to cut bracken before 30 September; 'that none Cut noe Brakens before the sun-rising and that none Cary above one sithe for one Tenement'. As with peat-cutting, cottagers were to wait until three days after the bracken day before starting to mow, to allow the farming community priority. The penalty imposed (20 shillings) was far above the general level of sanctions for breaking the court's orders, underlining the seriousness with which the court was attempting to resolve points of contention. Similar tight restrictions are found in the records of other courts across the Lake District in the later seventeenth and eighteenth centuries.

By that date, much of the competition for bracken was driven by the market for bracken ash. Although taking bracken for commercial purposes broke one of the principles governing the use of the commons (that resources could only be taken for 'necessary use' within the manor), a blind eye seems to have been turned to harvesting bracken for burning, which was widespread across the Lake District in the seventeenth and eighteenth centuries. The market for potash derived from both the manufacture of glass and from soap-making, where bracken ash provided a cheap and effective ingredient for washing cloth. References to bracken burning in the Lake District go back to the early sixteenth century and demand increased, probably reaching a peak in the eighteenth century, when substantial quantities of 'fern ash' were exported to Liverpool. On Stockdale Moor, between Ennerdale and Wasdale, where bracken was burnt under licence rather than through the exercise of common rights, burning continued regularly until 1785, after which no further payments are recorded. By the 1830s the trade in bracken ash had been killed off by the availability of cheap alternative sources of alkali. Only the harvesting of bracken for livestock bedding continued until the second half of the twentieth century.

***

Driving horses, cattle and sheep to and from the fells; trekking to the peat pots to cut fuel in the May sunshine and bringing it home once dry; the urgent mowing and gathering of bracken as autumn closed in – each operation took the local community out onto the fellsides so that the commons became a working landscape humming with activity at points across the year fixed by custom and byelaw. Sometimes gatherings on the commons also had a social dimension. Thomas Rawling of Lanthwaite Green, who died in 1918 aged 88, recalled how a sheep fair which had formerly been held each year on Brackenthwaite common at the foot of Grasmoor had been accompanied by sports, which included wrestling and fell-running (a race up and down Grasmoor).

Gathering other resources from common land also punctuated the seasons. The name Candleseaves Bog, a hollow on the north side of Skiddaw, refers to the collection of 'seaves' (rushes) to make rushlight candles, a regular, mundane part of the annual round, when rushes were gathered each summer in readiness for the shortening days to come. Another raw material, recorded in minor names such as Bayston Bank near Millom and Beckstones Gill at Thornthwaite, beside Bassenthwaite Lake, for example, was stone for use as 'bake stones', the flat stone slabs on which oat bread (the 'havver cakes' which formed the staple of the Lakeland diet) was baked. A stream side where suitably thin slabs outcropped would be an important local resource, visited sporadically, in order to obtain this essential, if simple, piece of kit for the kitchen. Through the name preserved on the map we can visualise a man and his boy leading a pack pony up the steep beckside and imagine the striking of the chisel ringing out across the valley.

Movement of people onto and across the open fells created a network of tracks and paths across common land. Ways led out to the common from the farmland of the valley floors, becoming stony, rough tracks or miry, wet lines beside a beck or up and across the hills. Many of these routes were 'outrakes', along which flocks and herds were driven at the key points in the farming year, or 'peat ways' leading up to the peat mosses where fuel was cut and dried in the summer. In Eskdale, the sheep drifts assigned to each farm by the manor court, dictating the route each flock was to take to its heaf, doubled up as a track to the peat banks on the low fells and the small stone hut (the 'peat scale') in which cut fuel was stored. There, as elsewhere in the Lake District, the routes up the hillsides behind the farms were carefully graded in a series of zig-zags, either short, narrow and steep for packhorses and their panniers, or (later) longer and wider to enable sled-fulls of peat and bracken to be brought down from the fell.

The commons were also crossed by other, longer-distance routes. In the heart of the fells, they included the mountain passes linking the daleheads. Perhaps the best known of these is the Styhead route from Borrowdale to Wasdale, which was recognised as the highway from Ravenglass and Millom to Keswick in the seventeenth century, when it was described as 'so very precipicious as is scarce passable'. These routes over the mountains, through saddles hemmed in by the high fells, were dictated by terrain; on the more featureless moorland commons of the fringes of the Lake District comparable routes across the rough grazings, linking villages and hamlets on the lower land, could be little more than lines marked only by the wear of repeated use. Before enclosure confined them between walls or hedge banks, such tracks were difficult to follow when bad weather closed in or as night fell. If a traveller was expected after dark, a lantern might be hung on the gate at the edge of the common, a frail glimmer to guide him back to hearth and home.

Some of the tracks across the commons have entered popular imagination as 'corpse roads', tracks across wild country along which the inhabitants of a community lacking a churchyard were carried to their final resting place. The two best-known corpse roads both linked an isolated dalehead with no burial ground to a churchyard in a neighbouring valley. One ran from Wasdale Head (where the tiny barn-like chapel did not have its own graveyard until 1901) to Eskdale, five miles away across the windswept saddle in the fells around Burnmoor Tarn. A ghostly tale of horses bolting and coffins lost in mist and snow has served to keep alive in popular imagination the vision of bleak journeys of mourning and loss across that moorland track. The other corpse road, still named as such on the modern map, ran from Mardale at the head of Haweswater across the fells to the parish church at Shap, its first section zig-zagging up the steep valley side from the now-drowned farms. Others have been claimed, largely spuriously, including one from Loweswater, where the fairly level track above Holme Wood on the slopes of Burnbank Fell and Carling Knott is said to have been the road along which bodies were carried to the mother church of St Bees, something which would have been necessary only before the church at Loweswater gained burial rights in the fifteenth century.

The past two centuries have seen a gradual withdrawal of labour from the fell commons: peat fires, rushlights and bakestones have become things of the past and the harvesting of bracken has almost ceased. In the twentieth century the herding of livestock became less intensive as cattle and horses all but disappeared from the common grazings, and the number of farms and, more recently, the number of sheep declined. Seasonal gathering of the sheep on the common fells continues to take place, shepherds on quad bikes speeding up the outrakes to tend their flocks. But fell walkers far outnumber farmers; the fell commons have become primarily places of recreation.

Cinderdale Beck.

CHAPTER 8

WATER

Loweswater

Water is synonymous with the Lakeland scene – in the lakes, in the tumbling becks and waterfalls, and in drenching rain falling from leaden skies. It is easy to take it for granted until confronted by the raw power of moving water or the drowning depths of lake and tarn. Water, flowing and standing, has been a rich resource, yielding fish and possessing the potential to be harnessed as a source of great energy. But it is also, ultimately, untameable – even a modest beck in spate can prevent travel or claim a life; flooding and sometimes wholesale destruction have been a perennial danger. Both its ubiquity and its unpredictability have led to a constant tussle between humanity and hydrology across the centuries.

Loweswater (a Norse name meaning the 'leafy lake') is the only lake to drain inwards, towards the heart of the Lake District (Plate 6). The lake is hemmed in between the steep slopes of comparatively low hills, Darling Fell to the north and Burnbank Fell to the south-west, from which descend fast-flowing becks, Crabtree Beck and Holme Beck. At the foot of the lake, the valley widens into a bowl of farmland, second only in size to the vale around Lorton. The valley-bottom stream both above and below the lake bears the name Dub Beck, referring to its lazy nature (a 'dub' being a pool). After it trickles out of the lake, it is swollen by the waters of two larger mountain becks, Whiteoak Beck and Mosedale Beck, which flow down from deep in the fells behind Melbreak. Gaining momentum, it changes its name, becoming Park Beck as it runs past the church and the Kirkstile Inn. It takes its name in this final section from the thirteenth-century deer park, which stretched back from the north-west shore of Crummock Water around the hamlets of Lowpark and Highpark. Winding, tree-lined, through the fields north of Lowpark, the beck slips into Crummock Water not far from the foot of the lake. Here, it has been tamed: canalised between concrete walls to keep it in its course after the level of Crummock was raised in the late nineteenth century, reducing the stream's fall.

Watercourses are in a constant state of flux, eroding their courses and depositing their burden of silt and shingle. Lakeland becks respond quickly to rainfall and are subject to sudden, sometimes catastrophic floods. On steep slopes with bare rock and thin soils water runs off swiftly to be carried away in surface runnels and trickles and thence to a stream; a cloudburst over the fells can turn a comparatively small beck into a raging torrent. Flash flooding is a constant danger in the Lake District: torrential summer rains or prolonged downpours falling on saturated ground in the autumn can result in dramatic change in the landscape.

Liza Beck, across the valley from Loweswater, like its namesake, the wild tumbling river in Ennerdale, takes its name from the Old Norse word *ljóss* ('light'). Its bright waters struck early settlers as its most noteworthy characteristic, standing out as a shining ribbon of white pouring down from the fells. In its upper reaches Liza Beck rushes down Gasgale Gill, the deep, scree-sided cleft between the bulks of Grasmoor and Whiteside, hidden in the fells. It emerges out of the mountains through a series of waterfalls, breaking milky white over the rocks. Revisiting Liza Beck a few years ago, it took me some time to gain my bearings. The floods of November 2009, which wrought such havoc downstream in Cockermouth, had wiped away the beckside landscape I played in as a child. Near Lanthwaite Green, on the common just above the fell wall, the beck had been dammed and dredged, probably in the 1940s or 50s, to create a pool to act as a 'shilly trap' to prevent torrents of shingle ('shilly' is the dialect term), brought down from Gasgale Gill in times of flood, from being deposited in fields further downstream. The pool was a favourite picnicking spot but, as its water came straight from the fells through the sunless Gasgale Gill, it was invariably piercingly cold; only the boldest dared to bathe. Now the pool is no more. Vestiges of the retaining dam survive in the eroded banks in a desert of boulders and gravel deposited by the flood. It was a similar story up the valley at Rannerdale. The familiar landmarks I remembered there from the picnic places and pools of my childhood had also been swept away, to be replaced by a raw, freshly-cut and rearranged watercourse, carving through rafts of newly-deposited gravel.

The 2009 floods brought back memories of an earlier cloudburst in August 1966, when huge quantities of boulders and gravel were dumped on the meadows and pastures in Borrowdale and Wasdale Head: such was the devastation that the army was brought in to help clear the fields of stones, rebuild walls and repair roads. Similar episodes have formed part of Lake District lore since the region first attracted visitors; they were part of its 'otherness', a terrifying natural wonder, adding a frisson of fear to a tour of the Lakes.

A flood on Liza Beck, often mentioned in travel literature, was 'the bursting of a water-spout' on Grasmoor in September

1760, when water pouring out of Gasgale Gill wrought destruction on the farmland at its foot. Robert Dixon's eye-witness account, published in *The Gentleman's Magazine* later that autumn, described how the water swept away field walls, tore up vegetation and soil, stripping one field to the bare rock, and deposited great quantities of sand and stones. William Gilpin, visiting the scene twelve years later, observed 'many marks remained, still flagrant, of this scene of ruin'. At the foot of Gasgale Gill, he wrote, Liza Beck 'was received by a piece of arable ground; on which its violence first broke. Here it tore away trees, soil and gravel; and laid all bare, many feet in depth, to the naked rock.' It then deposited its burden, covering the ground with 'so vast a bed of stones, that no human art can ever again restore the soil.' Yet, today, the smooth, improved grass of the fields within the intake wall show that the flood's damage was repaired. On close inspection, some of the field walls between Liza Beck and Lanthwaite Gate are 'consumption' walls, around twice the thickness of normal dry stone walls, built to consume stone from the fields. It is tempting to associate these bloated walls with the work of clearing up the stones and restoring the farmland after the events of 1760.

Perhaps the earliest Lake District deluge to be broadcast to a wide audience was the cloudburst at St Johns-in-the-Vale, near Keswick, in August 1749, which destroyed the mill there, cutting a new channel through the rocks and forcing those in its track to climb trees and clamber onto haystacks for safety. George Smith of Wigton gave an account of it in *The Gentleman's Magazine* under the title 'Dreadful storm in Cumberland'. Glimpses of similar events survive in the older written records, one of the earliest being from 1470, when a reduction in rent from a meadow at Wasdale Head was explained by its having been 'wasted by the water'.

Such events became part of communal memory, repeated and passed down across the generations. At Loweswater one particularly tragic flood, at Crabtree Beck early one morning in July 1828, cast a long shadow. The beck had been dammed to supply water to a lead mine, creating a small reservoir on the fellside, about 15 feet deep and over an acre in extent, several hundred feet above the farm of Crabtreebeck. After heavy rains, the dam burst, bringing a cascade of water, earth, trees and rocks tearing down the gill. Hitting the barn at Crabtreebeck, part of the torrent was diverted into the fold in front of the house. A servant girl, hearing the rumble and roar, leapt into the house just in time but her master, Joseph Turrell, carrying his toddler son in his arms, ran out into the yard on hearing the noise. Both were swept away and drowned.

This sad episode illustrates one of the truisms surrounding watercourses – that intervention by someone at one point can have profound consequences for others further downstream (or, in other circumstances, upstream). The mining company who had built the dam for their own purposes had not foreseen (or had chosen to ignore) the potential for catastrophe to the farmhouse beside the beck at the bottom of the fell.

It is not surprising that some of the earliest environmental regulation concerned modifications to watercourses. The principal value of water from the medieval period, for fisheries and as a source of power to drive water mills, involved placing barriers across a stream to divert its flow. As early as 1278, fish weirs on the River Derwent between Workington and Cockermouth were deemed to have infringed the ancient custom that a gap be left, wide enough for a sow and her five piglets to pass through. Almost a century later, in a dispute about a mill dam on the Derwent, it was alleged that the required gap 24 feet wide, known as the 'free water', had not been left. It was important that action downstream should not be to the detriment of others upstream. Maintaining the flow mitigated flooding and allowed valuable fish to pass to traps further up the river.

Fish traps in the rivers and becks (usually termed 'fishgarths') ranged from stone and brushwood banks placed in estuaries to trap fish as the tide receded, to substantial fish weirs to catch salmon in the Derwent and Eden. Smaller 'eel garths' on the lesser rivers of the Lake District proper were typically placed at the point where a beck drained out of a lake. One of the earliest to be recorded was in the fells south of Eskdale, where Linbeck drains Devoke Water. In the late thirteenth century there was a *vallatio ayguillarum* (literally 'embankment of eels') there, containing an 'eel ark' (*arca aygullarum*), a wickerwork trunk or chest in which the eels were held. Many of the 'elyings', 'eel arks' and 'eel garths' recorded in later centuries were probably similar. At Buttermere the 'Elyng' recorded in 1478 was in Buttermere Dubs, the stream flowing between the lakes; a memory of its location was preserved in the nineteenth century in the field-name 'Eel Garth' at the point where the Dubs flows out of the foot of Buttermere.

Mills also involved modifying flow, by diverting part of the stream into a man-made channel to feed the mill wheel, either directly or via a millpond. Most agricultural communities possessed a corn mill by 1300, to which the manorial tenants were bound by custom to go to grind their corn. In the Cocker valley each of the three main areas of ploughland (in the wide Vale of Lorton, at Loweswater and on the flats between the lakes at Buttermere) had its own watermill by an early date. A mill at High Lorton was mentioned in the mid-twelfth century, that at Buttermere some time before 1215 and that at Loweswater by 1305. Water was also used

1. **Buttermere from Melbreak.** The village and its former open fields lie between the lakes; at the head of the valley is the sharp prow of Fleetwith Pike with Gatesgarth at its foot.

2. **Crummock Water from Low Fell**, with the bulk of Grasmoor to the left and Melbreak on the right. At the foot of the lake the valley broadens out to the farms in Brackenthwaite and Loweswater townships.

3. Lorton Park looking towards the distinctive saddle of the peak known locally as Hobcarton but to the Ordnance Survey as Hopegill Head.

4. Palacehow at the foot of Brackenthwaite Hows with Grasmoor towering behind. The name Palacehow replaced the older name, 'Withebeckraine' or 'Withmoorcrane' in around 1800.

5. Memorial to the Mirehouse family of Miresyke in Loweswater churchyard.
The Mirehouses were at Miresyke by 1614 and continued to hold the farm until the 20th century.

6. Loweswater from Melbreak. The lost farmsteads of High Iredale and Stockbridge stood somewhe
in the fields in the foreground. The fellside to the right was the disputed ground of 'Waterendwood'

7. Godferhead, Loweswater. The mullion-windowed farmhouse dating from
the 17th century is dwarfed by the Georgian wing dated 1773.

8. The Vale of Lorton from near Swinside, looking over the irregular fields around Scales to the villages of High and Low Lorton, with the Cumberland Plain beyond.

9. Hatteringill, Whinfell. Plough ridges and circular stack stands surviving from the 1840s when the former common was cultivated after enclosure.

10. Cottages in High Lorton, built in the early 19th century
for workers in the brewery there, established by the Jennings family.

11. Meregill Beck, the boundary between Whinfell and Loweswater.

12. Looking down to Rannerdale and across Crummock Water from Grasmoor.

13. Buttermere church

14. Memorial to Fanny Mercer below Low Raven Crag on Fleetwith Edge.

15. Innominate Tarn

to power fulling mills which beat and thickened woollen cloth. Some were recorded in the century before the Black Death (one was built at Whinfell around 1282; there was another at Embleton in the early fourteenth century), but the number grew in the fifteenth century. There were two fulling mills at Brackenthwaite by 1437 and a licence had been granted by then for a third. At Loweswater, land beside Mosedale Beck had been set aside for building a second fulling mill. At Lorton the 'Overcornemylne' (later known as High Mill) had been converted into a fulling mill by 1478 and a new fulling mill was built at Tenters (the name recording the stretching of woollen cloth on hooked tenter frames after it had been fulled) around 1480. At each mill site, part of the flow was diverted by means of a weir to flow down a narrow artificial trench – the mill leat – falling less steeply than the beck itself to a point where it could be directed to turn the mill wheel before being returned to the beck below the mill. Damming a watercourse in this way inevitably affected the flow of water. When, around 1517, a new corn mill was built on the River Cocker (the mill later known at Lorton Low Mill) it was reported that 'in time of storm' the weir across the river 'obstructs the water so that it overflows ... in Whinfell and destroys and devastates the corn and meadow and grazing grounds of the tenants there to their grave damage and nuisance.'

Maintaining watercourses in good order was one of the areas overseen by the manorial courts, since it concerned the common good. Failure to keep water in its correct channel fell into the category of 'common nuisance', that is 'things done to the common grievances of many'. A lawyer's court-keeping manual of the seventeenth century notes that a court leet should sanction those who offended 'in the common waters, by stopping, turning, or corrupting [i.e. polluting] them, to the hurt of them that use them'. Responsibility for keeping the water in its 'right course' lay with the community. In 1503 the tenants of High Lorton were brought before Derwentfells court for failing to confine Whit Beck in its course; in 1723 the tenants of Thackthwaite were required by Loweswater court to keep Thackthwaite Beck in 'the antient and right course'. At Whinfell court in 1518 it was reported that the tenants of Low Lorton had failed to clear the course of Whit Beck at 'Whitebekfute', so that 'the said water in time of spate overflows the lord of the manor's land in Whinfell held by Richard Allenson'. Within the community, responsibility lay with the individuals through whose land a watercourse flowed: as it was put in a later case (in 1681), maintenance of the 'water races' in the fields belonging to Low Lorton 'hath beene usually carried along from neighbour to neighbour'. In the vicinity of Braithwaite, where several becks pouring out of the fells converged onto the wide flat valley floor between Derwent Water and Bassenthwaite Lake, keeping the water out of the roads and fields was a perennial challenge. The manor court there appointed 'watter lookers' to ensure that individuals fulfilled their responsibilities for turning the water and cleansing watercourses.

Keeping the water in its right course involved a range of operations: scouring or dredging to keep the channel clear, cutting back vegetation, strengthening the banks by facing them with stones or interwoven hurdles (the latter being termed 'wyndyng and spylyng' at Millom in the early sixteenth century). The cumulative effect of these obligations was to contain becks within their channels from the moment they left the open fell and entered farmland. Channels grew deeper and the flow faster; an untamed mountain beck became part of the controlled and managed landscape of the fields. And the fields themselves channelled the flow of water. The ridge and furrow of ploughing created parallel furrows into which water inevitably migrated, while banked and ditched field boundaries drew water to the ditch which sometimes became an open gutter. As a result, natural patterns of drainage were altered to conform to the shape of the fields. This can be seen on the Ordnance Survey's 25-Inch plans where a field bank and a stream running side-by-side often appear as parallel lines. Springs were captured in troughs to provide drinking water for homes and livestock in farmsteads and villages. Much of the pattern of drainage on the valley floors and lower slopes of the fells is the creation of human activity across many centuries.

In a land of high rainfall and mountain becks, crossing watercourses safely determined the routes of the network of roads and lanes. Small streams running by field sides – now culverted so that most travellers cross them unawares – could be left to flow across a lane, or partly covered with a 'rammel stone', a large flat flagstone, to keep foot passengers dry. But larger watercourses could only be crossed at a point where a ford or a bridge could be established. Between Crummock Water and the outskirts of Cockermouth the Cocker is crossed by only three bridges, two of which were fording points of great antiquity. The first coming upstream from the town was at Southwaite, where there was a bridge by the mid-seventeenth century. The earliest record of the name, written as 'Sowewad' in 1308, shows that the second part of the name was not 'thwaite' but 'wath', the Old Norse term for a ford; the name may have meant 'sheep ford'. The seventeenth-century bridge at Southwaite was later washed away: the crossing was a ford again for much of the nineteenth century, until the present bridge was built in 1890.

At Scale Hill, near the foot of Crummock, was a second early fording point. Scalehill Bridge was formerly known as 'Deepa Bridge'; somewhere nearby was 'Depewathcrag', recorded in 1525. The name occurs earlier as 'Dupwath', a place recorded in 1286, when there had been a dispute relating to obstruction of the way which led 'from the chapel of Loweswater to Dupwath towards Brackenthwaite'. 'Dupwath'/ 'Deepa' probably means 'deep ford', the second element again being 'wath'. It describes a deep fording place in the Cocker at the foot of Brackenthwaite Hows, across which men and horses were passing seven hundred and more years ago. In both cases, the names predate the bridges, recording their precursors in the road network, rare and valuable places where the river could be traversed in comparative safety. It is not clear whether the third bridging point on the Cocker, at Lorton, was similarly ancient. There was a bridge there by at least 1630 (the first record of the farm-name Bridgend in the parish register) but no hint of a place-name indicating a ford.

When bridges replaced fords over smaller streams is less easy to discover. Many would at first have been of wooden construction, some as simple as a log or two thrown across a beck. Such structures seem to be recorded in the name 'Stockbridge', which occurs several times across the Lake District, 'stock' being an Old English term meaning 'log'. It was the earlier name for Maggie's Bridge at Loweswater, recorded in adjacent field-names. The name occurs again near Low Lorton, recorded fleetingly in 1640. When the county bridges were surveyed in 1764, all three in the Cocker valley – Deepa Bridge, Low Lorton Bridge and the bridge over Whit Beck at High Lorton, which carried the pre-turnpike road over the fells to Keswick – were of mortared stone with 'battlements' on each side. Both bridges over the Cocker were narrow, two-arched structures, only 6 feet wide. Deepa Bridge, said the surveyors, 'consists of two arches, the western one 24 feet long. The pillar 9 feet thick. East arch

25 feet 6 inches long. Breadth between the battlements 6 feet. Height of battlements 1 foot 6 inches'. Less important bridges were the responsibility of local communities. In 1682 manor court orders record that the bridge over Sandy Beck was the responsibility of the inhabitants of Whinfell township and that, over the fells in the Braithwaite area, the township supervisors of highways could require individuals to cart a share of the stone needed to repair the bridges there.

From the nineteenth century the scale of the modification of watercourses escalated. As bridges were rebuilt and widened and their abutments strengthened, streams were channelled and constrained further, confining and increasing their flow and often causing scouring downstream from the bridge piers. Where field boundaries were redrawn to create straight-sided parcels of land, streams were often modified to fit the new boundaries. The final section of Whit Beck, where it crossed the former open fields of Low Lorton, was straightened when the fields boundaries were rearranged, probably in the 1840s, for example, as was Warnscale Beck at the head of Buttermere. The increased flow brought problems, not least in times of spate, when retaining walls might be undercut and fans of gravel deposited on the fields. A century and a half later, canalised streams are being 're-wilded'. A programme of restoration work on the straightened section of Whit Beck in 2014 has re-introduced curves in order to reduce erosion.

More dramatic changes to the hydrological system came in the creation of reservoirs for industrial use and to supply drinking water. The damming of Crabtree Beck to serve the lead mine at Loweswater in the 1820s, which had such fatal consequences, is just one instance. A reservoir was built beside High Nook Beck on the fells opposite, later in the Victorian period, to serve the lead mines there. Another was constructed on the slopes of Kirk Fell in 1935 to supply water to the villages of High and Low Lorton. But the biggest scheme was the raising of the level of Crummock Water under an act of Parliament of 1878, to supply drinking water to Workington and Cockermouth. A low dam at the lake's foot raised the surface of the water by around 3 feet. A salmon ladder was incorporated, to allow fish to swim from the Cocker up into the lake, and a pump house (of municipal sandstone) was later built. The boathouse in Lanthwaite woods, which had stood on the lake shore, was now almost surrounded by the lake. Low-lying fields north-west of the lake were drowned and rush-infested, despite being protected by a low retaining wall along the shore, as the higher lake level impeded drainage. Although this was not the transformation of a natural lake into a man-made reservoir on the scale seen at Thirlmere or Haweswater, Crummock is one of a large number of lakes and tarns in the Lake District to have been modified by damming to supply water for villages, towns and industrial purposes.

Largely hidden from view, but profound in its consequences, has been the introduction of field under-drainage across the past two centuries, to reduce waterlogging of soils and improve the land. The furrows between the ridges in ploughland and the ditches along field boundaries were early ways of improving drainage, channelling water away from growing crops. But a more determined effort to improve drainage by constructing underground channels began in the eighteenth century. Early field drains took the form of hollow drains, filled with stone or brushwood and covered with soil, to carry water away. At Mosser, Isaac Fletcher installed brushwood drains in one of his meadows in 1756 and also experimented with stone drains ('Intend to cobble the drains', he wrote in 1773) and sod drains. In 1778 he had three drainers cutting drains in another of his meadows: 'They make them slouping above to the shoulder and open below, putting in the top sod as it came out, green side up' but the following year he was again gathering stones for filling the drains.

A revolution in field drainage came in the first half of the nineteenth century with the introduction of tile drains. At first these were horseshoe drains, where a sheet of clay was folded so that its cross-section formed a horseshoe shape. After firing, horseshoe tiles were set lengthways end-to-end to form the drain, the open sides placed downwards, resting on the subsoil or on a 'sole' of slate. The manufacture of drainage tiles reached Cumberland around 1820; as in other counties, horseshoe tiles were superseded by circular pipes in the 1840s and mechanisation of production led to a rapid expansion of under-drainage in the same decade. Tile works sprang up wherever a suitable source of clay could be found. Near Aikbank in Mosser, Jonah Dixon of Toddell set up a tilery which operated during the 1840s; waterlogged depressions in the field still mark the site of the clay pits. Another tilery had been established at Hundith Hill in Embleton by 1839; it was operated in the 1840s by John Murray. Both were short-lived ventures run by local farmers during the first phases of mass drainage, before large-scale mechanised production took over; they had gone by the 1860s.

The scale of under-drainage reached a remarkable degree of sophistication in the Vale of Lorton during the later Victorian era, through the energy and commitment of one man, William Lancaster Alexander (1821-1910) of Oak Hill. The son of a Liverpool merchant and shipping inspector who had inherited property at Shatton through his mother, he became the unofficial squire of High Lorton and a prominent local philanthropist. His most visible legacies are public watering troughs, substantial structures providing an essential service in the days of horse-drawn vehicles. One beside the road near Casshow Wood carries the date 1873; another in a field by the lane from High Lorton to Scales is inscribed 'This watering place was erected by W. L. and Frances Alexander in the year of Queen Victoria's jubilee 1887'.

But his most lasting legacy lies below ground. This is the 'Lorton Main Drain', a complex of field drains carrying sub-surface water from the low-lying fields on the valley floor north of Low Lorton, and from the boggy ground in Whinfell between Sandy Beck and the northern flank of the fells. Alexander was the driving force behind the project, which required sophisticated engineering and a high degree of organising and coordination. A total of eight drains flowed into the Main Drain which ran beside the River Cocker, eventually emptying into the river near Stanger. The scheme involved three river crossings, where the drain ran beneath the Cocker, and the construction of drains through the land of no fewer than fourteen landowners. A deed to regulate the drainage system was drawn up on 31 December 1881, naming the landowners responsible for maintaining each section of the drains and the vitally important junctions between the pipes. Each landowner could add new field drains to the system (as long as they were for under-drainage and were not used to carry off surface water). To protect the system, trees were not to be planted within 25 yards of the drains. A set of memoranda accompanying the deed, recorded that the drain lay between 5 and 9 feet below the ground surface, with a fall varying between 1 in 100 and 1 in 1,000. The final section was a culvert 22 inches wide by 30 high. As the branch drains peeled away, the diameter of the drain gradually reduced, first to a 24-inch glazed sewage pipe, then gradually to pipes of 6-inch bore. One hundred and forty years later, the drain continues to function, though the lower sections back up when the river level is high. W. L. Alexander recognised that the outfall was a weak point, suggesting in the memoranda that if Southwaite Mill, half a mile downstream from the outfall, could be bought by local landowners and the mill weir removed, the river would be deepened and the outfall improved.

* * *

'Eternity flows in a mountain beck', wrote the poet Norman Nicholson. The power of water (vital for life, yet possessing great destructive force and capable of taking life away) endows it with symbolic potency most clearly seen in the ceremony of baptism. Places where water emerges from underground have had a powerful draw for many centuries and springs and wells have been considered holy places. The British landscape is dotted with such sites, born of a veneration for water found in pagan Celtic and Anglo-Saxon belief and adopted by a millennium and a half of Christian tradition.

Compared to the richness of spiritual association in the landscapes of the Celtic west, the Lake District is distinctly lacking in springs and holy wells bearing saints' names. There are a few. St Oswald's Well at Grasmere and St Patrick's Well at Patterdale were both recorded in the late seventeenth century, although their names may have been borrowed from the dedication of the local churches, rather than recording ancient sites of water veneration. Two 'holy well' sites have been claimed in the catchment of the Cocker but one of them is almost certainly spurious. That is the well at Stanger Spa, in the wettest corner of a damp field beside the Cocker at the foot of the Vale of Lorton, confidently marked in Gothic lettering as a holy well on the modern Ordnance Survey map. The saline well at Stanger, known for its supposed medicinal qualities, was drawing visitors by 1738, when a 'shelter' of some description had already been built over it. Despite attempts to suggest that the name Stanger is a corruption of 'St Anna' (place-name scholars are fairly confident that it actually derives from the Old Norse *stangir*, 'the posts or stakes'), there is no real evidence that this was ever a holy site. The more likely candidate as a holy well is not even marked on the modern map. This is 'St Ringan's Well' at the head of Loweswater beside Fangs Brow, the steep road leading over to Mockerkin. It is recorded on the tithe plan of 1839 as the name of a small field behind a watering trough on the roadside below the farm at Fangs. 'Ringan' is a variant form of Ninian, the name of the British saint associated with Whithorn in Galloway, whose cult extended into Cumbria in the Middle Ages. This shadowy evidence linked to a roadside cattle trough is the only hint we have of an early sacred watery place in the Cocker's catchment. But the power of water has held a fascination that transcends its utilitarian value. Land and water may have been tamed and exploited to provide a living throughout history but this is only part of the story.

Scale Force.

CHAPTER 9

WOOD AND ROCK

Scales

Heading upstream towards Buttermere the fells press in more closely. The western side of the valley from Melbreak to Warnscale Bottom is now devoid of settlement; it is a place of rock and water and, beyond Scale Beck, of woodland on the lower slopes. The geology changes: the journey from Cockermouth has so far been through country underlain by the Skiddaw Slates, the purple-grey, thinly fissured rocks which form the smooth, whale-backed fells of the northern Lake District. At the head of the valley the underlying rock is the craggier Borrowdale Volcanic series of the central Lake District. The boundary sweeps around the dalehead – the summits of Fleetwith, Haystacks, High Crag and High Stile are formed of the Borrowdale Volcanics. Between the two rock types, around Red Pike, the rocks are different again, composed of a pink granite known as syenite or 'Ennerdale granophyre'.

Scale Beck rises in a hanging valley between Red Pike and Gale Fell, drops over the steep northern flank of the fells as the dramatic waterfall of Scale Force, hidden in a deeply-incised chasm, then runs through boulders of the pinkish-orange granophyre over wet ground, glistening with a sheen of oil from the peaty soil, to Crummock Water. In autumn sunshine it is a place rich in colours: the pink of the granophyre; the golden brown of the bracken; rowans heavy with red berries; the gorse still flowering, buttercup-yellow. A range of colours occurs in minor place-names on the fellsides nearby, picking out distinctive hues in the landscape: Black Beck, Ruddy Beck, Blea Crag ('blea', a word with no direct equivalent in modern English, meaning 'dark' or 'bruise-coloured'), Grey Crag and White Cove. Over them stands Red Pike, named from the reddish hue of the granophyre, accentuated by the raw red scar up the scree to the summit, eroded by fell walkers.

Below Scale Force, Scale Beck divides into two distributaries which hug the sides of a fairly level delta spreading to the shore of Crummock. When the bracken is down, the tumbled walls of a medieval settlement can be seen, spread out along the flanks of the beck and across the delta inland from the lakeshore. If the bracken is low enough, the shapes of simple rectangular buildings, the small enclosures surrounding them and the trackways linking them can be picked out.

Exploring the site in the early 1970s, I stumbled on the remains of an amateurish excavation which had thrown up small pieces of green-glazed medieval pottery and lumps of iron slag. These finds provide clues to the use of the tumbled buildings, which give the name to the whole of the walled stretch of fellside between Scale Beck and Sourmilk Gill. 'Scales' or, more precisely, 'Buttermere Scales', takes its name from these tumbled huts, 'scale' being the dialect term for a hut, derived from the Old Norse *skali*. It seems very likely that these particular 'scales' are referred to in medieval documentation. Despite being closer to Buttermere, Scales was within the bounds of the manor of Loweswater. The survey of Loweswater on the death of Thomas de Lucy, in 1305, included income from four 'Skale'. 'Scales' are usually thought to mean shieling huts, seasonal dwellings on summer grazing grounds, where herdsmen and milk maids camped while tending the livestock, but the term could be used for a range of structures, such as the sheds or 'peat scales' in which cut peat was stored. It could also be applied to the huts of industrial workers, as it was in the case of the medieval lead miners on Alston Moor in the Pennines. If the 'scales' in Loweswater manor were indeed here, it seems most likely that the term in this instance referred to a cluster of industrial workers' huts. The iron slag among the footings of the huts suggests this, as does their location: the fellsides around Scale Beck yielded the raw materials for iron working. Small veins of iron ore outcrop around Scale Force, showing as a red stain among the screes. Trial diggings in the early 1870s revealed them to be too small to warrant the capital investment needed for modern mining but they may well have provided sufficient ore for the much smaller-scale medieval iron industry. Woodland on the lower slopes of the fells would have provided the charcoal needed to smelt the ore – the tell-tale circular platforms ('pitsteads') on which charcoal was made survive a couple of miles away in Flass Wood and a few can be found on what are now the treeless slopes of Melbreak overlooking Scale Beck. The iron industry of the southern parts of the Lake District is well-known and was far more extensive and of longer duration than here in the Buttermere valley, but charcoal burners and bloomery forges were in these valleys in the Middle Ages as well, not only here beside Scale Beck but also across the lake by Cinderdale Beck near Rannerdale.

It is a long jump back in time to the iron smelters of the era before the Black Death, when the sound of their hammering would have rung out across the valley and smoke from their charcoal pits might be seen rising from the woods. When the huts were abandoned is not known, but they had probably gone by the sixteenth century. It is tempting to think that Scales was the location of some 'scalings' (huts) on the common where two miscreants, hauled before the manor court in 1519, were suspected of harbouring 'wicked thieves'. Perhaps these were the last flickerings of life in the cluster of 'scales' beside Crummock, by then little-used and falling to ruin, a remote place for people on the margins of society.

The remains of the huts below Scale Force lie within an enclosure covering more than 300 acres, separated from the open fells above by a wall which follows Scale Beck and then runs across the slopes of Red Pike from Scale Force to Sourmilk Gill. It encloses both woodland (at the southern end) and open rough grazing. In manorial records, under the name Buttermere Scales or its alternative name, 'Green Lussack' (or variants such as 'Greynlussoke' and 'Graynlusseck'), the history of this bank of fellside can be traced back to the fifteenth century. 'Green Lussack' was part of the mountainous tongue of Loweswater manor, which stretched from the shores of the lakes to the crest of the fells from Haystacks and High Crag to Red Pike. Like other banks of mountainside deep in the heart of the Lakeland fells, the area was not normal common land but private pasture belonging to the lord of the manor which would be leased for a money rent. The grazing of Birkness (corrupted on the modern map to 'Burtness') was so leased in the fifteenth century and 'Graylussok' enters the written record in 1453, when it was described as a 'close in Lowsewaterdale' and was leased for an annual rent of 20 shillings. In the earliest surviving account roll for Loweswater, dating from 1437, it is perhaps to be identified with land called 'lez Cowmes' for which the same sum of rent was paid. 'The Combs' would be an appropriate name for the steep fellside containing the sculpted corries of Bleaberry Tarn and Ling Comb. It is likely that charcoal burning was still taking place there at this period, as the previous entry in the 1437 account records a payment for 'winning coal' from William Rawlynson (a significant surname, as it is common in Furness Fells, the heartland of Lakeland charcoal-burning).

However, it is as grazing ground rather than woodland that Buttermere Scales comes into focus in the historical record. By 1614 it was a pasture in which thirteen tenants from Loweswater held grazing rights, for cows in the summer months from 1 May to 15 August and for young sheep ('hoggs') across the winter from 1 November to 25 March. Although it was described as a 'close' in 1478 and had presumably been demarcated in some way, the boundaries of 'Green Lussack otherwise Scale' were confirmed by the manor court jury in 1740 when they ordered a new wall to be built, very probably the wall which today weaves across the fellside from Scale Force to Sourmilk Gill. The boundary described in 1740 picks out the subtleties of the fellside topography. Starting below Scale Force (at 'the Force-foot'), it ran to the foot of Blea Crag 'and so up a Green Slack to a Level a little above', then across to the head of Far Ruddy Beck 'in the most convenient place where a Wall or Hedge may be sett'. It then ran on the level through 'Latten hows' (a name now lost) to the middle of 'Blaiday-Beck', the older name of Sourmilk Gill. The wallers working across that rough terrain, fitting the wall where it was most 'convenient' across the two years from 1740, created the framework of the landscape we have today. The controlled grazing regime within those boundaries, literally fixed in stone by the new wall, may have helped to preserve the woodland in Scales.

Today, Scale Wood, hanging on the steep fellside between the lakes, is one of the larger blocks of deciduous woodland in the valley. The oaks of the lower slopes give way to a more open woodland of rowan and birch – not the shimmering and elegant silver birch but the more sombre and dowdy downy birch – on the upper slopes. How old the wood is in its present form is unclear. Writing in 1800, John Housman noted that, from a distance, the slopes 'appear covered with a thick wood' but, on closer inspection contained 'only a few straggling trees, interspersed among the rocks'.

Until the nineteenth century the valley as a whole contained comparatively little woodland, though hedgerow timber across the farmland of Loweswater and the Vale of Lorton exaggerated the wooded character of the lower sections. Woodland survived mainly where land was unsuitable for other uses – in gills on the fellsides and on rocky knolls on the valley floor, such as Casshow, Redhow and Brackenthwaite Hows, and on the broken land around Wood House in Buttermere. As elsewhere in the Lake District, where woodland on the tenants' farms belonged to the lord of the manor, its use was governed by custom. Typically, a distinction was drawn between large timber of oak and ash ('woods of warrant'), which could only be cut for house-building and repair by licence from the lord's bailiff, and 'underwood', the smaller wood of species such as hazel, alder and birch, which tenants could cut for fuel and other necessary uses. Rights to woodland on the tenants' farms were one of the areas of contention between lord and tenants in the late sixteenth and early seventeenth centuries. In 1597 the lord of the manor of Loweswater claimed that the tenants could only take underwood, although, after seeking legal advice, it was agreed that they had rights to the traditional 'botes' from trees growing on their own farms: 'house-boote' (timber for the repair of houses), 'fire-boote' (fuel for the hearth), 'plough-boote', 'cart-boote' and 'hedge-boote' (wood necessary for farming, as their names imply). When the customs of Loweswater manor were agreed between lord and tenants in 1619, the tenants' rights were confirmed but a piece of woodland near Bargate was set aside as the lord's wood.

As demand for charcoal increased, many patches of woodland were enclosed to protect them from livestock and were managed on a coppice rotation. This enabled a lord of the manor to raise income by selling the coppice crop for charcoal, which may have been the way in which most woods in the valley were being managed by the eighteenth century. When William Gilpin visited Buttermere in 1772, he noted that the north-east side of the valley was more wooded than the other and that the woodland was 'of that kind, which is periodically cut down' – in other words, coppiced. Such a strategy seems to have been under discussion in 1718 when Henry Westray was commissioned to report to the estate office at Cockermouth Castle on the potential value of woods for charcoal. In Buttermere, he wrote, there was 'wood both for Cole and thriving wood but [it is] Damnyfied by topping'. He seems to be describing a mixture of coppice ('Cole' wood), standards for timber ('thriving wood') and pollards (trees which had been 'topped' several feet above the ground to enable a crop of poles to sprout out of danger from grazing animals). From a forestry perspective, as Westray said, pollarding damaged the trees by preventing them growing into timber – as he put it elsewhere in his report, 'when the tops is cut of[f] the tree generly takes water & when they are watered it hinders them to thrive'. Pollarding had been a long-established practice, particularly for ash trees, which yielded a crop of poles for use about the farm, as well as nutritious leaves and bark as fodder for livestock. It had ceased by the mid-twentieth century. Ancient ash pollards survive across the Lake District on the edges of fields, some now hollow trunks, split apart by the weight of overgrown, uncut poles. Others have been re-pollarded in recent decades, reviving this part of the Lake District's farming heritage.

* * *

The history of how woodland and rock have been used in the Lake District are intertwined. Both were essential raw materials in the traditional economy. The rock of the fells yielded not only stone for building but, in places, precious veins of metal ore. In the 'wood age' before the era of iron and coal in Victorian times, the uses of woodland extended from timber for buildings and the making of tools and utensils, to fuel for the home and – importantly – for industrial hearths as well. Releasing the minerals locked up in the fells required wood to create the charcoal needed to smelt the ore. Woodland and minerals were high-value raw materials, controlled by those in power. Access to both was governed by lords of the manor, who possessed the mineral rights to stone and ore across their estates and retained ownership of all woodland, even when it grew on the farms of their tenants. The story of the exploitation of rock and wood is thus bound up with landownership and, because mining and quarrying were expensive operations, it is also a story of external influences.

Though mineral rights (which embraced both rights to rock and to the valuable ore-bearing veins) belonged to the lords of the manors, tenants might possess limited customary rights to take stone. Until the twentieth century most of the materials for construction were obtained locally – building stone, sand and gravel, clay for field drains, and so on. The easily-worked sandstone required for quoins, lintels, sills and mullions had to be brought in from the lowlands of west Cumberland but much other stone could be sourced locally: not only walling stone but roofing slate, cobbles for the yard and stable, and the larger slabs needed as flagstones for the kitchen floor, gate posts and 'booses' (stall divisions) in the byre. In a valley where most of the bedrock consisted of the cracked and fissured Skiddaw Slates, places where such large slabs of rock could be obtained were particularly sought after. The memory of one such quarry, in a field near Lowpark at Loweswater, survived among older members of the local community in the 1970s. Here the bedrock breaks through the surface on the crest of a swelling ridge. The smooth, ice-worn curve of the rock has been cut away on one side as workmen levered out huge slabs from the rock face. The outcrop was said to be prized particularly for 'booses', some of which survived in the 1970s in the byres at Highpark. Such quarrying produced very little waste material, so there is no spoil heap to draw attention to the workings.

Who controlled that small quarry is not known: if the slates it yielded were taken for use by the farmer in whose field the outcrop stood, it may have been worked as a customary right. But if it was worked as a commercial venture, albeit a small one, the lord of the manor would almost certainly have had an interest. Lordly income from slate quarries in the valley can be traced back to 1500 when the earl of Northumberland as lord of Derwentfells leased a 'quarry of Slatestons' near 'Swarebek' (now Sware Gill) in Lorton to Richard Alanson. The location suggests that this may have been the forerunner of the quarries near Scawgill Bridge on the Whinlatter road, which continued to be active into the twentieth century. In 1649 the estate granted licences to work slate in a quarry at Brackenthwaite and to make trials in Embleton as well.

At Loweswater the balance of interests in a slate quarry is illustrated in a memo entitled 'What I have in Lowswater' written in 1693 by the then lord of the manor, Sir Wilfrid Lawson. The fifth item on the list (after a farm he owned and let, his private enclosed pasture of Holme, and the corn mill), was 'A slate Quarry. Some tymes got nothing for it; this yeare Lett for £4'. It was of limited value: he could 'make nothing of it unlese the slaters take it' and he went on to note that 'the tenante[s] hath Previlige there to Git slate.' It sounds as though it was a small quarry largely serving local needs, to which the community had access by custom, perhaps akin to the outcrop yielding large slabs near Lowpark. By the time he was writing, slate quarries across the fells to the east, around Skiddaw, were thriving and the local market for slate appears to have been buoyant. When Thomas Denton described Bassenthwaite in 1688, he noted that the area around Skiddaw contained 'the best blew slate quarries in England … which are thin & light for covering of houses, & as smooth as glass; and all people covet to have them, who live within any convenient distance'.

By Victorian times, by far the largest slate quarries in the area were those at the head of the Buttermere valley at the summit of Honister Pass, where the blue-green slate of the fine-grained Borrowdale Volcanic series was extracted on an industrial scale. There were several separate quarries: Honister quarry and Dubs quarry on the back of Fleetwith and Yew Crag quarry on the slopes of Dale Head on the northern flank of the pass. The story of quarrying there can be traced in a series of leases stretching back to 1728. The scale of operations appears to have expanded when Charles Norman of Buttermere took out a 17-year lease in 1753. At that time the Honister quarries were meeting local demand: when Loweswater church needed re-roofing in 1751, the south side was slated with 'Ewecragg Slate'. By the early nineteenth century the quarry had become a tourist attraction. At the sound of a tourist guide's 'halloo', the quarrymen would answer with 'the shrill echoes of a horn' and gratify the visitors' curiosity by 'bringing down a load of slate through the almost imperceptible mazes of the rocks'. Major investment in the mid-nineteenth century expanded the scale of operations when new tramways were built to carry slate mined underground down the steep fellsides.

The cracked and twisted Skiddaw slates are criss-crossed with veins carrying a range of valuable minerals, especially lead and copper ores, and small lodes of iron ore around the edges of the intrusion of Ennerdale granophyre. Unlike the neighbouring Newlands valley, the mineral wealth of the Cocker valley was modest but that did not prevent every possible vein being explored in the hope of striking rich. At some point, probably in the 1680s, a group of Quakers opened a copper mine near Gatesgarth, on the slopes of High Crag, close to the track over Scarth Gap. Francis Allason, one of the miners, describing the venture as an elderly man in 1738, recalled that 'they got great Quantitys of very good Ore which they carried to Langdale Forges', fifteen miles or so across the fells, to be smelted. A second level was opened near Scale Beck but the company failed and, he recalled, the Quakers emigrated to Pennsylvania. Further attempts at mining, both for copper and lead, in Birkness and Warnscale (the slopes of High Stile, High Crag and Haystacks) were made in the early nineteenth century.

A second area where mining proved successful was Loweswater, where lead was mined over several decades in the nineteenth century. A vein was exposed during drainage works at Godferhead farm in 1816 and eventually a mine was opened near Netherclose in the 1820s. This was deep shaft work, mining ore from levels down to 40 fathoms (240 feet) deep. But it was short-lived; the mine closed in 1841. Two further lead mines were opened in Loweswater, one at Kirkgill Wood, near the Kirkstile Inn, opened in 1839, and another in the 1860s beside Whiteoak Beck, on the opposite side of the valley. The Whiteoak mine was also of limited success; a burst of activity from 1888 was short-lived and all the mine's equipment was sold at auction in 1892.

Those operations apart, most other attempts to mine metal ore from the valley's rocks failed. Where a mineral outcrop was discovered in the side of a gill, the lure of riches would lead to trial workings but the results were rarely successful. Isaac Fletcher expended considerable energy and money on attempting to mine lead ore on his property in Mosser between 1765 and 1773, having found a lead vein in a gill side. Several trial pits were dug, one (which had to be abandoned because of flooding) reaching a depth of 12 fathoms (72 feet). Little lead seems to have been obtained. It was a similar story when iron ore was discovered at several places between Floutern Tarn and Red Pike in the 1870s. Great expectations were followed by disappointment. The prospectus issued by Whitehaven Mines Ltd in 1871 anticipated that over 100,000 tons of ore could be raised each year and that the mine would be 'almost inexhaustible'. Small trials were made on Gale Fell and close to Scale Force, but two years later it was all over: 'a few tons of ore of fair quality' had been obtained but an inspector concluded that 'There is nothing here that would warrant any outlay of capital'.

* * *

The later years of the eighteenth century brought new people and capital to the upper reaches of the valley. Attracted by the 'discovery' of the Lake District by travel writers, tourists arrived, eager to experience the excitement and drama of the lakes and fells. They represented a new sensibility and a different perception of the value of rock and woodland. The earliest writing on the Lakes had focused on Keswick and Derwent Water, where the combination of the lake and its islands, the pastoral valley, the wooded hillsides, and the 'sublime' grandeur of fells behind perfectly met the taste for idealised picturesque beauty. An excursion to Buttermere quickly became a standard ingredient of a tour to the Lakes.

Visitors approached from Keswick by what was then a narrow grassy track over Newlands Hause. Buttermere village and its green fields on the valley floor between the two lakes appeared, dwarfed by the surrounding fells. Approaching the village, the sound of water intensified and, directly across the valley, Sourmilk Gill came into view – a white braid of water tumbling through the rocks from Bleaberry Comb, the corrie between High Stile and Red Pike. The pastoral scene, the lakes, the wooded lower slopes, the waterfalls and, towering over them all, the mist-shrouded high fells – Buttermere possessed all the key ingredients sought out by the early tourists.

Thomas West's first guide to the Lakes, published in 1778, concentrated on the main north-south axis through the fells, providing details of 'stations' from which the best views could be obtained around Windermere, Derwent Water and Bassenthwaite Lake. By the 1790s the Buttermere valley was sufficiently popular for Peter Crosthwaite to include a map of it, surveyed in 1793, in his *Series of Accurate Maps of the Principal Lakes of Cumberland, Westmorland and Lancashire*. In the absence of 'stations' identified by West, Crosthwaite marked six of his own to guide the tourist to the best views between Loweswater and the head of the valley. His first viewpoint was from 'High Gap Yeat', near High Cross in Loweswater, facing the austere north face of Melbreak; the second from Flass Wood above Highpark, looking over to the towering rock-strewn front of Grasmoor; the third from 'Dob Ley Head' on Brackenthwaite Hows, for the view up Crummock Water. Moving towards the head of the valley, he picked out further 'stations' from the road over Rannerdale Knotts at Buttermere Hause, from the hillside above Buttermere chapel, and from the slopes behind Gatesgarth farm at the head of the valley.

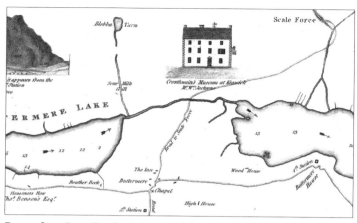

Extract from Peter Crosthwaite's map of Buttermere and Crummock, surveyed 1793, showing Scale Force and the viewing 'stations' at Buttermere Hause and above Buttermere chapel *(from An Accurate Map of Buttermere, Crummock and Lowes-Water Lakes, Scale Force &c, published 1794).*

Sourmilk Gill and Scale Force were at first the key attractions in the locality for the Lakes tourist. The prominent Sourmilk Gill gained fame early: William Gilpin, who visited in 1772, described it as being 'like a white ribbon bisecting the mountain'. Scale Force, by contrast, a pencil of water falling a total of 170 feet in a deep wooded cleft, had to be sought out. The walls of the north-facing chasm are permanently clammy and glistening in the spray, their surfaces softened by a profusion of ferns and liverworts. This waterfall became one of the wonders of the Lake District. In his guidebook of 1778, Thomas West drew attention to Scale Force without naming it. Where the road to Buttermere rounds Rannerdale Knotts, he wrote, 'the hoarse resounding noise of a water-fall is heard across the lake, concealed within the bosom of the cliff, through which it has forced its way, and when viewed from the foot of the fall, is a most astonishing phaenomenon'. By the middle of the following decade, a description of Scale Force, from the pen of 'some gentlemen' who had visited it, was being reprinted in provincial newspapers: 'the approach to it is a most curious chasm, between perpendicular rocks, from 30 to 50 yards high on each side, and from 8 to 10 yards apart. At the distance of about 50 yards up this chasm is a fall of water 162 feet perpendicular, … an entire white sheet of water from top to bottom, and … perhaps the most curious and beautiful cataract in the three kingdoms'. The artist, William Green, in his illustrated tourist guide published in 1819, likened it to 'a white ribband, stretched upon a piece of black velvet'. The numbers visiting Scale Force in the early days of the Lakes tour probably remained low, owing to its distance from the village and the rough ground which needed to be traversed – Sourmilk Gill, in contrast, could be seen by all from the road. John Housman, writing in 1800, advised that, when undertaking the walk to Scale Force, 'every stranger should be accompanied with a guide' and noted that, because of the difficult terrain, 'Scale-force … has hitherto been little known, or visited, by strangers'. A new path was planned but the road was still in a 'miserable condition' in 1819. Many visitors continued to take a boat across the lake to the foot of Scale Beck, to avoid the stony path from Buttermere, which passed from woodland to the rock-strewn, wet and sour slopes of Red Pike, which Harriet Martineau described as 'too swampy to be agreeable'.

One early visitor, Captain Joseph Budworth, touring the Lakes in 1792, included a visit to Scale Force in his itinerary. Returning to the inn at Buttermere, he was captivated by the beauty of the teenage waitress, Mary Robinson, and included a lyrical pen portrait of her looks in the account of his tour, published the same year. The 'beauty of Buttermere' quickly became an added attraction of the place. Mary's unsought fame led to an unhappy outcome, still well-known. Her renown spread, not least as a result of a later account by

Budworth, which included an update on Mary's appearance. In 1802 a smooth-tongued fraudster, announcing himself as 'The Hon. Augustus Hope', brother to the Scots aristocrat Lord Hopetoun, wooed Mary and, within three months of their meeting, married her at Lorton church. He was an imposter, already a married man and deeply in debt, who had committed what was then the capital offence of defrauding the Crown by franking letters to avoid postage. His real name was John Hatfield and he was hanged at Carlisle in September 1803 for this crime, less than a year after marrying Mary. The name of Buttermere and the tragedy that befell its innocent beauty spread far and wide. Mary left the valley, marrying a farmer from Caldbeck and raising a family out of the unwanted limelight. But these events added to the allure of Buttermere.

The 'discovery' of the Lakes led in Buttermere, as elsewhere, to landscape change, as new landowners sought to claim and capture the views and, indeed, to improve them. The impetus and the money were both new: in contrast to the landscape created by yeoman farming, this change, driven by aesthetics, was funded by external finance. Lakeside villas, situated to capture a view of the fells across water, sprang up beside most of the lakes from the 1770s onwards. Buttermere was no exception. By 1803 Thomas Benson, a wealthy Cockermouth lawyer, had built a lakeside house at Hassness, with large windows looking down the lake towards Sourmilk Gill. It was set in newly planted woodland of exotic species. At about the same time, the duke of Norfolk, who owned Gatesgarth, planted the strip of trees at the head of the lake, forerunners of the Scots pines which, reflected in the water of the lake, continue to form one of the iconic images of the Lake District.

Further tree planting followed, slowly increasing the woodland and giving more of the valley its modern wooded character. Much was the work of John Marshall, the Leeds millowner who accumulated a vast estate across the Lake District between 1811 and 1845. He bought the manor of Loweswater in 1814, Gatesgarth, Birkness and Hassness the following year and an estate in Brackenthwaite at the foot of Crummock in 1824. As Derek Denman, who has researched Marshall's purchases, puts it, 'Woodland was Marshall's main interest'. Marshall took advice from William Wordsworth about how to improve and manage his new property, spending three days with him at the inn at Scale Hill in 1816. Sara Hutchinson reported that Wordsworth was reassured that Marshall would 'in no wise sacrifice beauty to convenience' in his plans for planting. He planted Holme Wood on the dark side of Loweswater (native species on the lakeside; larch further up the fellside) and Burtness Wood on the banks of Buttermere (larch), as well as creating several other smaller woods around Buttermere. Marshall would have liked to extend his plantations through Buttermere Scales, offering to exchange the graziers' rights for pasture elsewhere on the commons, but was unable to gain their agreement. Lanthwaite Woods, on the opposite shore of Crummock by the foot of the lake, had already been planted with oak and larch before 1804 and Marshall continued to drive the management towards timber production rather than coppice, as long as his forestry could be done 'without hurting the appearance of the wood'.

This concern for aesthetic quality and the management of the landscape to maintain it were something completely new in the history of the Cocker valley, as elsewhere in the Lake District. To Marshall and those visiting the Lakes, the landscape was no longer simply an environment yielding physical resources but part of a visual, sensory experience to be relished and taken away in memory. Its rocks, woods and waters had now acquired a cultural value, setting in train new perceptions of the Lake District which resonate today.

Rannerdale in bluebell time.

CHAPTER 10

STORIED GROUND

Rannerdale

In an old-settled land, centuries – millennia – of physical toil have created the ground over which we pass, and have left a litter of relics, great and small, which form a link to previous generations. Every fragment of dry stone wall, every footing of a lost building, every drainage ditch, gatepost, levelled patch of ground is the result of a deliberate act of physical labour and of a decision behind it to expend time and energy on shaping the environment. Such legacies of the past have long been places which can act as points where the veil of time thins, bringing us closer to those who were here before. They also pose questions: who built, dug or hewed here; when and why? And they often elicit a response in the form of myths and stories to offer explanations of the inexplicable.

Stories which were long ago attached to prehistoric earthworks and rings of stones are remembered in the names given to them. Sampson's Bratfull, a prehistoric long cairn on the remote fells between Ennerdale and Wasdale, gained its name from a bible character: the cairn was explained as a load of stones which spilt when the strongman Samson's apron strings (a 'brat' is an apron) snapped as he carried them to a building site. At King Arthur's Round Table, the circular earthwork of a Neolithic henge near Penrith, the allusion is to the popular medieval romance – several Arthurian stories are set in the area. The supernatural explanation of the stone circle at Elva Plain, a much more modest site of antiquity, is recorded in the reference to elves in its name.

Recent and more mundane relics of the past also tug at the imagination. Ruined dwellings, in particular, have the power to evoke an immediate connection with the past and thereby to attract myth and story-telling. In the half-light of dusk, when adrenalin heightens the senses, they become places of mystery. One such place is Miterdale Head, a remote valley in the fells between Eskdale and Wasdale, where life ebbed away between the sixteenth and the nineteenth centuries as farms were deserted, leaving ruined houses and the tumbled footings of walls. I spent many hours exploring Miterdale in the 1960s, taking advantage of lifts from my father who was overseeing the planting of conifers in the intakes on the valley sides. Back among the archives, I unravelled the history of each farm – but imagination was forever pulling at my shoulder. In the quiet, as the Mite trickled beneath the sycamores, I peopled the ruins with the families whose names I had collected from the records and I fancied that I heard the knock of clogs on the cobbles, the jink of a chain from stable or byre, or children calling across the fields in the gloaming.

Myth accrued to the ruins at the head of Miterdale as a result of the publication in 1886 of a ghost story, set in an imaginary inn, 'Nanny Horns'. Written by Alice Rea of Gatehouse in Eskdale, the daughter of the family who owned the farmland in Miterdale, *The Beckside Boggle*, told of a stranger disguised as a woman, who arrived at Miterdale Head one evening when the man of the house was away and his wife was boiling tallow for making rushlight candles. When the stranger's disguise slipped, the woman panicked and the stranger met a grisly end from a ladle of boiling fat. The couple buried him in the ruins of the inn and hauntings began, continuing each year on the anniversary of the murder. The book's frontispiece was a photograph of the uninhabited farmstead at Miterdale Head, under the caption 'The Scene of Desolation'. In *Below Scafell* (1955), his memoir of life in Eskdale, Dudley Hoys captured the aura of Miterdale Head perfectly:

> To sit here in silence for a while is to sense soundless movement and grow aware that you are not quite alone. The shadows of history still creep invisibly around. Where men have once lived, and gone, there always lingers a feeling of their presence.

Another such place, where story has been even more powerful, is Rannerdale.

* * *

From Lanthwaite Green the road to Buttermere twists along the edge of the common below the bulk of Grasmoor, separated from the shore of Crummock Water by no more than a narrow strip of fields. It opens to a view up the lake with Rannerdale Knotts projecting into it, which must be one of the most photographed and painted scenes in the Lake District. Beside the lake, in front of Rannerdale Knotts, lies a triangle of bright green, stone-walled fields where Rannerdale Beck comes down from the slopes of Whiteless Pike (Plate 12). Rannerdale proper lies behind the green fields, tucked away behind the craggy Knotts. It is a stone-walled pasture, named on the map as High Rannerdale, dotted with the remains of woodland. And it is a place where people 'have once lived and gone': remains of what are probably medieval dwellings survive not far from the beckside, shaded by an ancient spreading crab apple tree, just above the limit of the cultivated land.

In May the valley is carpeted with bluebells, giving Rannerdale its popular name, 'the bluebell valley'. To sit there on a breezy day in the spring sunshine is to be assailed by a feast for the senses: patches of golden gorse blaze out from the soft mauve carpet of bluebells which clothe the valley, running up the lower slopes until they fade out into the browns of last year's bracken and rushes, not yet replaced by new growth. The pungent smell of fox, carried on the breeze, cuts through the heavy scent of the rowans as they come into flower. In the background is the sound of constant movement: the wind in the trees, the beck tumbling over rocks; lambs bleating; the croak of a raven over the crags.

Many visitors also know Rannerdale by another name – 'the secret valley'. The name was the product of the imagination of one man, Nicholas Size (1866-1953), the proprietor of the Victoria Hotel (now the Bridge Hotel) at Buttermere. A Liverpudlian by birth, Nicholas Size had been a railway manager whose love of the Lake District brought him to the then-derelict hotel at Buttermere around 1920. He was an energetic promoter of tourism and had ambitions to develop Buttermere to rival Alpine resorts, with a chairlift, beer garden and brass band, and a fully-equipped service station for motor cars. Not surprisingly, his plans were unpopular with neighbours and local landowners, who nicknamed him 'Old Nick'. In 1929 he published a slim volume under the title, *The Secret Valley: a picture of the great events which took place in unconquered Lakeland during Norman times.* The story told of a Norman attempt to subdue Lakeland and of how Earl Boethar, leader of the native Norse, held out against them from his stronghold in a 'secret valley', deep in the fells. It culminated in a final push by Ranulf le Meschin, the Norman lord of Cumberland under Henry I, whose army, coming up the valley from Cockermouth, were tricked into moving up Rannerdale where they were surrounded by Boethar's forces and cut to pieces. It is a vivid, gruesome tale – and also the hotelier's clever, barely-disguised advertisement for Buttermere. Size claimed that the remains of Earl Boethar's mill could 'still be traced in a beautiful glen which lies in front of the windows of the modern Victoria Hotel at Buttermere'. A footnote in the second edition states that the 'surprise view' down Rannerdale and across Loweswater to the Solway is twenty minutes' walk from the hotel. Printed in Kendal by Titus Wilson, the first edition of the book mimicked in format, font and layout the earnest publications of the Cumberland & Westmorland Antiquarian & Archaeological Society, also printed by Titus Wilson. Size presented his story as history, even trying to substantiate specific points by citing the Victoria County History of Cumberland. Words on the cover and title page were contradictory pointers: 'Truth is stranger than fiction' appeared above the author's name, and 'No good story is ever wholly true' beneath it. Size tempted his readers to believe what was no more than a figment of his imagination.

In 1930 he produced an enlarged edition of *The Secret Valley*, with the subtitle *The Real Romance of Unconquered Lakeland*, embellishing the new edition with further garbled references to recorded history. This time it was published by Frederick Warne, Beatrix Potter's publisher. The book carried a foreword by the novelist Hugh Walpole, who skirted around the question of the tale's historical veracity: 'It is not for me to say whether or no his history is accurate. In history I have always considered the spirit of the law more than the letter', concluding, rather limply, 'For myself, I *am* a believer because the atmosphere is here'.

Nicholas Size was tapping into the zeitgeist of the interwar years; the story ends thus:

The bravery and generalship of the great Earl Boethar and his generation had saved a section of our race from extermination – and it is not surprising that even to this day many of us make an instinctive yearly pilgrimage to Lakeland, conscious that we owe something to the mountains, and that from them alone the very best that is in us can draw strength and inspiration.

Nearly thirty years later, Nicholas Size's tale was given new life for a younger readership by Rosemary Sutcliff (1920-1992). In *The Shield Ring* (1956) she retold the story through the eyes of a young Saxon girl living in a Norse stronghold at Buttermere, weaving a love story into the tale of battles and bloodshed. In the names of people and places, Sutcliff's version of the tale is more specifically Norse: 'Earl Boethar' becomes 'Jarl Buthar'; Buttermere becomes 'Butharsmere'; Crummock Water 'Crumbeck Water'. Her 'Author's Note' adds to the supposed blurring of history and fiction. 'Save for Ranulf le Meschin', she wrote, 'I do not think that you will find the people of this story mentioned in any history book. Nevertheless, they were real people, though the trace of them and their long-drawn fight for freedom is in local tradition, not in written history …'. In truth, the 'local tradition' almost certainly stretched no further back in time than Size's original book. Among the natives in both Size's and Sutcliff's stories, only 'Earl Boethar'/'Jarl Buthar' draws on the name of an historical figure. This is Bueth, who is known only through the name of his son, Gille son of Bueth (who makes an appearance, as 'Gille Butharson', in Rosemary Sutcliff's story). The historical Gille was a native landowner in twelfth-century Cumberland, whose name is preserved in the name of Gilsland barony in the north-east of the county, around Brampton. Nothing is known of Bueth, nor is Gille known to have had any connection with the Lake District, let alone Buttermere. What is more, far from being a Norse name suitable to be borne by a Viking chief in Buttermere, 'Bueth' is generally considered to have been a version of the Gaelic name *Buide*, linking Gille's father to western Scotland rather than Scandinavia.

Size was writing an heroic story to help give Buttermere and Rannerdale a pseudo-history. He plucked place-names from the map, linking them to his fanciful chronicle: Butterwick in Mardale, Brotherilkeld ('Butterilkelt') and Boot in Eskdale, Butterlyp Howe at Grasmere and Buttermere itself were all linked, sometimes cleverly only implicitly, with the name of Earl Boethar. (To modern place-name scholars, Buttermere and Butterwick contain the Old English *butere* 'butter'; Boot is the Middle English word for a bend in the river; and the first element of Brotherilkeld is the Old Norse *buðir*, 'booths or huts'). For Nicholas Size, Wood House at Buttermere recalled the site of Boethar's 'great manor house built of wood', while Aikin Knott in Newlands was 'Ackin's Howe', the burial place of Boethar's henchman, Earl Ackin, rather than the more mundane interpretation in which the first element refers to oak trees.

What is remarkable about Size's slim flight of fancy is how the story of *The Secret Valley* has fused with Rannerdale, to become part of the spirit of the place, carrying the visitor's imagination into a purely fictional past. It was believed and, indeed, has been embellished. Rannerdale has become the 'Secret Valley' – although in Size's story the secret valley was Boethar's stronghold at Buttermere, hidden at the head of Crummock around the corner of Rannerdale Knotts. Rannerdale was merely 'the battlefield'. In popular imagination the bluebells have become the annual efflorescence of the blood of the slain Normans. In the first edition of the story, Size wrote merely that 'Rannerdale was like a charnel house but ... to-day all you can say is that there are more bluebells there than anywhere else', but in the second edition he added 'and perhaps there may be something in Omar Khayyám's idea that the loveliest flowers may spring from some dead Caesar's breast.' It is a skilful suggestion which was quickly taken up as fact. Just as Nicholas Size seized on and manipulated snatches of history and the richness of place-names to weave his fiction, so his story has become indelibly linked with Rannerdale. Such is the fame of the carpet of bluebells today that the hidden valley can scarcely cope with the number of visitors in May each year. The bluebells are now roped off, signs urging visitors to keep to the paths.

***

In weaving a story around place-names and in romanticising the Viking settlers of the Lake District, Nicholas Size and Rosemary Sutcliff were following a well-trodden path. The role of the Vikings had been an accepted theme in the region's history for many years. The key figure in the creation of a Viking past in the Lake District was W. G. Collingwood who dominated antiquarian and archaeological study in Cumbria in the early twentieth century and whose views of Cumbrian history remain highly influential today. In his *Lake District History*, first published in 1925, Collingwood painted a picture of Norse settlers opening up the Lake District, drawing parallels with the Scandinavian settlement of Iceland:

> We must consider that the dales were quite wild, but for a few British homesteads; and that the colonists began by settling outside the district and gradually worked up into the fells. We must take the analogies of Norse farming as we gather them from the early history of the parallel settlement in Iceland ... a chief established himself in a 'baer' or 'by' in a readily accessible spot: his thralls took the cattle and

sheep to summer pastures further inland and these in time
became fixed farms; and his descendants cut up the original
great land-take with its back-blocks until all available ground
was covered.'

Collingwood went so far as to provide the Lake District
with its own Viking sagas in his historical novels *Thorstein of
the Mere: a saga of the Northmen in Lakeland* (1895) and *The
Bondwoman* (1896). He originally conceived of *Thorstein of
the Mere* as 'the Fornesinga saga' (the saga of the Furness folk),
telling of the land-taking by the Vikings and of their relations
with 'the old inhabitants who lived in the fells'. At the heart
of the tale is a love story between Thorstein, the Viking, and
Raineach, one of the Celtic fell-folk – Collingwood was
fully aware of the ethnic and linguistic mix of pre-Conquest
Cumbria. However, he included two place-name maps in the
first edition of the book, one of the Furness peninsula ('The
Northmen in Hougun'), the other of the central Lake District
('The Northmen in the Fells'). Both are populated with
modern place-names reconstructed in Old Norse, a remarkable
feat which bears little resemblance to the interpretation of
the names by modern place-name scholars and presents the
Lake District as wholly Scandinavian territory. Again and
again, Collingwood chooses an Old Norse root for place-
names which almost certainly came from Old English: on
his maps, the second element of Grasmere (Old English
mere, 'a lake') becomes Old Norse *myrr* ('swampy ground');
Keswick (Old English *cēse-wīc*, 'cheese farm') becomes the
Old Norse *Ketelsveggr* ('Ketel's wall'); Broughton (in Furness)
(Old English *brōc -tūn*, 'village by a stream') becomes Old
Norse *Borgtun* ('fortified village').

Collingwood's books represented the full flowering of the
idea that it was the Vikings who settled the Lake District. He
was building on a tradition that can be traced back almost

to the time that the Lakes were first visited by tourists in the eighteenth century. The understanding of Viking roots came in two phases: first, the identification of what was claimed to be a Danish inheritance in Lakeland dialect and then a revised view, focusing on place-names as well as dialect, which recognised Norse influence as paramount. One of the earliest references to a Danish past comes in an account of a tour of the Lakes published in 1792 by Adam Walker, a native of Patterdale, who claimed that:

> In Westmoreland there were whole vallies of DANES, all relations, and known, when they could get out of their native hollows, by their red heads, and their language being like the baaing of sheep.

His comment came in an extended aside about the way 'provincial manners and provincial dialects' were being destroyed by modern developments, such as turnpike roads and the arrival of tourists. It is not clear whether Walker was passing on a commonly-held local belief in a Danish heritage or making his own assumptions, perhaps developing the ideas of linguists who, since the seventeenth century, had detected Scandinavian influence in northern English speech. The claim to Danish roots was given a boost by the essayist, Thomas de Quincey, who contributed a series of letters on the Danish origins of Lake Country dialect to *The Westmorland Gazette* in the winter of 1819-20. Moving in local circles (he was married to the daughter of a Westmorland statesman) and having knowledge of modern Danish, he was able to cite specific examples of dialect words with their Danish parallels. Later, he went so far as to claim that the Danish language was 'the master key for unlocking the peculiarities of the Lake District'.

The switch to identifying Norse, rather than Danish, as

the key to Lake District history came in Victoria's reign. In *The Northmen in Cumberland and Westmorland* (1856), Robert Ferguson used the evidence of place-names and dialect to argue that the Scandinavian presence in Cumbria was predominantly Norwegian, rather than Danish, and came from across the Irish Sea, rather than from the Danelaw. He maintained that Norse settlers were attracted by a mountainous environment, similar to that which they had left behind in Norway. From their base in the Isle of Man, he wrote, they 'beheld the blue outlines of a land like their own land – a land of mountains and valleys – a land waiting for people.' Attracted by this other Norway, 'a wandering settler saw the blue lake gleaming through the trees – and thought of his native land – and said "this shall be my home."' Ferguson hammered his argument home by claiming that the 'Characteristics, Manners and Customs of the Inhabitants' of the Lake District continued to exhibit Norse characteristics: 'caution and shrewdness' and 'a coldness and reserve of manner, which ... is apt to be mistaken for churlishness' were shared by Norwegian and Lakelander alike. The sturdy independence of the Lakeland statesmen, he argued, was a product of their distinctive ethnic origins as descendants of Viking settlers. It was a wonderfully romantic vision of the Lakeland past and one which has stuck.

A flowering of antiquarian and scholarly work between around 1890 and the outbreak of the First World War, led by Collingwood, laid bare the Norse roots of Lakeland dialect and recognised the Viking influence in the art of the pre-Conquest stone crosses in Cumbrian churchyards, notably the pagan Norse imagery on the Gosforth cross. By the time Nicholas Size came to write *The Secret Valley*, belief in the pre-eminence of Viking heritage had become fixed. We now know that the place-name assemblage of the Lake District is much richer, containing many names with roots stretching back centuries before the Scandinavian settlement, while the adoption of Scandinavian words into the local dialect means that a place-name containing a Scandinavian element may, in some cases, have been coined centuries after the Viking Age. Despite this, the Viking hold on the popular imagination is so strong that the notion that the Vikings settled the Lake District reaches deep into conceptions of the region's past. The idea that a Norse warlord based in Buttermere might have fought off the Normans fits the mould.

* * *

Rannerdale's true history is less romantic than the myth created by Nicholas Size but nevertheless contains elements of mystery. The place enters the written record around 1170 simply as a place-name, 'Ravenerhals', which refers not to the valley itself but to the 'hause' (the *-hals* element of the name), the pass over the shoulder of Rannerdale Knotts leading across the headland to Buttermere. The ancient route survives as a bridle way higher up the hillside than the narrow, crag-bound modern road around the point, described as 'new' in 1819. It seems likely that the first part of the place-name, 'Ravener' (meaning 'the summer pasture ground frequented by ravens'), applied originally to the green triangle where Rannerdale opens to the lake. At that early point, it would have been a remote outpost of settlement – a cluster of herdsmen's huts, occupied only in summer – on the track up to the head of the lake, where ravens called from the crags. Perhaps, like other summer pastures, the valley had been settled permanently by 1300 – the written record is silent. There was also industrial activity by the lakeside near Rannerdale. The name of Cinderdale Beck, the small stream tumbling off the southern slopes of Grasmoor just north of Rannerdale, refers to the 'cinder' or slag found nearby, which was the waste from a bloomery, where iron was smelted with charcoal. It is quite probable that this is a legacy of the 'woodland forges' in Brackenthwaite, for which rent was paid in the decades either side of 1300.

By the later Middle Ages some form of farming settlement had grown up, taking advantage of the flat triangle of ploughable land and hay meadow by the lakeshore with the fellside pastures behind. There is even a reference to a chapel of St Mary Magdalene at Rannerdale in 1508, the site of which is perhaps recorded in 'Chapel Field', the nineteenth-century name of a field near Rannerdale Bridge, where the road crosses the beck. But something happened. By 1547 there was no longer a settlement at Rannerdale – the farm there and the 'close' (probably High Rannerdale) were by then divided into seven parts, shared by people whose main holdings were in Brackenthwaite, further down the valley.

What happened to cause the desertion of the settlement that existed in Rannerdale in the later Middle Ages? It is tempting to link it to events surrounding a certain John 'alias Jak' Newcom, who lived at Rannerdale around 1500. He seems to have been a thorn in the side of his neighbours, taking land in from the common, not keeping his fences in repair, chasing his neighbours' cattle, and obstructing the highway. His unneighbourly actions culminated in 1516 when he killed a man. The manor court recorded that Jak Newcom struck Robert Thomson with an 'irnefork' on the common at Rannerdale Knotts and Robert died. Accessories to the crime were his children, Richard, Agnes and Elizabeth, along with Margaret Mirehus of Rannerdale, perhaps his servant, and John Peill of Buttermere (all of whom were described as 'labourers'). Jak Newcom fled. Perhaps these events left Rannerdale uninhabited. Could it be that the footings of the rectangular buildings and walls beside the track into High Rannerdale close to the edge of the green, cultivated fields are the site of Jak Newcom's farm? Or am I just succumbing to the temptation to attach a story to an abandoned dwelling?

The shared ownership of Rannerdale by farms further down the dale continued for three centuries, until Victorian times. In 1844 the green fields beside the lake were held by four different farmers and the pasture of High Rannerdale by three. In summer, from May to October, High Rannerdale was a shared pasture for sheep and cattle, each grazier putting in as many heifers and calves as his stint allowed and taking turns to provide a bull. By a custom which was of long standing in 1757, the sheep grazing in High Rannerdale were marked with a particular 'by-mark' to distinguish them from the flocks on the common beyond the enclosure wall. 'Longcrofts', the green fields by the lake, were also farmed communally on a rotation of two years of grain crops followed by two years' grazing. Each of the owners had their own strips in the years the field was ploughed but they grazed bullocks and two-year-old heifers by stint in the pasture years. By the middle decades of the nineteenth century most of the fields had come into the hands of a single owner and a new farmstead, Rannerdale Farm (at first called 'Scale View Farm'), was built there in the 1860s. In 1938 Rannerdale Farm became one of the first farms to be purchased by an off-shoot of the Friends of the Lake District, Lake District Farm Estates Ltd, which bought up farms in order to protect their land from development and afforestation and to preserve traditional Lake District farming culture. There is an element of irony here, that Rannerdale Farm, created less than a century before, should be chosen to exemplify a long hill farming tradition, making it worthy of protection against an uncertain future.

Rannerdale is a place of two stories, a fairly prosaic historical one of hill farming and iron smelting, and an imaginary tale of heroic struggle and bloodshed. Many people today are beguiled by the latter, happy to accept the spurious explanation for the profusion of bluebells there in springtime. Myth has smothered history. Places accrue meanings – and in the case of Rannerdale much of the popular meaning comes from an imagined past, mythical not historical. Nicholas Size's story of Earl Boethar's stand against the Normans was pure fiction (even if dressed up as fact) and the identification of Rannerdale as the 'secret valley' was a misunderstanding of Size's narrative – a double myth, if you like. Here, as elsewhere, historical reality is overlain by powerful stories which are now part of the spirit of the place. Place and story have fused, to the extent that the history is forgotten or ignored.

'Mill Beck & Buttermere Chapel' in the 1830s, drawn by George Pickering and engraved by M. J. Starling.

CHAPTER 11

PLACES OF PRAYER

Buttermere

In the 1860s, the Ordnance Survey described the village of Buttermere as 'a small village of five farm houses and some cottages, two Public houses and a chapel belonging to the Established Church'. The houses still cluster on the edge of level green fields between the lakes, where the deep, steep-sided valley of Sail Beck divides the Grasmoor massif from the fells surrounding Buttermere. Behind the village winds Newlands Pass, a ribbon of tarmac rising across the open fellside, and perched above the village on the edge of the common at the foot of the pass stands the church, a small rectangle of pink granite with a sandstone bellcote (Plate 13). The cool stillness of its interior and the material accoutrements of Anglican worship it contains combine to make this a place set apart, separate from the buzz of daily activity. In canon law it is consecrated ground – a building set aside as sacred.

Like most of the humble churches of the Lakeland dales, Buttermere's church was not in origin a parish church but, as the Ordnance Survey noted, a chapel. It was a 'chapel of ease', its purpose being to ease the religious obligations of folk dwelling at a distance from the parish church. Across the uplands of northern England medieval parishes were often vast territories embracing numerous communities, anchored to an ancient parish church site in the lowlands and running deep into the hills. Most of the Lake District valleys looked down-dale to a parish church out on the margins of the fells. Kendal, one of the largest parishes, embraced the valleys flowing south from Langdale round to Longsleddale, originally including the chapels at Grasmere and Windermere, which became parish churches in their own rights in the 1340s. The western valleys, from Eskdale to Loweswater, were within the bounds of the parish of St Bees, down on the coast; Buttermere and the rest of the Cocker valley fell within the parish of Brigham, in the low country just west of Cockermouth. The churches of Barton, Ulverston and Millom all had long, thin parishes reaching far into the fells. The only ancient parish church in the Lake District proper was that at Crosthwaite by Keswick and its territory extended up the valleys to Newlands, Borrowdale and the head of Thirlmere.

Obligations – to pay tithes and other dues, to take the sacraments, to bury the dead and to go to be married – bound the remotest part of a parish to the mother church, but for practical purposes church buildings were needed to serve the outlying communities from Sunday to Sunday and, from medieval times, chapels of ease were built. Early chapels often acquired quasi-parochial rights, with burial grounds and some form of endowment to provide for a priest to administer the sacraments. At Eskdale, for example, the inhabitants petitioned the pope in 1445 for their chapel of St Catherine to be raised to parochial status with a cemetery and a baptismal font, on the grounds that their dwellings were ten miles or more from the parish church of St Bees. The church at St Bees lay on the far side of two wide rivers and three smaller streams which swelled in rain and in winter, hindering them from making their way to attend christenings, burials, services and sacraments. Like Eskdale, other medieval chapels serving far-flung parts of an ancient parish had gained the status of parochial chapelries by the Reformation and were parishes in all but name: they included Loweswater, Lorton and Embleton. But others, many of which were probably founded in the sixteenth or seventeenth centuries, remained simple chapels of ease, in which the prayer book service was heard each week but where sacraments were rarely administered. Some were chapels within a parochial chapelry, in other words at one remove from a direct link to the ancient parish church. Buttermere chapel was such a place, as was the tiny chapel at Wythop; both were chapels within the chapelry of Lorton. The old church at Wythop, now no more than ruined walls beside the track near Kelswick farm, was probably built in the seventeenth century (its lintel dated 1673 survives in the modern church built in 1865 on the other side of Sale Fell). The Ordnance Survey, recording it on the first edition maps surveyed just before it was replaced, noted that 'there is no graveyard attached to the chapel, which it is said was never dedicated nor even consecrated'.

When Wordsworth wrote of chapels such as these being 'the only edifice that presided' over the dwellings of the 'Perfect Republic' at the head of the Lakeland dales, he might have been thinking of Buttermere. An early engraving shows the chapel gleaming white on the hillside above the village, as mist swirls around the fell tops and the waters of Mill Beck pour out beneath the bridge. The present chapel dates from 1840 but there had been a chapel at Buttermere for several centuries, certainly by 1594 when money was left for its maintenance. It was described as a 'very ancient chapel' in 1714 and was remembered as being so small that it could seat no more than half a dozen families. Of the old chapel only the font bowl and a pair of white sandstone columns, now serving as gate piers into the grassy garth surrounding the church, survive. The modern church, which was built a few yards below the site of its predecessor, stands in a tiny stone-walled garth (again, there's no burial ground), reached by a steep flight of sandstone steps between railings, across the rough rocky bank from the road. Inside it has the normal furnishings of a Victorian church: pews, organ, embroidered hassocks, stained glass in the east window, four oak coat pegs and a two-celled brolly stand in the porch. Apart from the absence of a graveyard, it is a parish church in miniature – indeed, it was elevated to that status in 1884.

Small and simple as the church at Buttermere is, one has to visit the churches which were not completely rebuilt in the nineteenth century to gain the full flavour of the Lakeland chapels of ease. They are simple, low, sometimes whitewashed buildings, often in a remote location. Among the most memorable perhaps are the old church at Martindale (replaced by another on a new site in 1882), which lies on the edge of the common; Mosser old church, reached only by muddy footpaths across the fields; and Newlands chapel, cupped by the surrounding fells, with daffodils among the graves. Perhaps most evocative of all is the tiny chapel at Wasdale Head, a chapel within the chapelry of Eskdale, which claims to be the smallest church in England. So small and so low that it seems to crouch in its little burial ground shaded by yew trees, it barely rises above the maze of field walls on the valley floor, surrounding which rise the high fells of central Lakeland.

These chapels possess a rare stillness; they seem to be quietly waiting. They call to mind e. e. cummings' poem 'i am a little church'. Though his inspiration is said to have been a church at Madison, on the edge of the White Mountain National Forest in New Hampshire, parts of the poem might have been written of the fell chapels:

> i am a little church (no great cathedral)
> far from the splendor and squalor of hurrying cities
> - i do not worry if briefer days grow briefest,
> i am not sorry when sun and rain make april
>
> ...
>
> around me surges a miracle of unceasing
> birth and glory and death and resurrection:
> over my sleeping self float flaming symbols
> of hope, and i wake to a perfect patience of mountains

In the words of Bishop William Nicolson, describing the chapel at Mungrisdale in 1703, the Lakeland chapels are 'long and built Barn-wise; without any Distinction of Church and Quire' – in other words a simple rectangle, with no division between nave and chancel, as the absence of sacraments meant that no chancel was required. One such chapel of ease in the Pennines, near Middleton-in-Teesdale, carries its barn-like character into its name: Laithkirk, literally 'barn church', 'laith' or 'leath' being the dialect (ultimately Scandinavian) word for a barn. Most chapels had a small stone porch and simple 'domestic' windows, sometimes with stone mullions, akin to those in a farmhouse or cottage. Only the bellcote, a stone frame usually holding a single bell, open to the air, identified the building as a church. Thomas Machell, the seventeenth-century antiquary, said of Martindale chapel, 'It differs little from a barne, but a bell hanging at the west end of it'. The early Quakers, who, in the 1650s insisted on calling churches 'steeple houses' (reserving 'church' to refer to the worshipping community), tellingly called Embleton chapel a 'Bell house', because it lacked a steeple.

In the vernacular, while simple chapels like Buttermere's

were referred to as such, parochial chapels such as those at Lorton and Loweswater often acquired the dignity of being styled 'kirk' – after all, these were parish churches in all but official status. Hence, place-names like Kirkstile, beside the church at Loweswater, and Kirkhead nearby (a name recorded from the thirteenth century), which used 'kirk' in a general sense. The status of some pre-Reformation chapels was enhanced by dedication to a patron saint: Lorton's chapel was dedicated to St Cuthbert; Eskdale's to St Catherine, for example. But in the Popery-fearing centuries after the Reformation most chapels – particularly those which were not parochial – carried no dedication and were simply referred to as the chapel of the community in which they lay. Only with the renewed willingness to adopt saints in Victorian times did the dales chapels gain dedications – Buttermere's is to St James.

Until the nineteenth century, the institutional scaffolding which supported the religious life of these chapels of ease was rudimentary. There was generally no living for a clergyman in the normal sense of the word: no glebe land (or only a right to dig peat for the fire or to graze a few sheep on the fell) and no right to take tithes. Such endowments as there were were very small and other income – often small contributions paid by each family by custom – could be uncertain. The curate's income in several chapelries was under £5 a year in the early eighteenth century. At Wythop it was £2 7s 0d, coming partly from the inhabitants and partly from interest from bequests; at Wythburn it was £3 8s 2d, most of which came from the inhabitants who paid two shillings for every pound of rent they paid to the lord of the manor. At Satterthwaite in Furness Fells a mere £2 was paid by the inhabitants and this was fixed by custom, while at Seathwaite in Dunnerdale the income was £3 12s

6d paid by the inhabitants. At Mungrisdale the salary ought to have been £5 but almost one-third of the inhabitants were Dissenters (largely Quakers) who refused to pay. One way of supporting the curate was the ancient system of 'whittlegate', whereby the clergyman received board and lodging by turn from each house in the chapelry. This was the system at Buttermere in the early eighteenth century: in 1714 it was said that Buttermere chapel had 'nothing belonging to it, the Curate going from house to house in the chapelry, having no settled maintenance'. The term 'whittlegate' is said to refer to the curate using his 'whittle' or knife as he went from lodging to lodging. With such poor endowments, the curates in the fell chapels often supplemented their income by serving as schoolmaster or drawing up wills, deeds and financial papers, providing some rudimentary legal services for the local community.

An autobiographical account left by John Banks who was curate and schoolmaster at Mosser chapel in 1653, when he was fifteen, recalls how he went to

> teach school at Mosser-chappel ... where I read the Scriptures also [on Sundays] and Homily ... and sung Psalms and prayed ... for which service my wages from the people was to be 12d every house of them that came to hear me by the year (and a fleece of wool) and my table free; besides 12d a quarter for every scholar, [there] being 24.

Here we see both local control in action and a young man trying to cobble together a living: a shilling a year from each household who came to the chapel, free board, presumably on the 'whittlegate' system, and the income he could get from teaching. He also received a fleece from each household – it may not have been a coincidence that his father was a 'fellmonger', that is a dealer in fleeces and skins. The custom of schoolmasters receiving wool from each family yearly at clipping time is recorded in eighteenth-century Loweswater. It would probably have given him an income of around £5 a year, over and above board and lodging, at a time when a live-in farm servant's wage in Cumberland was about £2 a year.

Curates were generally readers, the lowest clerical order, whose role was to read the Prayer Book service but who were not licensed to christen, marry or celebrate communion. The parson would sometimes come out from the parish church to preach and perhaps baptise. At Buttermere the incumbent of Lorton came to preach no more than three or four times a year in the early eighteenth century. Many of the readers in the chapels were drawn from the community in which they served: where their names are known they frequently bear local surnames. They were often nominated by the inhabitants, a right described at Embleton in the sixteenth century as 'the nameinge, placeinge or displaceinge' of the curate. This was grassroots religion. The person officiating in the chapel from Sunday to Sunday was not an external representative of the established church but a local man performing a service for his neighbours. Few readers were university-educated and they were often young men like John Banks – sometimes still teenagers – who might double up as schoolmaster, using the chapel to teach school. For some, it was the first step on a clerical or schoolmastering career and the turnover of readers could be rapid. At Buttermere, where the inhabitants still nominated the curate in the later eighteenth century, a dozen men served the chapel in the twenty years before 1780.

Perhaps encouraged by the inbuilt conservatism of these valley communities, older practices survived in some chapels long after they had fallen into disuse elsewhere. In the process of making notes on all the churches in Carlisle diocese in the years running up to 1820, the diocesan chancellor, Walter Fletcher, noted that, on the few occasions each year when the parish priest came to celebrate communion, the congregations in the chapels of Mungrisdale, Newlands and Thornthwaite received the bread and wine while they were seated in their pews, rather than coming up to the communion rail (if, indeed, there was one). This was a survival of Calvinist practice from the sixteenth and seventeenth centuries, frowned on by the church authorities of the nineteenth – but it also hints at an egalitarian, communitarian ethos in the fell chapels.

Distance from the parish church, the meagre stipend and the low qualifications of many of the readers combined to make the life of these chapels one of 'self-help' religion in the seventeenth and eighteenth centuries. These were the community's communal spaces, and there are instances of tensions between localities and the ecclesiastical hierarchy as it attempted to impose its authority on these far-flung churches. There were battles over the appointment of readers (the Church attempting to wrest the right of nomination from local communities) as increases in the funding of a living came with strings attached. By 1800 stipends were more generous and incumbencies frequently longer. Sometimes they were much longer, thirty, forty or even fifty years being not uncommon.

By mid-Victorian times, the homespun clergy of the dales chapels a few decades earlier appeared quaintly out-of-date. William Dickinson's 'Reminiscences of Clerical Life in the Early Part of the 19th Century', published in 1875, includes an account of Osborne Littledale, who served as assistant curate at Buttermere for almost a quarter of a century, from 1804 to 1828. He was a native of Arlecdon parish, near Lamplugh, the son of a dry stone waller who managed to afford him clerical training at St Bees. But he remained a practical countryman, which made him popular in Buttermere. 'His manners were of the homeliest character ... he was strong and active, willing, and ready to put his hand to work when his neighbours were in need of help; and having been brought up on a farm, nothing of that kind came amiss to him.' His clothing was that of his neighbours: 'a drab fustian coat, corduroy knee-breeches, grey stockings of the coarsest yarn', clogs stuffed with bracken and a hat 'brown, bare and crumpled'. He was physically strong ('of burly frame and spirit') – he had been a prize wrestler in his youth – and laboured side by side with his parishioners, cutting peat on the fell-tops for the poor, felling trees, helping out with sheep clipping and at hay-time.

For more than half a century from 1816 two men served the tiny chapel at Swindale, hidden in an unfrequented valley between Haweswater and Shap. Stephen Walker, son of a local farmer, arrived in 1816, first as assistant to his uncle, and remained there until his death in 1850. Thomas Sewell, born in Shap, served for the next twenty years until his death in 1870. Both were remembered for their Westmorland speech and as 'grand old dale priests, in full sympathy with their neighbours'. The hint of nostalgia in this retrospective view was a product of a later age when a social chasm had opened up between priest and people. Sewell, a 'tall, good-looking, square-shouldered, long-legged, big-striding man', was a keen follower of fox hunts, knowing every inch of crag and fell. A story told of his brother William, when preaching at Wythburn, at the head of Thirlmere, epitomises the down-to-earth, homely character of life in the chapels at this time. William is said to have lost his sermon, dropping it down a crack out of reach, but rose to the occasion by telling his congregation, 'T'sarmont's slipt doon i' t' neuk and I can't git it oot; but I'll tell ye what – I'se read ye a chapter i' t' Bible 'at's worth three on't'.

On Sundays, small groups would converge on the chapel from farms and cottages as the bell rang out across the valley, to hear and share in the time-hallowed words of Matins or Evening Prayer, week in, week out, except when 'the rigours of winter' – storms, floods, snow and ice – prevented them. On weekdays in the seventeenth and eighteenth centuries, the chapel would have possessed little of the reverential hush it would come to gain in the Victorian era. As a young reader taught school in the chapel to help make ends meet, the damp air would be filled with the clump of clog sole on flagstone floor; the squeal of chalk on slate; the whispering and chatter of children and, on occasion no doubt, the wrath of the master. Over time, separate schoolrooms became more common, but in several of the chapels within Crosthwaite parish children continued to be taught in the west end of the chapel until the nineteenth century. The schoolroom at Newlands was partitioned off but one still had to go through it to enter the chapel until a new schoolroom (even then, still attached to the church) was built in 1877.

In the Victorian era the status of the fell chapels changed as they became parish churches in their own right and were sometimes rebuilt. They were elevated to become independent livings, more formally controlled by the church authorities. In place of a home-grown reader, the church would be served by a vicar, usually an offcomer, frequently M.A. Oxon or Cantab. Roomy vicarages were built to house the incumbent and his family in a manner appropriate to their increased status, the residence sometimes exceeding in size the small building in which the parish community worshipped. In response to the growth of ritual in the nineteenth century – and to the elevation of the chapel into a church in which the sacraments could be celebrated – chancels were built. At Buttermere a sanctuary was added, one step higher and fractionally narrower than the nave. At Borrowdale and at Wythburn disproportionately large chancels were added at the east end, attached uncomfortably to the low, barn-like body of the church. In their fittings and furnishings the chapels copied churches the country over – stained glass in the windows, pitch pine pews and polished brass.

Since the Second World War, the fell chapels, in common with churches across the country, have seen a falling away of congregations, so that the burden of responsibility for church life and fabric has been carried on the shoulders of fewer and fewer loyal souls. A dearth of ordained priests and the struggle to balance the books has resulted here, as elsewhere, in the grouping of livings under a single member of the clergy and less regular services. The recent past of the fell chapels might be written as a history of decline. And yet ....

In this seemingly secular age, Lakeland chapels have been quietly reclaimed as communal places and gained a new life. They have become places of pilgrimage for visitors to the Lake District, providing a cool, light pool of silence in which to pause after a day's walking in the fells. Most have visitors' books, recording innumerable brief detours through the creaking door, separating the ceaseless change of the outdoors from the stillness within. Many years ago I called into the chapel at Newlands on an autumn day of bright, low sunshine and cold showers, with the first scattering of snow on the fell tops. As usual, the visitors' book lay open on the table, containing the names of literally hundreds of people who had visited the church that year. Hardly a day had gone by without at least a handful of visitors; men, women and children (the outsized, effort-filled signatures of the youngsters sprawling across several lines) from all over the world. The most common comments were 'peaceful', 'beautiful', 'serene'. Some simply recorded the occasion of their visit ('a wet and exhausted mountain-biker'); others expressed deeper feelings. One entry read 'In memory of the sailor who drowned on Derwent Water on 12th May 1992'; another stated simply, 'I found the peace of God in this valley'. In the smallest chapel of all, at Wasdale Head, a book provided for people to request prayers contained at least one entry every day of the year when I flicked through it.

The old chapels possess an air of quiet tranquility, drawing visitors in. Some, no doubt, come 'to kneel where prayer has been valid' (in T. S. Eliot's words), spending a few minutes themselves in prayer. But many come out of curiosity, seeking something but perhaps not knowing what or why. As Philip Larkin put it in 'Church Going', churches will continue to draw people towards them: '... someone will forever be surprising / A hunger in himself to be more serious, / And gravitating with it to this ground'. The records in the visitors' books speak of reverence, of worship even. For how many, I wonder, is a visit to one of the old dales chapels the culmination of a day worshipping in the fells?

To Larkin, the ultimate draw of a church's sacred ground was that it was 'proper to grow wise in, / If only that so many dead lie round.' In this respect, however, some fell chapels were different. At Buttermere there is still no burial ground – being built directly onto the rock, there can be none; in most of the chapels the graveyard is small and the practice of burying beside the church came late. Providing burial space (and receiving the dues paid for burying the dead) remained the prerogative of parish churches and parochial chapels, often until the nineteenth century. So, at chapels like Wythburn and Newlands the graves and the tombstones are recent. To walk through the memorials is to be reminded of the widening horizons of the communities who claim some sense of ownership of these places of prayer. As surnames tended to be rooted in place, the turnover of local residents can be traced on the stones. Older surnames linked by the inscriptions on large Victorian headstones to particular farms disappear to be replaced by new names, still recognisably Cumbrian. And offcomers arrive, bringing surnames from across the British Isles and from mainland Europe. As in graveyards the length of Britain, the story of Lakeland communities across the past two centuries can be told from the memorials in their chapel garths.

Lake District churchyards also tell another story. For more than a century, the patch of walled graveyard around the tiny church at Wasdale Head has received the bodies of rock climbers who have died on the fells. One of the earliest burials was that of three young men in their twenties, from Croydon, Devon and Kew Gardens, who lost their lives on Sca Fell in 1903 and rest together under a single headstone. They lie close to where they fell. Another of the stones at Wasdale Head, to Claud Frankland, killed on Great Gable in 1927, sums it up simply but profoundly: 'Here he lies where he loved to be'.

Now notions of ownership and the purpose of the chapels are changing once more. In the tender care of small but dedicated bands of helpers, who polish wood and brass, embroider hassocks and bring flowers, with an incumbent rarely resident, the fell churches are once again becoming the preserve of the laity. Practices such as the holding of informal worship in summer in the chapel at Wasdale Head mark a return to the 'self-help', grassroots religious life of the seventeenth and eighteenth centuries. Now that the Lake District has become an international property of the heart, the old chapels, waiting quietly amid a 'perfect patience of mountains', reach out to a much wider world, claiming ties of deep meaning to many. As the parish authorities at Wasdale Head put it, 'the church building, which is always open, provides its own ministry to visitors'.

Detail from the tombstone of Edward Nelson and family of Gatesgarth in Lorton churchyard. The carving is an early work by Josefina de Vasconcellos (1904-2005).

CHAPTER 12

BREEDING GROUNDS

Gatesgarth

At the head of the lake of Buttermere the sharp, chiselled gable of Fleetwith Pike forms a prow pointing down-dale (Plate 1). At its foot stands Gatesgarth, one of the great sheep farms of the Lake District and one of the best documented in the written record. It is the last human habitation a visitor passes at the head of the valley before entering a world of rock, wind, and the constant sound of water.

Not long before my family left Lorton, my mother and I drove up to Gatesgarth to call on Annie Nelson (1887-1970), whose family had lived there for more than a century. It was the day after the catastrophic storm of 15 January 1968, when 20 people were killed in Scotland. The Crummock valley was wind-battered and rain-sluiced, debris from the storm scattered across road and fields. Gatesgarth Cottage, huddled beside the road at the foot of Honister Pass, was warm and dark. We found Annie in a state of some agitation as a limb of a tree had crashed down on her hen house and she had brought the hens inside 'to keep them warm'. Her care for animals was legendary: in her youth the cattle in the byre were her domain and in the 1930s she had raised a pair of orphaned fox cubs, which would follow her about the yard at the farm and were eventually sent to London Zoo when grown. That afternoon in 1968 the cottage was a cosy shelter from the gale: worn easy chairs either side of the fire; a treasured oak bread cupboard, inscribed 'F/H E 1722', opposite, which, Annie told us, had come from Lanthwaite Green. We had tea sitting close to the open fire as the wind rattled around outside.

Annie was a link to a remarkable depth of history there at the head of the dale. Her grandfather and father, both called Edward Nelson ('Old Ned' and 'Young Ned'), had farmed Gatesgarth for more than eighty years, from 1850 until 1934, when 'Young Ned' gave up farming at the age of 87. During the Nelsons' time Gatesgarth became one of the engines driving the improved and now iconic breed of Herdwick sheep, their genes spreading from Gatesgarth and a handful of other farms out across the Lakeland fells.

The ancestors of modern Herdwicks were found mostly in the western valleys of the Lake District, particularly in Wasdale, Eskdale and Dunnerdale. Before refinement by selective breeding in the nineteenth century, their particular distinguishing characteristic was that the ewes were polled (hornless). A young Bristolian visiting the Lake District in 1774 was struck by the contrast between the sheep of the Ambleside area ('Their sheep have small horns & black faces' – like the modern Swaledales) and those near Cockermouth, probably Herdwicks, some of which '[had] horns and some none; all with grey faces & legs'. The distinctiveness and the restricted distribution of the Herdwicks have made them part of the otherness of Lakeland, complete with their own origin myths. They were said to have been brought to the Lakes by Viking settlers, or to have come ashore on the west Cumberland coast from a wrecked ship from the Spanish Armada (a variant of this story has them being cast ashore from a 'Danish East Indiaman'). Modern genetic study lends some weight to the story of Viking origins. The Herdwicks were probably descended from early native breeds of sheep, possibly from the prehistoric period, as their genetic makeup contains vestiges of primitive genomes from the earliest domesticated sheep. But they also share genetic markers with far-flung sheep populations in Sweden, Finland and Iceland, separating them from other British breeds. This and a rare gene which they and the neighbouring Rough Fell sheep of southern Cumbria share only with an ancient breed from Texel, one of the Frisian Islands off the Dutch coast, perhaps hints at links to the Frisian and Viking traders of early medieval northern Europe. Some of the ancestors of the modern Herdwicks may indeed have arrived with Scandinavian settlers in the tenth century. When Herdwicks were first mentioned by name as a distinctive breed in the late eighteenth century, it was their 'hardiness of constitution', fitting them for the fierce weather of their mountain home, which drew comment.

Another of the puzzles of the breed lies in its name, 'Herdwick'. It is essentially the same as the place-name Hardwick, meaning 'stock farm', which is found widely across England and has no connection with the grey-fleeced sheep of the fells; it was used to identify livestock farms as opposed to arable farms. The earliest use of the term 'herdwick' in the Lake District is found in the survey of the estates of the newly-dissolved monastery of Furness Abbey in 1537, which describes several of the monks' farms in Furness Fells and at Brotherilkeld in Eskdale as 'herdwyks'. They were not specifically stated to be sheep farms but the name of the breed presumably comes from this use of the term for a large livestock farm. In the 1680s there was a 'Herd-wick of sheep' on Muncaster Fell and another 'herdwick' on the Dalegarth estate in Eskdale. As the name of the breed, it seems to have been firmly established by the time James Clarke first used it in print in the 1780s: 'there is a kind of sheep in these mountains called Herdwicks ...', he wrote.

The modern character of the breed is largely a product of selective breeding across the nineteenth century by a few Lakeland farmers, including the Nelsons at Gatesgarth. The process had begun by 1844 when the West Cumberland Fell Dales Sheep Association was formed to enable breeders to have access to good rams. That was six years before 'Old' Ned Nelson took over the tenancy of Gatesgarth. He arrived there at the age of 35, bringing 200 sheep with him from his former home, the Kirkstile at Loweswater, to add to the three flocks, totalling 1,200 sheep, which were let with the farm. Through careful and persistent stockmanship he refined the breed and won prizes for his improved sheep. One of his Herdwicks won the sheep championship at the Royal Show in 1864 and, by the 1870s, Nelson is said to have had 150 Herdwick rams for hire at Gatesgarth, ensuring that genes from his improved breed entered nearly every Herdwick flock in the Lake District. 'Young' Ned Nelson took over the farm in 1887 and continued the work, further refining the breed, even as the economic winter of the interwar years closed in. The Nelsons and a handful of like-minded stockmen worked determinedly to transform the Herdwick breed into the sturdy animal which adorns so many Lakeland images today. They aimed for a barrel-shaped body and sturdy legs set towards the outside. The fleece, purple-black in newborn lambs, should be thick and dense, fading to an even browny or silvery grey in the adult sheep; the head and legs are a 'clear, hoar-frosted colour' of white. The ewes are now uniformly polled, the rams carrying thick, curving horns on a broad head, which is covered in bristly hair and free from wool.

Lakeland shepherds like the Nelsons came to be treated

with a kind of reverence. Visitors increasingly saw them, like their sheep, as part of the otherness of the Lake District. Terry McCormick has recently traced the nuances of these developing views, from the backward look of Wordsworth and others who saw a fading world of lost purity as the statesmen declined, to the idealising of Lake District farmers in the late-Victorian years, notably in the writings of H. D. Rawnsley, vicar of Crosthwaite and co-founder of the National Trust. Rawnsley wrote of 'the quiet patience and honour of a shepherd's life, of the power of the Cumberland hills to make trusted and generous, to educate and refine' and deemed himself 'not a little privileged to have been admitted among [them]'. Lakeland shepherds were sought out – conversing with them, the visitor was humbled, as he fleetingly shared the 'mountain purity' of their way of life.

For Rawnsley the virtuous character and life of Lakeland shepherds was inseparable from the supposed Viking roots of the fell-farming communities. His ideas are epitomised in a green slate memorial to Edward and Joseph Hawell, two shepherds, father and son, which he erected on Lonscale Fell near Keswick, beside the main path up Skiddaw where all could see it. It takes the form of a round-headed cross, modelled on the Viking Age stones in west Cumbrian churchyards. 'On it', wrote Rawnsley, 'is carved, in symbol of eternity, the endless knot their Norse forefathers used'. Although modern scholarship suggests that the round-headed crosses and panels of interlace are not purely Norse but derive from a fusion of Celtic and Scandinavian cultures in tenth-century Cumbria, Rawnsley's intention was clear – he wanted to express an unbroken chain linking Lakeland shepherds to the Viking world, adding a further dimension to the otherness of their fell-farming culture.

During the years of depression in the 1920s and 1930s,

when times were hard for sheep farmers, those who sought to protect the Lake District recognised the need to preserve the fell farming way of life. The period saw Beatrix Potter's acquisition of the large herdwick farm at Troutbeck Park in 1923 and the purchase of three farms, including Rannerdale, by Lake District Farm Estates in 1938. Gatesgarth, too, was gathered in to preserve it for posterity, the primary impetus here being landscape preservation. When the Marshall family's large estate in the Buttermere valley (which included Gatesgarth) was broken up in 1934, Gatesgarth was bought by the historian G. M. Trevelyan, who placed it under covenant with the National Trust to protect it for the future. Trevelyan, Regius Professor of Modern History at Cambridge, was an ardent campaigner for the preservation of the English countryside, which he saw as 'the repository of national identity, "spiritual values", and liberty and freedom'. His tenet was that 'the countryside was made for man, if only man would learn to love and respect it'. His was an influential voice, as chairman of the estates committee of the National Trust and president of the Youth Hostel Association, and he had a particular love of the Lake District. In the early 1930s he bought a string of farms in Langdale, making several of them over to the National Trust, and when the deal to buy Gatesgarth was sealed in 1935 his excitement at his purchase was palpable. He spent two days 'scrambling about in [the] innermost recesses' of the fells which made up the bulk of the estate: 'There is a wonderful high lonely tarn called Bleaberry Tarn in the arms of the crags of High Style, where I bathed. I never saw it before. It's a great land.' Under his tenants, the Richardson family (who eventually bought the farm in 1963 and farmed there until 2016), Gatesgarth continued to be one of the pre-eminent Herdwick farms.

***

Gatesgarth's history as a powerhouse of stock breeding is a long one. It was already one of the largest sheep farms in the Lake District before the Nelsons took it over. On Peter Crosthwaite's map of Buttermere published in 1794, Gatesgarth is flagged 'The D[uke] of Norfolk's Great Sheep Farm'. Four years before 'Old Ned' Nelson arrived in 1850, it had been let with 1,479 sheep, divided into three separate flocks grazing the three banks of high fellside surrounding the farm: first, Gatesgarthside, the northern flank of Gatesgarthdale Beck which was freehold pasture belonging to the farm; then Fleetwith, part of Buttermere common; and finally 'Burtness' (more correctly, Birkness), another area of freehold pasture, across the valley in Loweswater manor on the slopes of Haystacks and High Stile. Earlier in the nineteenth century the number of sheep was even higher, being estimated variously as 1,800 or over 2,000 in the years around 1800. When William Green drew up a list of the largest sheep flocks in the Lake District for his guidebook published in 1819, Gatesgarth was in the top ten, along with other dalehead farms – Taw House and Brotherilkeld in Eskdale, Black Hall at the head of Dunnerdale, Patterdale Hall at the head of Ullswater and Troutbeck Park.

If we were to go back a century before 'Old' Ned Nelson arrived at Gatesgarth, the landscape would have appeared wilder. Warnscale Beck meandered across the dale bottom (described in 1750 as 'pasture & wett meadow ground'), its alternative name 'Crooked Beck' describing its winding route in its natural state. The plantations and new walls and the beck's straightened course were yet to come – it would have appeared a more open, less tended scene. In 1750 there were two farms at Gatesgarth, one on the site of the present farm; the other (according to Annie, the one her grandfather took over) on the site of the car park opposite her cottage. Even in 1750, both were large sheep farms, one running 1,000 sheep; the other 600. There were a few acres of ploughable ground around the farmsteads but most of the 'low grounds' were hay meadows – it was said that the tenant of one of the farms 'buys the greatest part of his bread Corn'. The valley bottom was more valuable for the vital crop of grass needed to make the hay to feed the sheep through winter. Surrounding the fields were the sheep heafs on the open fells, at that date listed under six names: Gatesgarthside, Green and Fleetwith on the east; Birkness, Warnscale and Dalehead on the south and west.

Almost thirty years earlier, a glimpse of farming practice at Gatesgarth can be caught in a rare flash of detail provided by an inventory drawn up when one of the farms there changed hands in 1722. Shepherding items head the list: 'tipp couples' (chains to tie two rams together to control them); two pairs of 'Wool Shears (old)'; the wherewithal for 'salving' the sheep (by spreading a mixture of butter and tar on the skin in autumn to keep down parasites): 'butter kitts', 'salve kitts', 'tarr dishes', 'greasing forms' and the 'smitt potts' for renewing the sheep marks on the fleece. 'Husbandry Gear' included a 'graveing spade' for digging peat for fuel, a 'turf spade' and 'gripe' (i.e. muck fork) and a 'Gavelock', the dialect term explained in parentheses as 'Iron Crow'. Conspicuous by its absence is any mention of a plough or harrow – this was a stock farm through and through. But it was not only a sheep farm: in the kitchen, alongside the tableware for the family and farm servants (coarse earthenware plates, porringers and posset cups, three dozen trenchers and two dozen 'piggins'), were the tools of dairying, including 14 wooden milk bowls ('of which 6 are thrown & 8 girded'), two milking pails, four cheese rums and a churn. We even know the names of the seven milk cows on the farm at that date. Five were black cows: Bony (6 years old; 'calves a fortnight hence', that is, in November), Lovely (6 years old; calves in March); Stubby (10 years old; calves in April); Langhorns (12 years old; 'has a calve three weeks old'); and Old Pegg (14 years old; due to calve in the spring). The others, also in calf for the spring, were a red cow, Langhorn'd Redd (11 years old), and a 'branded' cow called Brandy (7 years old).

Much of the world of stock farming at Gatesgarth described in the survey of 1750 and the inventory from 1722 would have been familiar to Annie Nelson and her family. There had been changes of course, particularly in the livestock themselves, not only the improvements to the Herdwick breed but also the replacement of longhorn cattle by the new shorthorn breed in the nineteenth century. Other changes included the arrival of sheep dips in the later nineteenth century, but second-hand memories of older practices (washing sheep in summer in a 'wash dub' in a beck before clipping, and salving them in autumn to protect against parasites) survived. Continuities in hill farming practice flowed down to the middle decades of the twentieth century, only being finally dislodged by the tractor and the quad bike and increasing external regulation.

***

Gatesgarth had an even earlier incarnation, a faint echo of which seems to have reached down to Annie's time. In the field behind her cottage Annie was aware of traces of past buildings, surviving as faint earthworks. She knew the field as 'Chapel Close' (the name was already in use by 1750) and she believed the earthworks to be the remains of a long-lost chapel. This seems to be an example of a tendency found elsewhere in the Lake District to identify unexplained, forgotten footings or heaps of stones as religious sites – the 'Chapel in the Hause' at Boredale at the head of Martindale, and Towtop Kirk, the stone circle near Bampton, are other examples. However, when the earthworks at Gatesgarth were excavated in the winter of 2007-8, they were revealed to be the remains, not of a religious building but of a medieval longhouse, a tangible survival of the farm that stood there in the Middle Ages.

Uniquely for the Lake District, records allow us to recapture life at Gatesgarth in the late 1200s. At that time, Gatesgarth was a cattle-breeding farm or 'vaccary' (from the Latin *vacca*, a cow) run as part of a wider stock-rearing enterprise centred on Cockermouth Castle. Such livestock farms were numerous in the Pennines and areas like the Bowland fells in the Middle Ages but were less common in the Lake District. There were a few and where they are mentioned explicitly, it is striking that they are found at the heads of the valleys. The barons of Egremont had vaccaries at the head of Ennerdale and at Wasdale Head, for example, and monastic vaccaries were found high up Borrowdale, at Stonethwaite, and at Brotherilkeld at the head of Eskdale. In each of these other examples, we know nothing of the workings of the vaccaries; merely the fact that farms described as such stood in those locations. Detailed farm accounts from Gatesgarth, however, give a first-hand description of farming at the dalehead over a period of almost thirty years from 1267.

As is so often the case with historical records, the world of this thirteenth-century farming enterprise can be recaptured only because a quirk of history resulted in the survival of documents which would otherwise almost certainly have been lost long ago. With the rest of the southern half of Derwentfells, Gatesgarth lay in the part of the honour of Cockermouth belonging to William de Fortibus, earl of Albemarle. When he died in 1260 his share of the Cockermouth estate formed part of the dower of his widow Isabella, becoming a distant outpost of the countess's landed inheritance which was centred in the East

Riding of Yorkshire and in Northamptonshire. Records of the farming enterprise at Gatesgarth were kept meticulously and fed into the management of this vast estate. When the Fortibus line ended with Countess Isabella's death in 1293, her estates – and, importantly, the parchment rolls recording the estate's accounts – passed to the Crown. Although the earl's Cumberland estate was granted back to the de Lucy family in 1323, thus reuniting the two halves of the honour of Cockermouth, the records from the countess's time remained stashed away in a corner of the Tower of London, preserved for posterity to become a tiny part of a huge collection of account rolls now preserved in The National Archives. Had any of Isabella's children outlived her (her son, William's heir, had died young in 1269), it is unlikely that these account rolls would have survived; we have the bureaucratic inertia of medieval royal administrators to thank for forgetting about them and letting them languish in a dusty recess.

The list of grazing grounds in Derwentfells retained in hand by the countess as private pastures, drawn up in 1270, was headed by Gatesgarth, which was a pasture not for sheep but for cattle: it could support 60 cows and their young. These were part of a large, integrated stock-breeding business, which included another upland cattle pasture on Skiddaw (for oxen, bullocks and heifers) and a lowland stock farm at Birkby, on the coast near the modern town of Maryport. Gatesgarth's role in this medieval agri-business was as a breeding ground for cattle.

The ten account rolls which survive from the days of the dowager countess, scattered across the years between 1267 and 1290, record a herd of upwards of 40 cows at Gatesgarth, with two bulls and their young up to two years old, making a total herd of around 100 beasts. In the 1280s they were in the care of an estate official, Adam Fordles or Forthles, the 'keeper' of the vaccary, who was a local man who held property in Buttermere. He was assisted at Gatesgarth by a 'cow keeper in winter'. As well as providing bullocks to be grown on as draught oxen and heifers to replenish the breeding stock, the vaccary generated income by selling milk, suggesting that it supported local dairying. A vital component of the vaccary was the level meadow land at the head of the lake, from which hay was cut each year to provide the feed to see the cattle through the winter. Across the dark months of the year, the stock were housed indoors (a cow house 67 feet long was built in 1282-3) and their dung collected, to be spread on the meadows to replenish fertility each spring. When the grass began to grow again, the herd was put out to graze in what is variously called the 'wood' or the 'park' of Gatesgarth, which was enclosed by palings. This was almost certainly the precursor of Gatesgarthside (termed the 'forest of Gatesgarth' in the sixteenth century), which remained one of the private pastures belonging to the farm in the nineteenth century. Its wall enclosing the vast bank of fellside on the slopes of Robinson, from Hassness to halfway up Gatesgarthdale, dates from the nineteenth century, but there are traces of an earlier bank and ditch in places. The wall fixed in stone the bounds of a pasture which had been the private ground of the lords of Cockermouth in the Middle Ages and was the last vestige of their active use of their forest of Derwentfells. In the countess's time, groups of grazing cattle would be seen moving slowly between the rocks and crags in open woodland across the 'park'; dairymaids would have been milking the cows; labourers mowing, spreading and bringing in the hay; others mending the park pale or repairing the cowsheds.

The world of the vaccary fades from view after the death of Countess Isabella in 1293. The even more distant managers of the Crown's estates had let the pasture of Gatesgarth to tenants by 1310 and, with the end of direct farming, the detailed accounts of the stock keeper ceased. The vaccary remained leased and was subdivided into several tenanted holdings: by the sixteenth century there were three farms at Gatesgarth, the ancestors of the holdings which eventually coalesced in 'Old' Ned Nelson's time into the single farm of today.

How was the dalehead used in the centuries before the vaccary and its remarkable records? We have to rely once again on the names of places to be able to say anything about the dalehead breeding grounds before the mid-thirteenth century. The name Buttermere suggests that the valley was rich in grazing: 'butter' may imply no more than rich pastures but it is conceivable that it might record a deep-seated dairying tradition, reaching back before the vaccary at Gatesgarth enters the written record. But there are other place-names which hint at an even earlier way of life, before the cattle arrived. 'Gatesgarth' itself means the 'mountain pass frequented by goats', the pass in question presumably being Honister. Like other Lakeland names referring to goats (the other Gatescarth, at the head of Longsleddale; Gaitscale at the head of the Duddon valley), it speaks of an untamed and remote wilderness, the stronghold of goats on the crags. Goats were part of the medieval pastoral world, in the Lake District as elsewhere in the upland north, particularly in the inner recesses of the fells, but they seem to have been part of an older pastoralism, pushed aside by cattle and sheep. The isolated Hobcarton valley near Whinlatter was identified as a grazing ground for a flock of goats in the list of 1270, but even by that date no goats are recorded on Countess Isabella's other fell pastures. By the sixteenth century attempts were being made to control or even ban goat-keeping (because of the damage they did to trees), but in the decades around 1500, inhabitants of Derwentfells and Loweswater were still occasionally brought before the manor courts for keeping goats and the name Goat Crag, overlooking the lake above Hassness, perhaps hints at their late survival.

If goats clung to the wild places, it was the pig which was central to an earlier world of pastoralism lower down the Lakeland valleys. Around the Lake District, particularly on the lower fells and in valleys tucked away on the edges of the hills are place-names containing the words *swīn* or *svín* ('swine') and *griss* (Old Norse for a 'young pig') – names like Swinside and Swindale, Grisedale and Grizebeck. When the first historian of Cumberland, John Denton, writing around 1600, attempted to explain the stem of the name Mungrisdale he probably wasn't far wrong. He described it as a 'store house' where the medieval lords of Greystoke kept livestock and 'suffered the porklins to run wylde in the woodes that grew in the skirtes and borders of the mountaines'. Pigs were woodland animals and were grazed in the surviving patches of woodland, which would have been more extensive in the Scandinavian and Norman periods than after the colonisation of the dales in the twelfth and thirteenth centuries. Such pig-grazed woods probably existed on the edge of the fells above Lorton, where two farms and a bank of fellside carry the name Swinside. The 'assarts' (woodland clearings) recorded there in 1259 suggest that the woods were being cleared for cultivation and that the pigs had perhaps already gone. Elsewhere in Derwentfells were the Grisedale on the northern slopes of Grisedale Pike and another Swinside in the fells behind Buttermere, near the pass over to Newlands. The use of woods as grazing grounds for pigs generated income for the lords in the form of 'pannage', a render paid specifically for putting pigs into woodland to feast on the acorn crop in autumn. Countess Isabella's estate accounts show that pigs continued to be pastured in the woods of Derwentfells even when sheep and cattle farming was well established: the 22 shillings paid in 1282 was for 171 pigs and 93 'hogs'. However, the accounts also show that receipts from pannage declined steeply across the later thirteenth century, the sum collected in 1289 being less than one-fifth of the figure for 1266. By the time of the Black Death pannage was largely a thing of the past in Cumbria, suggesting that the pigs had gone as the woods faced an onslaught from the hungry mouths of cattle and sheep, or were enclosed to protect them for coppicing.

***

Livestock husbandry also had an impact on the wildlife of the high fells, particularly those species deemed to be vermin and to pose a threat to sheep. Their presence is recorded in place-names across the Lake District, referring to wolf, fox and wild cat, and to eagle and raven. Of these, the wolf was the earliest to disappear and the species most deeply ingrained in folk memory. Wolf place-names in the Lake District are neither numerous nor completely certain – the difficulty for place-name scholars is that Old Norse *ulfr* ('wolf') is impossible to distinguish from the identical personal name *Ulfr*. Likely candidates for names referring to wolves are Ullock ('the place where wolves play') in the Newlands valley and Ulpha ('wolf hill') in Dunnerdale. How long wolves survived in the Lake District is difficult to say. It is generally agreed that they did not outlive the Middle Ages in England (though they clung on in the Scottish Highlands until perhaps the seventeenth century). The latest explicit mentions of wolves in England are from the northern counties: from the Bowland Fells in northern Lancashire around 1300 and from the North York Moors in the 1390s. Their demise has been put down, at least in part, to the decline in the population of deer in the later Middle Ages, as the financial potential of livestock farming in upland forests outweighed attempts to preserve game. It may be telling that the vaccary at Gatesgarth and the lordly sheep flocks in Derwentfells do not appear to have been troubled by wolves in the later thirteenth century. Perhaps they had gone by then.

But the wolf was the exception; most predators survived into much later centuries or are still present today. Among the place-names linking wildlife to particular places on the fells, the most numerous are those referring to ravens, as in the Raven Crags on Fleetwith, Melbreak and Low Fell, where ravens are still to be seen. Some crags deep in the heart of the fells are named from the eagle, the king of birds, now no longer present in the Lake District. These names often use the eagle's Old English name, *earn*, as in Erne Crag and (through a misunderstanding of its meaning) in Heron Crag and Aaron Crag (in Borrowdale). There were eagles at the head of Buttermere: 'Here Eagles Build' stated George Smith's map of 1751, in the wildness beneath Haystacks. Mammalian vermin included wild cats and 'marts' (whether the 'sweet mart' (pine marten) or the 'foul mart' (polecat) is often unclear). In his account of Westmorland in the late seventeenth century, the antiquary Thomas Machell recorded that 'Marts and wild cats are found all over' the Langdale area, while at Hartsop at the head of Ullswater, 'They have great store of Marts hereabouts, som of which are very perniciouse not only to their Lambs but old sheep too'. The last refuge of the reclusive wild cats was probably in hidden, wooded gills, as recorded in the name Catgill (found beside Derwent Water and near Mosser, for example). Then there was the fox, Beatrix Potter's 'Mr Tod', the species most associated as a threat to Lakeland sheep farming in the popular imagination.

The map is peppered with references to the fox in names such as Tod Crag, Tod Gill and Todholes.

All these species were subjected to sustained persecution. They were all listed in the Tudor vermin acts as creatures for which the churchwardens of every parish were to pay a bounty under the Act of 1566 (which was not repealed until 1863). In the comparatively few surviving records from Cumberland, payments for ravens and foxes top the lists, while the heads of wild cats and 'marts' were also frequently brought in. In a rare survival of early churchwardens' accounts for the Lake District proper, from the fell chapelries in St Bees parish in 1666, payments for 2 fox heads from Netherwasdale, 5 ravens and a fox cub from Eskdale, and 7 fox heads, 12 young ravens and a wild cat from Ennerdale are recorded. By 1800 it appears that the last of the wild cats and eagles had gone from the Buttermere valley. The killing of a wild cat at Waterendwood, Loweswater, probably in the 1770s, may well have been one of the last. At Buttermere, where eagles nested in Burtness Comb, the last breeding pair were said to have been shot around 1790 by the son of the farm manager at Gatesgarth. Pine martens just about clung on, particularly in the more remote dales. One was captured in Burtness Comb, probably in the early twentieth century – 'a mysterious animal like a very large weazel' – and taken down to Annie Nelson who kept it as a pet for several years. Like her pet fox cubs, it became a talking point among her many visitors.

Foxes survived. The distinctive tradition of Lake District foxhunting, where the hounds were followed on foot and the hunts were firmly rooted in the local farming culture, is well known. It would bring the valley to life on a cold winter's morning: a line of cars parked hurriedly on the roadside where a huddle of older men with binoculars scoured the fellside across the valley; younger men striding across the fell, following the pack in full cry, weaving in and out of the rocks in pursuit of their quarry. Packs such as the Melbreak, which hunted across the Buttermere valley, were founded in the nineteenth century, the Melbreak pack itself dating from about 1870. It has been estimated that around 350 foxes were killed each year by the six Lake District hunts in the mid-twentieth century, without any noticeable reduction in overall fox numbers. However, there had by then been a change in the character of the fox population – the dark grey, long-legged fell foxes of the nineteenth century, which roamed the higher fells, had gone, to be replaced by the smaller reddish breed which lurked mainly in wooded areas. The increase in the number of walkers on the fells at a time when woodland gamekeeping was in decline is thought to have driven the change.

Modern foxhunting packs built on a much longer tradition of organised hunting. The Cumbrian surname Todhunter, recorded from the fourteenth century, implies that huntsmen formed a separate occupation from an early date, and organised hunting is explicitly recorded by the later seventeenth century. In 1690 the court for the manor of Braithwaite and Coledale (which included Buttermere) noted that there had been 'great complainte' in the Newlands valley that 'sevarall within that neighbourhood has been very necligent when desired to goe to hunte the Fox' and the jury ordered 'that all the neighbourhood that has anye heafe goeing sheep [on the fells there] shall uppon notice given partikullarly send every one a man to hunte'. The following year the order was repeated and directed specifically at the community at Buttermere: when called, every household there was to send either 'the man of the house, his son or his servant … to the hunting of the fox'. How the hunt was organised is not stated, but it was clearly a communal event and an obligation. On the other side of the Lake District, at Thornthwaite, near Shap, further evidence of hunting survives in the records of the manor court. In 1678 the court there ordered that the bounties payable for killing foxes were to be divided between those killing the fox and 'the Huntsman and them that keeps the doggs', suggesting the presence of an organised pack there as well, more than three centuries ago.

For a thousand years and more the upper reaches of the Lake District valleys have served primarily as a breeding ground for domestic livestock. The animals put out to graze may have changed across the centuries, as the pigs of the Viking and Norman eras gave way to cattle and sheep of the later Middle Ages, with sheep coming to dominate in later centuries, but the imperative throughout has been to harvest a crop of young livestock bred on the fells. It has been a single-minded pursuit, particularly where young of sheep, susceptible to the depredations of both birds and mammals, were concerned. The names of high crags and hidden gills recording species of wildlife which have been hunted to extinction are a silent record of the losses which accompanied centuries of livestock farming on the Lakeland fells.

'Ready for a climb': Dick Hall in 1931 (photograph by his cousin, R. L. Hall).

CHAPTER 13

THE FREEDOM OF
THE FELLS

Warnscale Bottom

This journey upstream ends in the deep basin of Warnscale Bottom, hemmed in by walls of crag below Haystacks and Fleetwith Pike. Behind the crags lie the broken fell tops of the mountainous heart of the Lake District. These fells are the gathering ground for the streams feeding Buttermere and Crummock. As heaven deals the water, rain falling on the northern slopes of Brandreth and Grey Knotts seeps into the wet ground, to emerge in a host of infant streams which trickle across the surface, sometimes ponding in wet hollows or meandering around outcrops; in places sliding in a wet smear across a slab of rock, continually drawn down-slope by gravity. The trickles combine and gather speed, creating veins of pure water, glittering in the sunshine. These headwaters of Warnscale Beck then plunge over the crag into a steep-sided chasm overhung by rowan trees, below which they continue to fall through waterfalls and pools before reaching the valley floor, where they become a wide braided stream, dissipating their energy across a spreading bed of gravel. As the beck crosses Warnscale Bottom, its character changes again. Where it passes a small plantation of Scots pine and enters the farmland of Gatesgarth, its final reach has been straightened – and 'straitened' – in an attempt to improve the drainage of the waterlogged meadows on the valley floor.

Heading from Gatesgarth out into the fells, the silence is palpable – a silence accentuated by sound: distant tumbling water hundreds of feet away; sheep calling across the fellsides; the croak of a raven or mew of a buzzard high above. Three routes lead from Gatesgarth out and up across watersheds to the valleys beyond: the road over Honister Pass to Borrowdale, a quarrymen's track up Warnscale Bottom along the flank of Fleetwith Pike, and the mountain pass of Scarth Gap, the notch between High Crag and Haystacks, leading over to Ennerdale. These have long been part of the network of long-distance tracks through the high fells of the central Lake District, linking valleys which were only a few straight miles apart but were separated by inhospitable high rocky ground. Until the 1930s the mountain passes through the central Lake District were rough, stony tracks. The Ramblers' Federation yearbook, *The Lakeland Rambler*, for 1934 listed the passes and noted that only Kirkstone, Whinlatter and Dunmail Raise were 'good motoring roads'. Motorcycle trials, it said, were sometimes attempted over Hardknott and Wrynose but they were 'really only fit for walking'. Horse-drawn charabancs from Keswick had traversed Honister and Newlands passes in the summer months for many years and motorists soon began to tackle them, risking the steep gradients and tyre-shredding stones; 'some succeed in going over'. Pressure was building to convert the main mountain passes into made roads. Five improvement schemes were proposed in 1934, but only two of them, Honister pass and the Birker Moor road from Dunnerdale to Eskdale, were completed. Newlands pass followed shortly afterwards, the seven-foot grass track over the hause to Buttermere being replaced by tarmac in 1937. Other mountain routes survived in their pre-motor state, including Styhead pass, which had been listed for improvement in the 1934 proposals. But the importance of the unmade passes grew as fell walking and rock climbing gained in popularity from the Victorian period.

From the early days of Lake District tourism, travellers came not only to gaze at the landscape from vantage points in the valleys but began to head for the fell tops. An ascent of Skiddaw on horseback, accompanied by a guide, had become part of the tourist itinerary from Keswick by the 1770s. How many early visitors ventured into the more mountainous terrain of the central fells is unclear. Coleridge famously climbed Sca Fell in 1802 and Dorothy Wordsworth and her companion Mary Barker (whom Dorothy described as 'an active Climber of the hills') ascended Esk Hause and went on to Sca Fell, guided by a local shepherd, in 1818. By the mid-nineteenth century, visitors, often led by local guides, were crossing the fells on the mountain passes and reaching the summits, as J. B. Pyne's engraving of 1853 showing tourists on Brandreth, taking in the view down the Buttermere valley, demonstrates. The growth of rock climbing in the Lake District in the 1880s and the increasingly powerful draw of the fells to walkers and ramblers in the first half of the twentieth century swelled the numbers of visitors who now peopled the remote places which had for centuries been the preserve of shepherds, quarrymen and few others.

The passion with which fell walkers and rock climbers claimed the fells was part of a revolution in the way land was valued and perceived. At its heart lay a new idea, that the nation as a whole and the public at large had a valid interest in land and landscape. Its roots are often attributed to Wordsworth's famous rallying call that the Lake District was 'a sort of national property, in which every man has a right and interest who has an eye to perceive and a heart to enjoy' but, as Paul Readman has recently shown, they can be traced back even earlier, to 1802, when Richard Warner saw the beauty of Lakeland scenery as 'the common property of the people'. It was a change of view which gathered pace in the 1860s with the founding of the Commons Preservation Society in 1865 and came to the fore in the Lake District in fierce debates in the 1870s and 1880s over the proposal to dam Thirlmere to provide a water supply for Manchester, and over a succession of railway projects, including one to build a line from Keswick to Buttermere and Honister.

This new attitude was revolutionary because it led inexorably to the view that the public interest could limit the freedom of action of the owner of the land. It is something we take for granted today, when property rights are constrained by layers of legislation protecting wider interests – planning controls, conservation legislation, listed buildings and scheduled archaeological monuments, and so on – but it was radically new in the nineteenth century. From the 1860s the main public claim was access to common land for the purposes of recreation, the view being that open land should act as lungs for the swelling population of smoke-bound towns.

In the Lake District, the struggle over Thirlmere was more complex, as two different visions of the wider public interest collided. Manchester Corporation planned to exercise their property rights (they had bought up most of the Thirlmere valley) to satisfy one external interest – providing water to sustain life and improve sanitation in one of the nation's largest industrial cities. But the corporation's aims clashed with the aesthetic value claimed by sections of the nation as a whole. Harriet Ritvo has suggested that the revolutionary ideas about 'ownership' that were played out over Thirlmere, which led to the establishment of the first serious conservation body in the area, the Lake District Defence Society, were the foundation of modern 'green' ideas. The most vociferous opponents of Manchester's scheme 'had neither a legal right

... nor a direct financial stake' in the outcome, but there emerged from the battle over the dam a belief which has stuck: the public's interest in preserving the character of the Lake District was of sufficient weight to fetter the freedom of those with property rights there. By 1887 the *Manchester Guardian* could opine, 'The Lake District belongs to all England' and 'all England' increasingly meant the climbers and walkers who took to the fells.

* * *

In the story of the discovery of the fells by walkers and climbers, the mountain passes leading from Gatesgarth played a central role. Two routes became increasingly popular: the quarrymen's track that led up to Grey Knotts and Brandreth and on to Great Gable and the Sca Fell massif, and Scarth Gap pass which gave access both to Pillar Rock (a climbers' honeypot) and, by way of Black Sail pass, to Wasdale Head, the Mecca of early rock climbers. Gatesgarth farm played a part in this new passion for the fells. From the middle of the nineteenth century, the Nelson family acted as guides: 'young' Ned Nelson recalled that his mother's death, when he was a boy, coincided with him having taken a party over to Wasdale. The anonymous 'Volunteer Rifleman' on a walking tour through the western fells in the summer of 1859 found 'a good many tourists' staying at Wasdale Head and met other walkers as he made his way across Black Sail and Scarth Gap passes. Serious rock climbing took off in the Lakes in the early 1880s, when the educated upper middle-class pioneers of Alpine mountaineering turned their attention to rocks nearer home and the attraction of climbing spread to a wider, regional middle class. Wasdale Head became the focal point for these 'university men' and professionals, as the natural base for exploring the most promising rock-girthed fells, Great Gable and the Sca Fell group. To reach Wasdale, parties of visitors often crossed the fells from Keswick, coming via Scarth Gap and Black Sail, recording their journeys in the hotel visitors' book at Wasdale Head in the 1870s and 1880s. In 1878 a banker from Perth and his companion arrived there from Buttermere with Edward Nelson (presumably 'young' Ned), 'a trusty guide (without whom no-one should attempt wandering among these hills)', they wrote.

One of the increasing number who took the routes out from Gatesgarth in the early days of Lake District mountaineering was the local pioneer of rock climbing, John Wilson Robinson (1853-1907) of Whinfell Hall, near Lorton. He was part of the Wasdale Head brotherhood, a local cragsman whose prowess on rock was greatly respected and who forged a close climbing partnership with the young Walter Haskett-Smith, later considered to be 'the father of British rock climbing'. Their partnership on the rocks bridged a social divide and epitomised the ability of the new sport of rock climbing to break away from the exclusivity of the Alpine mountaineering tradition. Haskett-Smith, Eton- and Cambridge-educated, was a man of private means; Robinson, six years his senior, was a yeoman farmer and land agent. Robinson appears to have been a charismatic man, 'with smiling tanned face, sandy side whiskers, a bald head [and] a suit of good homespun tweed' – a man of a sunny nature, full of fun and a great raconteur. Indeed, in Robinson, the visiting climbers had as their guide, mentor and climbing partner a true representative of statesman stock, a north country yeoman, deeply rooted in the soil of the Lake District, whose lineage (both his Quaker forebears of longstanding and his presumed Scandinavian ancestry deeper in the past) linked him inextricably to contemporary idealised views of Lake District mountain society. He was the real thing: a Lakeland yeoman rock climber.

Robinson knew Gatesgarth and Warnscale Bottom well. It is said that it was not unknown for him to set out from his home, Whinfell Hall, at 3 o'clock in the morning in order to meet a Cambridge professor on Great Gable at 10 o'clock. Such excursions may have been uncommon, but Robinson pioneered routes up the crags around Buttermere which became recognised rock climbs, including Green Crag gully at the head of Warnscale Bottom in 1889 and chimneys on Chapel Crags on High Stile in 1893. His route to Pillar Rock in Ennerdale, with which his name is indelibly connected (he made over 100 ascents), also brought him to Gatesgarth and over Scarth Gap. Other climbers built on John W. Robinson's pioneering explorations, so that the crags surrounding Buttermere became a secondary centre for rock climbing. One Edwardian climber, Lehmann J. Oppenheimer (1868-1916), a Manchester mosaic artist and manufacturer, chronicled how he and his fellows conquered gullies on Haystacks and around High Stile across the first decade of the twentieth century. By then, the high fells had become a place of energetic recreation – 'a remote and secluded playground of extraordinary beauty and health-giving properties'.

***

As we were leaving Gatesgarth Cottage that stormy day in January 1968, Annie Nelson turned back into the house and brought out a slender, dark cane walking pole which she handed to me. It had belonged to my grandfather's elder brother, Richard Watson Hall (1882-1935), known universally as 'Dick', and had been given to Annie as a memento after his death. 'You'd better have it, lad', she said, 'in case something happens to me'. Gatesgarth had been a second home to Dick Hall, an ardent outdoor man who pioneered several climbs in the Buttermere and Crummock valley. Like his hero, John Wilson Robinson, whom he had known in his youth, he was a local man, not university-educated and thus socially on the fringes of the climbing elite. He had taken over the family grocery business in Cockermouth from his father, but he was a reluctant grocer, his heart being outdoors and on the fells, and he retired from the business in 1926, when he was in his forties.

His diaries – fourteen volumes recording his life from early manhood in 1904 until his premature death in 1935 – paint a vivid picture of someone driven by a passion for the outdoors. He was a sturdy man, 'exuding health and happiness', a man of 'radiant good-fellowship' and boundless boyish energy which spills out from the pages of his diary: he was 'a boy still growing up and a boy full of the enthusiasms of youth', as one obituarist put it in the local press after his death. He explored every crag and gully from Hobcarton to Haystacks, walking or cycling out from Cockermouth at every available opportunity, camping for a spell most summers with climbing companions on the common at Lanthwaite Green. Ever the adventurer, he built a coracle from a chicken swill and paddled it through Buttermere and Crummock and down the River Derwent (the *Daily Mirror* headed its report 'Voyage in a Hen Basket'!). After retiring from business, he led walking holidays to Switzerland and Andorra, was instrumental in the early days of the Youth Hostel Association, and wrote a homely handbook on hill camping, fell walking and rock climbing, *The Art of Mountain Tramping* (published in 1932). 'I have found my work', he confided to his diary in 1909, when he started writing regular newspaper pieces 'of free air & sun & fell' for the local press under the pen name 'Hobcarton', revelling in the joys and beauties of time spent on the fells.

'Dear old Gatesgarth' was Dick Hall's favourite base for excursions to the high fells. He knew the Nelsons well, the link between the two families going back to his parents' day. A visit at Easter, a vigorous climb followed by tea in the kitchen at Gatesgarth, had become an established annual event before the First World War. In 1906 Dick, then 24 years old, and my grandfather, with their young uncle Arthur Watson, cycled to Gatesgarth on Easter Tuesday and left word with Mrs Nelson 'for tea (ham & eggs!) at 3 o'clock for 6 people', as they were expecting to be joined by other members of the family. They climbed Haystacks and Brandreth, then, on a whim, decided to go further, to Green Gable and Great Gable, arriving back at Gatesgarth at 6 o'clock to discover that the rest of the family had eaten their tea – more ham and eggs were ordered. 'We are almost hysterical with fresh air & sun & roar & laugh very boisterously', Dick wrote. 'It is ripping being out in the air and we all enjoyed it immensely.' The Edwardian language may have dated but the exhilaration of a day on the fells is an experience many will recognise. The Easter visits continued for the rest of his life, usually on Good Friday, and when Dick, Kathleen Dixon of Toddell and a few friends formed an informal hiking club in 1928 they dubbed it the 'Gatesgarth Club'. Though the mode of transport had changed from bicycle to motorcycle to motor car by the 1930s, the format remained the same – a climb, usually an ascent of Great Gable, followed by tea at the farm.

Dick Hall and his circle were but a handful of the many regulars for whom tea at Gatesgarth was an integral part of a day on the fells. 'How many professors, public school boys, teachers, fell walkers and rock climbers, and ordinary folk have entered that home?' wrote 'a Mountaineer' in an appreciation of Mrs Nelson after her death in 1930. '[A]ll received a kindly welcome … [Mrs Nelson was] always ready … to enter into sympathy with our exploits among the hills and to provide us with food, shelter and warmth, after long days of rain and storm on the high fells'. Her husband, Ned, regaled visitors with stories of sheep and foxhunting and the olden days. The warmth of that farm kitchen spread far, linking Gatesgarth to an international community of cragsmen. The farm sale at Gatesgarth when Ned Nelson retired in March 1934 must have felt like the end of an era. Well-wishers, most of them visitors welcomed to the farm by the Nelson family over many years, collected the substantial sum of £110 as a gift for him. His funeral at Lorton six months later was large, the mourners including that champion breeder of Herdwicks, Mrs Heelis (Beatrix Potter). One of his many friends, the sculptor Josefina de Vasconcellos, carved him a fitting tombstone, a solid slab of slate, with a cameo at the top of a Herdwick ewe nursing two lambs.

After her parents' deaths Annie Nelson continued to serve teas at Gatesgarth Cottage well into old age, so the link between the Nelsons and the climbing community continued for more than a century. Recalling days on the rocks in the years after the Second World War, one climber remembered Annie Nelson's front room as 'the rendezvous for many a cheerful gathering of damp and pungent climbers, their patched knees stained with moss and their fingernails black with dirt and lichen'. Gatesgarth's place in the world of rock climbing continued in recent decades, throughout the Richardson family's time at the farm, as a rescue post for the Cockermouth Mountain Rescue team, of which Maureen Richardson became president.

The passion for the fells and, particularly, the rock climbers' close encounter with the micro-topography of a crag face spawned a host of new place-names, reflecting how a new social group was gaining finger-tip knowledge of every slab and crevice on the high crags and claiming the fells as their playground. As the gullies and chimneys up the crags surrounding Buttermere were explored, tested and designated as rock climbs in the first two decades of the twentieth century, new names proliferated. In 1922 Dick Hall produced 'A Memory Map of the Crummock Valley, showing Recognised Rock Climbs', a crude sketch map which he had printed as a quarto sheet. On the face of Haystacks were 'Green Crag Gully', 'Toreador Gully', 'The Y Gully', 'Wharn Ghyll' and 'Stack Ghyll'. Around Burtness Comb were 'Sheepbone Buttress', 'Barndoor Climb', 'Oxford and Cambridge', 'Bishops Arete' and 'The Mitre Climb'. The language of these new names was modern English – in many cases, no doubt, spoken with an Oxford drawl – setting them far apart from the dialect names of the working landscape. Where these names are not purely descriptive, they have the feeling of being clubbish, sometimes of being an in-joke among friends, now lost to us. Lehmann Oppenheimer confirmed that the name of 'Toreador Gully' on Green Crag was just that: Haskett-Smith had christened it as a result of 'a pleasant incident at the top after he, Scott-Tucker and I had been exploring it', he wrote coyly, without giving away what that incident was. 'Sheepbone Buttress' was a name associated (why is not clear) with A. C. Pigou, professor of Economics at Cambridge, who had built a house at Lower Gatesgarth in 1911 to give him immediate access to the climbs around Buttermere. Pigou was part of the university crowd which included G. M. Trevelyan, and Lower Gatesgarth (a spartan house for a bachelor professor) became a base for all-male climbing parties in the years when the climbs around Burtness Comb and Haystacks were being explored.

Learned allusions could lie behind some of the names dreamt up by the educated climbers. After conquering an unnamed gully on Haystacks on the last day of the nineteenth century, the pioneering party chewed over a suitable name

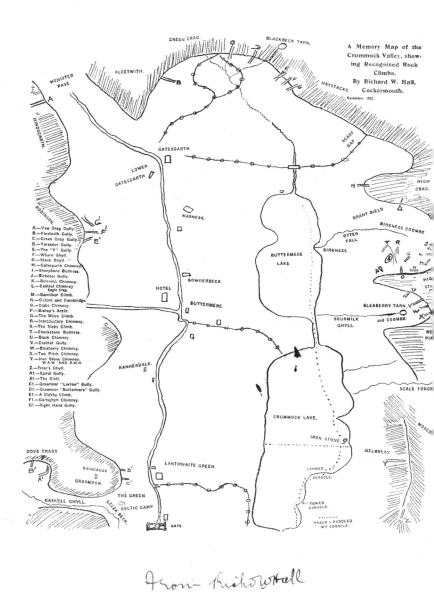

Richard W. Hall's 'Memory Map of the Crummock Valley, showing Recognised Rock Climbs', 1922

for the climb as they were returning to Gatesgarth in the moonlight. They thought of building on the legacy of Scandinavian place-names in the Lake District: 'Why not recall the old Norse name – High Stacken, the high cliffs – "High Stack Gill", how would that do, eh?' asked one; 'Too grandiose,' thought another. '"Stack Gill", then' – and so it was settled.

Just a few of these rock-climbers' names have made it onto the Ordnance Survey maps: Sheepbone Buttress on High Crag, Lorton Gully and Buttermere Gully on the steep front of Grasmoor, are examples. Perhaps the most striking new name from the earlier twentieth century – and probably the best known – is 'Innominate Tarn', the name of a small body of water in a hollow on the back of Haystacks, enclosed by rocky knolls on all sides (Plate 15). In summer dragonflies and damselflies play among the reeds and bog bean which fringe its glinting waters, and at lunchtime the edge of the tarn becomes a magnet for fell walkers to sit and eat their sandwiches. The name appears to have originated with Dick Hall, who, in 1933, wrote to John Bartholomew & Son, the Edinburgh mapmakers, suggesting that the tarn, then unnamed on Bartholomew's one-inch map of the Lake District, should be called 'the Innominate Tarn'. He had long called it that, he said, having once asked Allan Nelson of Gatesgarth the name of that small, dark pool among the rocks. 'It hes neah nyam', said Allan and so 'Innominate Tarn' it became.

***

A couple of hundred feet above Gatesgarth Cottage, on the sharp rocky front of Fleetwith Pike, a small white wooden cross has been secured to the crags by a metal stay (Plate 14). It bears the inscription 'Erected by friends of Fanny Mercer, accidentally killed 1887'. At first the white paint was kept fresh by Fanny Mercer's family; then Mrs Nelson at Gatesgarth Farm and subsequently her daughter Annie ensured that it was repainted at intervals – thus protecting and transmitting the memory of a particular event at a specific place on the fell. The modern cross is a replacement, maintained by the Cockermouth Mountain Rescue Team; its predecessor had been scarred by graffiti, the carved initials of those who had succeeded in scrambling up to its rocky ledge to take a closer look.

Fanny Mercer was a servant girl in the household of Revd Philip Bowden-Smith, a housemaster at Rugby School, who was staying on holiday at Wood House, Buttermere. On Thursday 8 September 1887 she and two other members of the household were coming down the front of Fleetwith Pike, having walked round the crest of the fells from Scarth Gap. She was carrying a long pole, an alpenstock, which she seems unwisely to have held in front of her. A witness to the accident, a farm worker at Gatesgarth who was raking bracken on the fellside, reported that, 'the end of her alpenstock having caught her in the stomach and given her a twist', she missed her footing and fell backwards, hitting her head on a rock and then rolling 130 feet down the fellside. Found unconscious, she was taken down to Gatesgarth and treated by a missionary skilled in surgery, who happened to be staying at Buttermere vicarage, but she died later that evening. For more than a century the simple memorial has bound to that one spot on the rocks the memory of a young girl now long departed. Few can have noticed the cross without recognising that it records a life cut short on the fells.

The fells can lay a claim on the heart, even if the body is spared. The rock-climbing pioneers, drawn to the freedom of the high places and the exhilaration of days spent on the fells, experienced something which went far beyond aesthetic pleasure in views revealed by breaking mist or low sun. Terry McCormick has described it as 'an individualistic, redemptive, mystical claiming of the Lake District'. The cragsman Lehmann Oppenheimer, who had an intense passion for the fells, found formal religion oppressive, a feeling which came to him suddenly during a memorial service for Queen Victoria in the church at Grasmere. The following day, which was a Sunday, he went out into the fells, to 'a church of a different kind'. It was 'A better church, this, than the one in the valley, and more inspiring,' he wrote, 'Here life was no dream-like interlude between two eternities … it was joy, reality, consciousness … of the vaster all-enfolding spirit'. He found communion in the fells.

The draw of the mountains probably became stronger in the 1920s in a society ravaged by the First World War. W. G. Collingwood 'could never be happy out of sight of mountains. Their absence was a kind of starvation to him'. In 1923 a friend advised Dick Hall to 'Take all openings that come to go off to the beloved fells. There lies healing and harmony'. The poet and cragsman Geoffrey Winthrop Young experienced a 'return to life' when he got out onto the fells again. To one young schoolmaster-climber, Richard B. Graham, chosen for the 1924 Everest expedition, the rocks and fells of Cumberland were his 'real & only home', from which nothing could sever him. Many people experience a sudden awareness of the transience of human life when confronted by the immensity of unchanging mountains – even the miniature mountains of the Lake District. We are locked in time while the mountains appear to be eternal. Perhaps it is not surprising that a glimpse of eternity gained on the high fells can produce an experience of transcendence.

So strong can be the call of the fells that some seek a resting place on the tops after death. Cremation, which became increasingly common from the early twentieth century, provided an opportunity for the physical remains of the departed to be cast to the winds on the fells, forging a perpetual link to a loved place. The view down the Buttermere valley from Haystacks or from Grey Knotts is one of the most breathtaking in the Lake District, making the peaks surrounding Gatesgarth some of the most loved of places. How many fell walkers have asked for their ashes to be scattered there, I do not know – certainly the best known walker of them all, Alfred Wainwright, did: 'All I ask for, at the end,' he wrote, 'is a last long resting place by the side of Innominate Tarn, on Haystacks, where the water gently laps the gravelly shore and the heather blooms and Pillar and Gable keep unfailing watch'. His widow duly honoured his request after his death in 1991.

There must have been numerous, similar quiet acts of remembrance as family members have carried out one last wish for a loved one, to bind them forever to a corner of the world that they loved in life. How many have stood for a moment in silence, shaking the ashes out into the wind, which blows them back into the moss and rock, sending a scattering across the jackets and faces of the bereaved? The songwriter Ewan MacColl speaks for many:

Take me to some high place of heather, rock and ling
Scatter my dust and ashes, feed me to the wind
So that I may be part of all you see, the air you are breathing
I'll be part of the curlew's cry and the soaring hawk,
The blue milkwort and the sundew hung with diamonds
I'll be riding the gentle breeze as it blows through your hair
Reminding you how we shared in the joy of living.

If 'death is no more than a turning of us over from time to eternity' (in the words of the early Quaker, William Penn), where better, then, to seek an eternal resting place than in the timelessness of the fells?

***

As this journey into Lake District history has shown, change has been constant; timelessness is an illusion. The landscape we know today has been moulded and given meaning through the interplay between people and place over many centuries, a span of time straddling countless generations but still a mere flash when set against geological time. Conceiving of this timespan of human history is hard. The past can never be fully recaptured and even comparatively recent chronology is sometimes difficult to grasp. Earlier times may be thought of simply as 'the olden days' – in the dialect of Cumberland, 'yance ower, lang sen' (once upon a time, long ago) – a time beyond personal memory, when things were different. My generation can imagine the era before the First World War in the sepia photographs from the youth of our grandparents, who told us how their world changed so utterly as a result of that war. Born in the later decades of Victoria's reign, they, in turn, could envisage the world about which they had heard when young, a time before the coming of railways and photography; the age of wigs, knee-breeches and buckled shoes. And so it would stretch back across the years. A hazy past hovers in the distance in memories passed down to us; behind that, older worlds are lost beyond the horizon. To recapture these requires a determined leap of the imagination.

Perhaps that imaginative leap can be made more readily when history is grounded in place and locality. The very permanence of place can collapse time and draw the far-distant past towards us. Past generations no longer seem separated by the passing of the years but united by having shared the experience of place. Pondering the enduring attraction of history, G. M. Trevelyan wrote:

> The poetry of history lies in the quasi-miraculous fact that once, on this earth, once, on this familiar spot of ground, walked other men and women, as actual as we are today, thinking their own thoughts, swayed by their own passions, but now all gone, one generation vanishing after another, gone as utterly as we ourselves shall shortly be gone, like ghost at cockcrow.

Such an awareness can be most immediate when the senses are jolted out of time by sudden beauty or by that experience of transcendence captured fleetingly on the fells. It may be caught at the end of a day on the high tops, when the evening sun throws a 'lingering light' on the craggy face of Grasmoor, flushing it pink. Or, again, in the sounds of a clear spring morning before the dull persistent rumble of traffic arrives. Across the lake come ageless sounds: a dog barking in a farmyard – as familiar five hundred years ago as today – and, even older, the call of a cuckoo in the woods. Old Ned Nelson would have heard the cuckoo as he sorted sheep at Gatesgarth in Victoria's reign; his predecessor, the keeper of the vaccary there six hundred years earlier, may also have raised his head to listen as he tended the beasts in the reign of Edward I. Had they been able to meet on that spring day in the farmyard, the vaccary keeper might have pointed out to Ned Nelson the lake, the farm, the track over to Borrowdale and the prow of fell towering above them, using names (Buttermere, Gatesgarth, Honister and Fleetwith) which Ned Nelson would have recognised, even if the vaccary keeper spoke them rather differently. The language of the landscape connects them – and us – to the past, dissolving the intervening centuries. Yet even the six centuries spanned by their shared experience of place shrinks when placed in the context of the totality of human history in the area. Beyond the chain of memory provided by the names, the sights and sounds of the landscape itself link us to the deeper human past. Who, I find myself wondering, was the very first person to set eyes on the lake which we now know as Buttermere on a May morning and to hear the cuckoo calling across the valley, perhaps five thousand and more years ago?

SOURCES AND BIBLIOGRAPHY

ABBREVIATIONS

CAS	Cumbria Archive Service
CCM	Cockermouth Castle Muniments (formerly CAS, DLEC)
CWAAS	Cumberland & Westmorland Antiquarian & Archaeological Society
CW	*Transactions of CWAAS: CW2* = new series, 1901-2000; *CW3* = third series, 2001- (searchable and available online at www.cumbriapast.com)
L&DFLHS	Lorton & Derwent Fells Local History Society
ODNB	*Oxford Dictionary of National Biography* (online at www.oxforddnb.com)
RWH Diary	Diaries of Richard Watson Hall (1882-1935), 1904-35: CAS, DX 1065.
TNA	The National Archives, Kew

NOTES ON SOURCES

The sources drawn on for each chapter are detailed below. Those wishing to explore further the local history of the Buttermere valley will find an impressive array of short papers in the Lorton & Derwent Fells Local History Society's erstwhile *Journal* (formerly *Newsletter*), running to sixty issues between 1994 and 2017 and now available online at www.derwentfells.com/journal.html. Brief factual historical summaries for each of the communities covered by this book, a detailed history of the township of Mosser, and links to other historical resources will be found on the website of the Cumbria County History Trust (www.cumbriacountyhistory.org.uk/places).

Place-names underpin the book and feature prominently in most chapters. Landscape historians using place-names as evidence must piggyback on the specialist expertise of place-name scholars, without whose work errors of interpretation would be legion. For Cumberland, the key sources are the English Place-Name Society's county survey (Armstrong *et al*, 1950-2) and Diana Whaley's superb *Dictionary of Lake District Place-Names* (Whaley, 2006). Material drawn from these works is not noted separately below.

Chapter 1. Introduction: A Lakeland Valley

The quotations about landscape are from Rob Cowen, *Common Ground* (Hutchinson, 2015), p. 205; Jonathan Bate, *The Song of the Earth* (Harvard University Press, 2000), p. 18 (quoting Thomas Hardy's *Far from the Madding Crowd*); Paul Readman, *Storied Ground: landscape and the shaping of English national identity* (Cambridge University Press, 2018), p. 16; and W. G. Hoskins, *The Making of the English Landscape*

(Hodder & Stoughton, 1955), pp. 13-14. The Lake District's World Heritage Site nomination document can be accessed from www. lakesworldheritage.co.uk. Oliver Rackham coined the terms 'planned' and 'ancient' countryside in Rackham 1986, pp. 3-5. Wordsworth's much-quoted description of the Lake District valleys is in his *Guide* (Wordsworth 2004, pp. 42-3). Collingwood's affectionate comment on the valley is from Collingwood 1932, p. 101; Heaton Cooper's from his *Mountain Painter: an autobiography* (Kendal: Frank Peters, 1984), pp. 71, 126; Wainwright's deep attachment is clear from Wainwright 1993. The litany of flood years at Cockermouth is from Bradbury 1981, pp. 4-6 and Fletcher 1994, pp. 112, 152.

Chapter 2. Place-Names (Bitter Beck)

The quotations about place-names are from Christopher Tilley, *A Phenomenology of Landscape: Places, Paths and Monuments* (Berg, 1994), pp. 18-19; Alasdair Maclean, *Night Falls on Ardnamurchan: the twilight of a crofting family* (Edinburgh: Birlinn, 2001), p. 185; Tim Robinson, *Stones of Aran: Pilgrimage* (Dublin: Lilliput Press, 1986), pp. 186, 188; and *Setting Foot on the Shores of Connemara & Other Writings* (Dublin: Lilliput Press, 1996), p. 156; and Simon Taylor (ed.), *The Uses of Place-Names* (Edinburgh: Scottish Cultural Press, 1998), p. 1. For Thomas Farrall (1837-1894), the author of *Betty Wilson's Cummerland Teáls* (Farrall, 1892), see Denwood and Thompson 1950, pp. 30-1. Dickinson's dialect *Glossary* (Dickinson 1859) was later substantially enlarged by Prevost 1905. John Bolton's lecture is reported in some detail in RWH Diary, Vol. 2 (11 Jan. 1909). Wakelin 1977 and Wales 2006 place Cumbrian dialect in a wider context. The Ordnance Survey's role in recording place-names is summarised in Oliver 1993, pp. 61-2; the 'Original Name Books' are in TNA, OS 34/20-21 (for Brigham parish), OS 34/79 (for part of St Bees parish including Loweswater). Sources for the unofficial or obsolete names referred to in this chapter include: Palmer (n.d.), p. 88 ('Noon Point'); CAS, DSO 331/1 ('Cut Cheese'); RWH Diary, Vol. 5, 28 Apr. 1921 ('Dick Robin'); CAS, DWM/2/96 ('Deepa Bridge'); CAS, YPR 7/1/1/2, 4 and Crosthwaite 1968 ('Withebeckraine'). For the lost medieval settlements of Ureby and 'Oustwic', see Winchester 1986; 1987, p. 95. 'Ingilberdhop' occurs in two 13th-century charters (Wilson 1915, pp. 566-7); the name appears to have survived as

'Inglebarrow', a field-name near Hopebeck recorded in 1844 (CAS, DRC/8/25, field no. 13). Elva Plain stone circle is described in the National Heritage List for England, entry no. 1013385, and (with a plan) in Anderson 1923.

Chapter 3. People (Tom Rudd Beck)

Patterns of personal names in northern England are discussed in Postles 2007; Redmonds 2004 and Winchester 2011a. Industries along the lower reaches of Tom Rudd Beck are described in Bradbury 1981, pp. 186-9; the idea of 'edgelands' is from Farley and Symmons Roberts 2012. The name Tom Rudd Beck occurs in 1778 in CCM, box 109, enfranchisement deed no. 11; the Thomas Rudd whose memory it may preserve is recorded in Wordsworth 2012, pp. 25, 52-6, 68, 125-6. Local medieval economy and society are discussed in Winchester 1987; the 1270 survey is in TNA, SC11/730. The discussion of 'statesman' society draws on Wordsworth 2004, p. 74, Marshall 1972 and Winchester 1998. William Green (1819, II, p. 224) and John Housman (in Hutchinson 1794, II, p. 135) commented on yeoman society at Loweswater. Surname persistence between 1535 and 1642 has been analysed using the Muster Rolls (TNA, E101/549/13) and Protestation Returns (Parliamentary Archives, HL/PO/JO/10/1/82). The figures are: Loweswater 15 (83 percent) of 18 surnames persisted; Lorton: 17 (77 percent) of 22 surnames; Mosser: 11 (69 percent) of 16 surnames. Data on 'yeoman dynasties' and on 'Place' and 'Ground' farm names derive from Winchester 1998 and further analysis of land tenure records. The survey of Greystoke barony in 1472 is CAS, DHG/16; that of the earl of Northumberland's estates in 1570 is TNA, E164/37 (quotation from f. 3). Population change between the 17th century and 1831 is based on the number of households recorded in the 1662 Hearth Tax assessments (TNA, E179/90/77), estimates of total population from the Protestation Returns of 1642 (arrived at using multipliers in the range of 2.77 to 3.33), and the printed 1831 Census report for Cumberland. For the villa at Hassness see below (sources for Chapter 9); for John Marshall's purchases, see Denman 2011; and for Mire Close, see CAS, YDX 366/15 (sales particulars. 1865). Population change across the 19th century draws on the Census Enumerators' Books, 1861-1891 (TNA, RG9/3934-6; RG10/5239-40; RG11/5173-4; RG12/4301-2). The decline in the number of farms since the 1960s is based on information from Arthur Reid, Lanthwaite Gate Farm, in 1969 and Kenneth Bell, Hudson Place Farm, in 2018. The figure for second homes and holiday accommodation is from https://melbreakcommunities.wordpress.com/community-issues/melbreak-communities-plan.

Chapter 4. Dwelling Places (Toddell)

Much of the material on the yeoman farms in Whinfell, Blindbothel and Mosser is drawn from my edition of the diary of Isaac Fletcher (Fletcher 1994), which contains extensive biographical notes and potted histories of many of the farms. Some family papers of the Dixons of Toddell are in CAS, YDX 159; others were made available to me by the late Bill Brooker of Aberdeen. The Whinfell rental of 1270 is in TNA, SC11/730. The description of the deserted farmstead at Cleaty Bank comes from TNA, OS 34/20, p. 88. Coleridge's description of Loweswater is in Hudson 1991, p. 68. Information on individual farmsteads there has been pieced together largely from manorial records in CAS, DLAW/1/248-252; DWM/11/121-127. Other sources include: Bargate: photograph in Southey 2008, p. 80; Mill Hill and Steel Bank: Denman and Asquith 2016; Loweswater parish register (CAS, PR/87/1); Rig Bank: CAS, DLAW (loose papers); Denman 2011, p. 284; 'Burnyate' (1521): CCM, box 299/18, m. 12; High Iredale (1616): TNA, C3/375/34. Vernacular buildings in the Lake District as a whole are discussed in Brunskill 2002 and Denyer 1991. Descriptions of the farmhouses mentioned here are on the National Heritage List for England, entry numbers: 1146497 and 1145157 (Lowpark), 1311790 (Godferhead), 1326862 (Whinfell Hall), 1137934 (Underwood); Whinfell Hall's history is told in Waller 2007, pp. 75-91.

Chapter 5. Farmland and Village (The Vale of Lorton)

The quotations on the annual rhythm of labour in the fields are from Patrick Kavanagh's poem 'The Great Hunger', section IV (in his *Collected Poems* (Martin Brian & O'Keefe, 1972), p. 40) and 'A Loweswater Dalesman's Reminiscences' (*Carlisle Journal*, 12 Jan. 1909), which reproduces extracts from an account by John Walker (1788-1842). For Lorton's field pattern and field-names the main sources are the enclosure award of 1832 (CAS, QRE 1/55) and tithe plan of 1840 (TNA IR30/7/107; CAS, DRC 8/118); field-names in 1578 are from the survey of the Percy estates in Cumberland (CCM, box 301). I reconstructed Lorton's medieval landscape in Winchester 1987, pp. 143-9 and have explored Lake District field-names and the history of dry stone walls more generally in Winchester 2016 and 2017. Material on the short-lived farm at Hatteringill comes from the Whinfell enclosure award (CAS, QRE 1/11), the recollections of William Walker Dixon (1817-1910) (in private hands) and census enumerators' books for 1841 and 1851 (TNA, HO107/2484; RG9/3936). The term 'beaten street' was used by John Denton (2010, p. 107). Jenat Birkett's evidence from 1602 is in TNA, E134/44 Eliz/H.18. The much-quoted description of roads as 'verie troublesome' will be found in Holinshed 1807, I, p. 191. Highway maintenance in the 18th century was recorded by Isaac Fletcher (1994, pp. 268, 285-6, 319-20); the condition of local lanes by Fletcher (1994, pp. 196, 278-9) and W. W. Dixon (memoirs, pp. 161-2). The survey of High Lorton in 1649 is in CAS, DCHA/8/8; social change in High Lorton across the 19th century is traced in George 2003 and in several articles by Derek Denman (Denman 2001; 2006; 2010).

Chapter 6. Boundaries (Meregill)

The tithe dispute concerning Thackthwaite and Mosser, settled in 1220, is recorded in Wilson 1915, no. 104 (pp. 142-3). Ordnance Survey 'Boundary Remark Books' are preserved in TNA, OS26. The boundary of Loweswater in 1614 is in CAS, D/LAW/1/248, m. 1, and the description of the 1792 boundary riding in CAS, DWM/11/172 (letter, J. Waite to M. Smith, 3 Feb. 1810). Aspects of prehistoric settlement in the Lake District are discussed in Edmonds 2004 and Quartermaine and Leech 2012. Faith 1997 explores Anglo-Saxon territoriality and the origins of manors. Medieval colonisation and boundary definition in Cumbria are discussed in Winchester 1987, pp. 27-31, 37-55. John Denton's interpretation of 'thwaite' place-names is in Denton 2010, pp. 37, 186. The boundary between Brackenthwaite and Lorton, defined loosely c.1170 (Wilson 1915, pp. 536-7), is discussed in Winchester 2000a, pp. 26-8. Sources for later boundary disputes are: Loweswater and Lamplugh, 1525: CCM, box 299/22, m. 17v; Lorton and Embleton, 1705: CCM, box 85, Derwentfells court leet, 1705; and for the long-running dispute between Loweswater and Mosser over 'Waterendwood': Winchester 1987, pp. 42-3; CAS, DLAW/1/261 (evidence c.1664); CAS, DWM/11/405 (1827 lawsuit).

Chapter 7. Common Land (Brackenthwaite Fell)

Much of this chapter draws on my previous work on the history of common land (Winchester 1987; 2000) and medieval stockrearing in Derwentfells (Winchester 2003). The early reference to heafing comes from CCM, box 299/6, Loweswater court, 24 Sept 1479. Details of heafs and gathering places on the fells around Buttermere are from CCM, box 120, Braithwaite & Coledale court leet verdicts, 1678, 1684, 1693, 1706. The 1847 evidence for the allowance of an overlap between sheep heafs is from CAS, DWM/11/408/2. The Westmorland dialect poem about heafs is from Garnett 1912, p. 17; and the remarkable first-hand account by Peter Fawcett of mischief on Mosser common is preserved in family papers which were in the possession of Diana Fawcett, Broughton, Hants, in 1991. Overgrazing in Wasdale and Eskdale is recorded in CCM, box 94, draft brief in case of R. Grave vs. I. Fletcher, and TNA, IR18/716. Sheep numbers at Loweswater since the 1870s are from the parish summaries of the annual agricultural statistics (TNA, MAF 68); figures on the reduction in sheep since the 1990s are from www.foundationforcommonland.org. uk/stories/buttermere-brackenthwaite-and-above-derwent-common-cumbria. Manorial byelaws governing turbary rights are from CAS, DWM/11/122 (Loweswater) and CCM, box 85, Derwentfells court leet verdicts (Lorton); the exploitation of bracken is discussed in Winchester 2006. Thomas Rawling's recollections of the sheep fair and sports are from RWH Diary, Vol. 3, 13-17 July 1915. The description of the Styhead route is from Denton 2003, p. 81; the story of the corpse road from Wasdale Head can be traced back to Rea 1886, pp. 297-308. Dickinson (1875, p. 216) tells of lanterns hung on the gate to the common to guide travellers home.

Chapter 8. Water (Loweswater)

Dixon 1760 and Gilpin 1808, II, pp. 4-7 report the Grasmoor 'water spout' of 1760; further details are given in Southey 2008, pp. 15-17. Smith 1754 describes the St John-in-the-Vale cloudburst of 1749; the meadow wasted by water at Wasdale Head in 1470 is from Alnwick Castle muniments, X.II.3, box 3/a. Details of the tragedy at Crabtree Beck come from *The Cumberland Pacquet*, 22 July 1828, p. 3 and Shaw 2015. Medieval fish weirs and fulling mills are discussed in Winchester 1987, pp. 107-13, 117-19; the evidence for the early 'eel ark' on Devoke Water is from Wilson 1915, p. 573; that for the new mill weir on the Cocker in 1517 from CCM, box 299/14, m. 15. The court-keeping manual quoted in relation to manorial oversight of watercourses is Sheppard 1654. Cases coming before local manor courts are in CCM, box 299/9 (High Lorton, 1503); box 299/15, m. 11v (Low Lorton, 1518); CAS, DWM/11/122 (Thackthwaite, 1723); CCM, box 85 (Derwentfells court leet verdicts) and box 120 (Braithwaite & Coledale court leet verdicts). Sources for 'Deepa Bridge' include CAS, 'A Survey of the Bridges in the County of Cumberland, 1764'; CCM, box 299/22, m. 25 ('Depewathcrag'); and Wilson 1915, p. 145. The orders about bridge repair in 1682 are from CCM, box 120, Braithwaite & Coledale court leet verdicts. Isaac Fletcher (1994, pp. 4, 265, 357) recorded his attempts at field drainage; the spread of tile drains in Cumbria is charted in Davis 2011. Aspects of the life of William Lancaster Alexander (1821-1910) are told in Jane 2010; copies of the deed and plan of Lorton Main Drain were kindly made available to me by Peter Kerr, Lower Stanger Farm. The quotation from Norman Nicholson's poem 'To the River Duddon' is from his *Collected Poems* (Faber & Faber, 1994), p. 25. The history of the saline well at Stanger Spa is told in Hudson 2013 and St Ringan's Well at Loweswater, recorded as a field-name on the Loweswater tithe plan (CAS, DRC/8/121, parcel no. 247), is listed in Fair 1952.

Chapter 9. Wood and Rock (Scales)

'Scales' place-names are discussed in Winchester 2011b. National Heritage List for England, entry no. 1014735, describes the deserted settlement site by Scale Beck. The reference to four 'Skale' in Loweswater in 1305 is from TNA, C133/119/9; that to 'scalings' there in 1519 from CCM, box 299/16, Loweswater court, 18 Oct. 1519. I have pieced together the history of the enclosed pasture of Buttermere Scales or 'Green Lussack' from 15th-century estate accounts (CCM, box 29), the survey of Loweswater manor in 1614

(CAS, DLAW/1/248) and the manor court order of 1740 (CAS, DWM/11/122). Housman's comment on Scales Wood is in Housman 1800, p. 312. Woodland management in medieval Lakeland is discussed in Winchester 1987, pp. 100-7; the agreement over rights to woodland in Loweswater in 1619 is in CAS, DLAW/1/255 (copy, c.1700); and the local evidence for coppicing and pollarding is from Gilpin 1808, Vol. I, pp. 232-3 and CCM, box 169, H. Westray to W. Coles, 3 March 1717/18. Early evidence for slate quarrying comes from CCM, box 29/9 (Lorton, 1500), and box 311 (licence, 1649); CAS, DLAW (loose paper) (Loweswater, 1693) and Denton 2003, p. 140. Tyler 1994 traces the history of the Honister mines; the quotation about early tourists is from Farington and Horne 1816, p. 52; the use of Yewcrag slate on Loweswater church is from Southey 2008, p. 39. The evidence for copper, lead and iron mining is from Denman 2013; Head 2005; Fletcher 1994 (summarised pp. xxv-xxvi); and Southey 2008, pp. 30-1. Ian Thompson (2010) charts the 'discovery' of the Lake District; Peter Crosthwaite's maps of the Lakes were reprinted in Crosthwaite 1968. The descriptions of Scale Force are from West 1778, para 214; 'some gentlemen' (printed in *Leeds Intelligencer*, 26 Oct. 1784; *Derby Mercury*, 28 Oct. 1784; and *Newcastle Chronicle*, 23 Oct. 1785); Green 1819, Vol. II, pp. 216-17; and Martineau 1858, p. 82. The story of the 'Beauty of Buttermere' is told by Thompson 2010, pp. 135-49. Benson's lakeside villa at Hassness (later demolished and rebuilt) is portrayed in a painting reproduced in *The Wanderer* (L&DFLHS, May 2015). John Marshall's role in tree-planting in the valley is discussed in Derek Denman's doctoral thesis (Denman 2011, especially pp. 234-92, from which the quotations are taken).

Chapter 10. Storied Ground. (Rannerdale)

The material on Miterdale Head is from Winchester 1979, Rea 1886 and Hoys 1955, p. 85. Rannerdale's pseudo-history is the creation of Nicholas Size (1866-1953), published first as Size 1929, embellished in Size 1930 and re-told by Sutcliff 1956. For the personal name Bueth, see Edmonds (forthcoming). W. G. Collingwood's role in developing the all-pervading story of the Lake District's Viking roots is explored in Townend 2009. The quotation from *Lake District History* is from Collingwood 1925, pp. 42-3. Notions of Scandinavian influence in Cumbria are traced from Walker 1792; through De Quincey (Janzow

1972; Roberts 1999) to Ferguson 1856. De Quincey's 'master key' claim is in an unpublished letter of c.1857 at www.gutenberg.org/files/18862/18862.txt. Sources for the more prosaic true history of Rannerdale include the first occurrence of the place-name c.1170 (Wilson 1915, pp. 536-7); reference to the chapel there (CCM, box 299/12, m. 3); the pattern of landholding in 1547 (CCM, box 314/38, Brackenthwaite); the activities of Jak Newcom (CCM, box 299, rolls 9-15, 22); the management of Rannerdale stinted pasture (lecture given by John Bolton in 1891 (transcript in L&DFLHS archive); and CCM, box 85, Derwentfells court leet, 1757); the purchase of Rannerdale Farm by Lake District Farm Estates (Cousins 2009, pp. 65-7). The dating of the new road round Buttermere Hause is from Green 1819, II, pp. 209-11.

Chapter 11. Places of Prayer. (Buttermere)

The Ordnance Survey's description of Buttermere is in TNA, OS34/21, p. 63. I discuss medieval parishes in Cumbria in Winchester 1987, pp. 22-7 and chapels of ease in Winchester 1998, pp. 97-100. Eskdale's petition for its chapel to be raised to parochial status in 1445 is in Wilson 1915, p. 369n. e. e. cummings' poem 'i am a little church' is in cummings 1960, p. 91. The descriptions of the fell chapels, their endowment and clergy in the 18th and early 19th centuries are from Nicolson 1877, Butler 1998 and Platt 2015. James Hudson made a bequest to Buttermere chapel in 1594 (Lancashire Archives, WRW/C/R220D/21); Bulmer 1901, p. 683 recorded the small size of the old chapel there. Machell's description of Martindale chapel is in CAS, DCHA/11/4/1, p. 698; Embleton chapel is termed a 'bellhouse' in Penney 1907, pp. 33-4. The personal testimony of the reader at Mosser chapel in the 1650s is in Banks 1712. William Dickinson's accounts of Osborne Littledale and William Sewell are in Dickinson 1875, pp. 126-9, 142-4. Littledale was nominated as assistant curate at Buttermere in 1804 (CAS, YDRC/10/5/104) and left to take up the curacy of Bleasdale, Lancashire, in 1828; he died in 1833 (Smith 1894, pp. 222-3). T. S. Eliot's 'to kneel where prayer has been valid' is from 'Little Gidding' in his *Four Quartets* (*The Complete Poems and Plays of T. S. Eliot* (Faber 1969), p. 192); Philip Larkin's poem 'Church Going' is widely anthologised, as in Rhys Jones 1999, pp. 147-9.

Chapter 12. Breeding Grounds. (Gatesgarth)

Annie Nelson's hand-reared fox cubs were noted in RWH Diary (Vol. 9, 11 Mar 1931) and by Cooper 1938, pp. 49-50. The evolution of the Herdwick breed is discussed in Brown 2009; recent work on their genetic distinctiveness in Bowles *et al* 2014. The descriptions of Lakeland sheep in 1774 are in Donaldson *et al* 2018, pp. 22, 39; the use of 'Herd-wick' in 1688 is in Denton 2003, pp. 79-80; and James Clarke's first use of 'Herdwick' as the name of the breed in Clarke 1787, p. 98. Terry McCormick (2018) traces how Lake District farmers have been viewed by outsiders since the 18th century (the quotations from Rawnsley are on p. 142). Rawnsley's comment on the memorial cross on Lonscale Fell is in Rawnsley 1903, p. 165. For G. M. Trevelyan's purchase of Gatesgarth, see Cannadine 2004 and Moorman 1980 (quotations pp. 219, 221). The history of Gatesgarth before the arrival of the Nelsons has been pieced together from William Green's list of sheep farms (Green 1819, II, pp. 265-7); early 19th century estate papers (CAS, DWM/11/226; 11/252; 408/2); deeds (CAS, DLONS/W/9/6); and the inventory of 1722 (CAS, DLONS/W/4/16). Warnscale Beck's alternative name is recorded on a plan of 1812: CAS, DWM/11/408/1. For the medieval vaccary see Winchester 2003 and Railton 2009. For goat-keeping and pannage, see Winchester 2000b, p. 104, and Winchester 1987, pp. 101-2. John Denton's interpretation of the place-name Mungrisdale is in Denton 2010, p. 107. The history of wild animal species draws on Yalden 1999, p. 168 and Pluskowski 2010 (for the wolf); Lovegrove 2007 (especially pp. 204, 226-7, 266 and Appendix I) and Addy 1976. Thomas Machell's comments about marts and wild cats are from Whaley 2006, p. 231 and Ewbank 1963, p. 139. The last vestiges of wild predators in the valley were recorded in Dickinson 1875, p. 166 (wild cat); Green 1819, II, p. 214 (eagles) and Cooper 1938, p. 49 (Annie Nelson's pine marten). Information on modern foxhunting is from www.melbreakcommunities.wordpress.com/parish-councils/ (for the Melbreak hunt) and Pearsall and Pennington 1973, pp. 187-8. Evidence of organised foxhunting in the 17th century is from CCM, box 120, Braithwaite & Coledale court leet verdicts, 30 May 1690, 15 Apr. 1691, and John Rylands Library, Manchester, English MS 1155, f. 11v, 9 Oct. 1678 (Thornthwaite).

Chapter 13. The Freedom of the Fells. (Warnscale Bottom)

The Lakeland Rambler 1934, p. 76, and Berry and Beard 1980, pp. 21-5 describe the state of mountain passes in the 1930s; Southey 2014 recounts the improving of Honister and Newlands passes. An early visitor's ascent of Skiddaw is recorded in Donaldson *et al* 2018, pp. 29-33; Dorothy Wordsworth's ascent of Esk Hause in McCracken 1984, pp. 163-4; Pyne's engraving of tourists on Brandreth is reproduced in Hodge 1957, opp. p. 131. The nation's claim on land and landscapes is explored in the context of the Lake District by Ritvo (2009) and by Readman (2018); the growth of rock-climbing is traced by Westaway (2013). The importance of the Scarth Gap-Black Sail route in mid-Victorian times is shown by A Volunteer Rifleman 1861, pp. 77, 79, 84, and Jackson 1980, p. 33 and *passim.* Ned Nelson's recollection of acting as a guide when a boy c.1860 is recorded in RWH Diary, Vol. 9, 27 Mar. 1930. The accounts of the early climbers John Wilson Robinson, Lehmann Oppenheimer and W. P. Haskett Smith draw on Waller 2007, Oppenheimer 1908 and Williams 2004; the story that Robinson would leave home at 3.00 a.m. is from RWH Diary, Vol. 6, Sept. 1922 (newspaper cutting). Richard W. Hall's character is drawn largely from family memory and obituaries pasted in RWH Diary, Vol. 13; typed minutes of the 'Gatesgarth Club' survive in CAS, DSO 331/1. Gatesgarth's importance among the wider rock-climbing fraternity is shown in Price 1986, p. 183 and its links with the mountain rescue service are recorded in the obituary to Maureen Richardson in *The Guardian*, 21 Nov. 2018. How 'Toreador Gully' and 'Stack Gill' received their names are in Oppenheimer 1908, pp. 58, 86, while the naming of Innominate Tarn is recorded in RWH Diary, Vol. 11 (annotated letter from John Bartholomew & Son Ltd, 18 Mar. 1933). Fanny Mercer's death was reported in *The Advertiser* (Leamington Spa), 17 Sept. 1887, p. 5. The section on the 'mystical claiming' of the fells (McCormick 2018, p. 122) and the passionate attachment expressed by walkers and climbers draws on Oppenheimer 1908, pp. 158-60; obituary to W. G. Collingwood in the *Alpine Journal*, 45 (1933), p. 150 (cited by Readman 2018, p. 143n); Westaway 2013, p. 177 (re Winthrop Young); and RWH Diary Vol. 6, letters from Eustace Charlton, 14 Oct. 1923 and R. B. Graham, 8 Nov. 1923. Graham did not make it to Everest: he resigned in the face of objections to his presence because he had been a conscientious objector during the War. Wainwright expressed his desire for his ashes to be scattered on Haystacks in 1966 (reprinted in his *Memoirs of a Fellwanderer* (Michael Joseph, 1993), p. 203). Ewan MacColl's song, 'The Joy of Living' is on the album *Black and White: Ewan MacColl – the Definitive Collection* (Cooking Vinyl, 1990. COOK CD 038). G. M. Trevelyan's reflection on 'the poetry of history' is from his autobiography (Trevelyan 1949, p. 13). The image of 'lingering light' thrown by the evening sun is borrowed from a youthful poem by Wordsworth (1930, pp. 2-3).

BIBLIOGRAPHY

This Bibliography includes printed works referred to in the text or in the 'Notes on Sources' above. Unless stated otherwise, the place of publication is London.

A Volunteer Rifleman (1861) *Rambling Notes of a Rambling Tour through some of the English Lake Scenery*, Sunderland: Wm Henry Hills and Windermere: J. Garnett.

Addy, John (1976) 'Financial problems of St Bees churchwardens', *CW2*, 76, pp. 133-43.

Anderson, W. D. (1923) 'Elva Stone Circle', *CW2*, 23, pp. 29-33.

Armstrong, A. M., Mawer, A., Stenton, F. M. and Dickens, Bruce (1950-2) *The Place-Names of Cumberland*, English Place-Name Society, Vols. XX-XXII. Cambridge University Press.

Banks, John (1712) *A Journal of the Life, Labours, Travels and Sufferings ... of ... John Banks*.

Bate, Jonathan (2000) *The Song of the Earth*, Harvard University Press.

Berry, Geoffrey and Beard, Geoffrey (1980) *The Lake District: a century of conservation*, Edinburgh: Bartholemew.

Bowles, D., Carson, A., and Isaac, P. (2014) 'Genetic distinctiveness of the Herdwick sheep breed and two other locally adapted hill breeds of the UK', *PLoS ONE*, 9 (1), e87823.

Bradbury, J. Bernard (1981) *A History of Cockermouth*, Chichester: Phillimore.

Brown, Geoff (2009) *Herdwicks: Herdwick sheep and the English Lake District*, Kirkby Stephen: Hayloft.

Brunskill, R. W. (2002) *Traditional Buildings of Cumbria, the county of the Lakes*, Cassell.

Bulmer, T. & Co. (1901) *History, Topography and Directory of Cumberland*, Penrith: Bulmer & Co.

Butler, L. A. S. (ed.) (1998) *The Cumbria Parishes 1714-1725 from Bishop Gastrell's Notitia*, Kendal: CWAAS Record Series XII.

Cannadine, David (2004) 'Trevelyan, George Macaulay (1876-1962), *ODNB*.

Clarke, James (1787) *A Survey of the Lakes of Cumberland, Westmorland and Lancashire*.

Collingwood, W. G. (1895) *Thorstein of the Mere: a saga of the Northmen in Lakeland*, Edward Arnold.

Collingwood, W. G. (1925) *Lake District History*, Kendal: Titus Wilson.

Collingwood, W. G. (1932) *The Lake Counties*, (new edition) Frederick Warne.

Cooper, W. Heaton (1938) *The Hills of Lakeland*, Frederick Warne.

Cooper, W. Heaton (1984) *Mountain Painter: an autobiography*, Kendal: Frank Peters.

Cousins, John (2009) *Friends of the Lake District: the early years*, Lancaster: Centre for North West Regional Studies.

Cowen, Rob (2015) *Common Ground*, Hutchinson.

Crosthwaite, Peter (1968) *A Series of Accurate Maps of the Principal Lakes of Cumberland, Westmorland and Lancashire, first surveyed and planned between 1783 and 1794*, with an introduction by William Rollinson, Newcastle: Frank Graham.

cummings, e.e. (1960) *Selected Poems 1923-1958*, Faber.

Davis, Edward and Stella B. (2011) *Draining the Cumbrian Landscape*, Kendal: CWAAS Research Series XI.

Denman, Derek (2001) 'Houses and occupiers in High Lorton village around 200 years ago from John Bolton's 1891 lecture', *The Newsletter* no. 24 (L&DFLHS, Sept. 2001), pp. 6-7.

Denman, Derek (2006) 'Peiles, Bowes, Jennings and mills: a history of the Tenters fulling and thread mills in Lorton, 1479-1912', *The Newsletter*, no. 38 (L&DFLHS, Aug. 2006), pp. 10-17.

Denman, Derek (2010) 'Lorton Park in the nineteenth century', *The Journal*, no. 45 (L&DFLHS, Feb. 2010), pp. 7-19.

Denman, Derek (2011) 'Materialising cultural value in the English Lakes, 1735-1845', unpublished PhD thesis, University of Lancaster.

Denman, Derek (2013) 'They wrought in the Buttermere copper mines', *The Journal*, no. 51 (L&DFLHS, Feb. 2013), pp. 13-19.

Denman, Derek, and Asquith, Roger (2016) 'An old plan of Mill Hill estate', *The Journal*, no. 58 (L&DFLHS, Aug. 2016), pp. 15-24.

Denton, John (2010) *John Denton's History of Cumberland*, ed. Angus J. L. Winchester, Woodbridge: Surtees Society 213.

Denton, Thomas (2003) *A Perambulation of Cumberland, 1687-8, including descriptions of Westmorland, the Isle of Man and Ireland*, ed. Angus J. L. Winchester with Mary Wane, Woodbridge: Surtees Society 207.

Denwood, M. and Thompson, T.W. (1950) *A Lafter o' Farleys in t' Dialects o' Lakeland 1760-1945*, Carlisle: Charles Thurnam.

Denyer, Susan (1991) *Traditional Buildings and Life in the Lake District*, Victor Gollancz.

Dickinson, William (1859) *Glossary of the Words and Phrases of Cumberland*; revised and enlarged as *A Glossary of the Dialect of Cumberland* (Carlisle, 1878).

Dickinson, William (1875) *Cumbriana, or Fragments of Cumbrian*

Life, Whitehaven: Callander & Dixon.

Dixon, Robert (1760) 'An authentic account of a water spout which mostly fell upon Brackenthwaite in the county of Cumberland, on Sept. 19 1760; by an eye-witness', *Gentleman's Magazine*, 30, pp. 520-2.

Donaldson, Christopher, Dunning, Robert W., and Winchester, Angus J. L., (eds) (2018) *Henry Hobhouse's Tour through Cumbria in 1774*, Kendal: CWAAS Tract Series 27.

Edmonds, Fiona (forthcoming) 'Names on the Norman edge: the persistence of Gaelic names in "Middle Britain"', in Keith J. Stringer and Andrew Jotischky (eds), *The Normans and the 'Norman Edge': peoples, polities and identities on the frontiers of Europe in the Central Middle Ages*, Routledge.

Edmonds, Mark (2004) *The Langdales: landscape and prehistory in a Lakeland valley*, Stroud: Tempus.

Eliot, T. S. (1969), *The Complete Poems and Plays of T. S. Eliot*, Faber.

Ewbank, Jane M. (ed.) (1963) *Antiquary on Horseback*, Kendal: CWAAS Extra Series XIX.

Fair, Mary (1952) 'Holy wells of west Cumberland', *CW2*, 52, p. 191.

Faith, Rosamund (1997) *The English Peasantry and the Growth of Lordship*, Leicester University Press.

Farington, Joseph, and Horne, Thomas Hartwell (1816) *The Lakes of Lancashire, Westmorland and Cumberland*.

Farley, Paul and Symmons Roberts, Michael (2012) *Edgelands: journeys into England's true wilderness*, Vintage Books.

Farrall, Thomas (1892) *Betty Wilson's Cummerland Teáls*, Carlisle: Charles Thurnam; 8th edn.

Ferguson, Robert (1856) *The Northmen in Cumberland and Westmorland*, Longman.

Fletcher, Isaac (1994) *The Diary of Isaac Fletcher of Underwood, Cumberland, 1756-1781*, ed. Angus J. L. Winchester, Kendal: CWAAS Extra Series XXVII.

Garnett, Frank W. (1912) *Westmorland Agriculture, 1800-1900*, Kendal: Titus Wilson.

George, Ron (2003) *A Cumberland Valley: a history of the parish of Lorton*, Markham, Ontario: Bovate Publications.

Gilpin, William (1808) *Observations on Several Parts of England, particularly the Mountains and Lakes of Cumberland and Westmorland, relative chiefly to Picturesque Beauty made in the year 1772*, Cadell & Davies (3rd edn).

Green, William (1819) *The Tourist's New Guide: a description of the Lakes, Mountains and Scenery in Cumberland, Westmorland and Lancashire*, Kendal: R. Lough.

Head, Walter (2005) 'Loweswater lead mines', *The Journal*, no. 36 (L&DFLHS, Aug. 2005), pp. 3-6.

Hodge, Edmund W. (1957) *Enjoying the Lakes from Post-chaise to National Park*, Oliver & Boyd.

Holinshed, Raphael (1807) *Holinshed's Chronicles: England, Scotland and Ireland*, 6 vols.

Hoskins, W. G. (1955) *The Making of the English Landscape*, Hodder & Stoughton.

Housman, John (1800) *A Topographical Description of Cumberland, Westmoreland, Lancashire and a part of the West Riding of Yorkshire*, Carlisle: Francis Jollie.

Hoys, Dudley (1955) *Below Scafell*, Oxford University Press.

Hudson, John (2013) 'Stanger Spa', *The Journal*, no. 52 (L&DFLHS, Aug. 2013), pp. 2-6.

Hudson, Roger (1991), *Coleridge among the Lakes and Mountains*, Folio Society.

Hutchinson, William (1794) *The History of the County of Cumberland* (2 vols), Carlisle: F. Jollie.

Jackson, Herbert and Mary (1980) *Lakeland's Pioneer Rock-Climbers: based on the visitors' book of the Tysons of Wasdale Head, 1876-86*, Dalesman.

Jane, Mick (2010) *Mr William Lancaster Alexander 1821-1910*, Aspatria: privately printed.

Janzow, F. Samuel (1972) 'De Quincey's "Danish origin of the Lake Country Dialect" republished,' *Costerus*, 1, pp. 139-59.

Kavanagh, Patrick (1972) *Collected Poems*, Martin Brian & O'Keefe.

Lovegrove, Roger (2007) *The Silent Fields: the long decline of a nation's wildlife*, Oxford University Press.

Macfarlane, Robert (2015) *Landmarks*, Hamish Hamilton.

Maclean, Alasdair (1984) *Night Falls on Ardnamurchan: the twilight of a crofting family*, Victor Gollancz (reprinted Edinburgh: Birlinn, 2001).

Marshall, J. D. (1972) '"Statesmen" in Cumbria: the vicissitudes of an expression', *CW2*, 72, pp. 248-73.

Martineau, Harriet (1858) *The English Lakes*, Windermere: John Garnett.

McCormick, Terry (2018) *Lake District Fell Farming: historical and literary perspectives, 1750-2017,* Carlisle: Bookcase.

McCracken, David (1984) *Wordsworth and the Lake District*, Oxford University Press.

Moorman, Mary (1980) *George Macaulay Trevelyan: a memoir by his daughter*, Hamish Hamilton.

Nicholson, Norman (1994) *Collected Poems*, ed. Neil Curry, Faber & Faber.

Nicolson, William (1877) *Miscellany Accounts of the Diocese of Carlile*, ed. R. S. Ferguson. Carlisle: CWAAS Extra Series I.

Oliver, Richard (1993) *Ordnance Survey Maps: a concise guide for historians*, Charles Close Society.

Oppenheimer, Lehmann J. (1908) *The Heart of Lakeland*, (facsimile edition Holyhead: The Ernest Press, 1988).

Palmer, W. T. (n.d.) *Things Seen at the English Lakes*, Seeley, Service & Co.

Pearsall, W. H., and Pennington, W. (1973) *The Lake District: a landscape history*, Collins New Naturalist Series 53.

Penney, Norman (ed.) (1907) *The First Publishers of Truth*, Headley Bros.

Platt, Jane (ed.) (2015) *The Diocese of Carlisle, 1814-1855: Chancellor Walter Fletcher's 'Diocesan Book' with additional material from Bishop Percy's parish notebooks*, Woodbridge: Surtees Society 219.

Pluskowski, Aleksander G. (2010) 'The Wolf', in Terry O'Connor and Naomi Sykes (ed.), *Extinctions and Invasions: a social history of British fauna* (Windgather Press), pp. 68-74.

Postles, Dave (2007) *The North through its Names: a phenomenology of medieval and early-modern Northern England*, Oxbow Books.

Prevost, E. W. (1905) *A Supplement to the Glossary of the Dialect of Cumberland*, Oxford University Press, and Carlisle: Thurnam & Son.

Price, Tom (1986), 'Way out West', in A. G. Cram (ed.), *100 Years of Rock Climbing in the Lake District* (Fell & Rock Club Journal XXIV (2), no. 70), pp. 181-6.

Quartermaine, Jamie, and Leech, Roger H. (2012) *Cairns, Fields and Cultivation: archaeological landscapes of the Lake District uplands*, Lancaster: Oxford Archaeology North.

Rackham, Oliver (1986) *The History of the Countryside*, J. M. Dent.

Railton, Martin (2009), 'Archaeological investigations of the remains of a medieval vaccary at Gatesgarth Farm, Buttermere', *CW3*, 9, pp. 57-67.

Rawnsley, H. D. (1903) *Lake Country Sketches*, Glasgow: James MacLehose.

Rea, Alice (1886) *The Beckside Boggle and other Lake Country Stories*, Fisher Unwin.

Readman, Paul (2018) *Storied Ground: landscape and the shaping of English national identity*, Cambridge University Press.

Rebanks, James (2015) *The Shepherd's Life: a tale of the Lake District*, Allen Lane.

Redmonds, George (2004) *Christian Names in Local and Family History*, The National Archives.

Rhys Jones, Griff (1999) *The Nation's Favourite Twentieth Century Poems*, BBC.

Ritvo, Harriet (2009) *The Dawn of Green: Manchester, Thirlmere, and Modern Environmentalism*, University of Chicago Press.

Roberts, D. S. (1999) 'Thomas De Quincey's "Danish Origins of the Lake Country Dialect"', *CW2*, 99, pp. 257-65.

Robinson, Tim (1986) *Stones of Aran: Pilgrimage*, Dublin: Lilliput Press.

Robinson, Tim (1996) *Setting Foot on the Shores of Connemara & Other Writings*, Dublin: Lilliput Press.

Shaw, Sandra (2015) 'The floods of Crabtree Beck', *The Journal*, no. 56 (L&DFLHS, Aug 2015), pp. 13-18.

Sheppard, William (1654) *The Court-Keeper's Guide*.

Size, Nicholas (1929) *The Secret Valley: a picture of the great events which took place in unconquered Lakeland during Norman times*, Kendal: Titus Wilson.

Size, Nicholas (1930) *The Secret Valley: the real romance of unconquered Lakeland*, Frederick Warne.

Smith, George (1754) 'Dreadful storm in Cumberland', *Gentleman's Magazine* 24, pp. 464-5.

Smith, Tom C. (1894) *History of the Parish of Chipping*, Preston: Whitehead.

Southey, Roz (2008) *Life in Old Loweswater*, Cockermouth: L&DFLHS.

Southey, Roz (2014) 'Taming the pass', *The Journal*, no. 54 (L&DFLHS, Aug 2014), pp. 4-9.

Sutcliff, Rosemary (1956) *The Shield Ring*, Oxford University Press.

Taylor, Simon (ed.) (1998) *The Uses of Place-Names*, Edinburgh: Scottish Cultural Press.

Thompson, Ian (2010) *The English Lakes: a history*, Bloomsbury.

Tilley, Christopher (1994) *A Phenomenology of Landscape: places, paths and monuments*, Berg.

Townend, Matthew (2009) *The Vikings and Victorian Lakeland: the Norse medievalism of W. G. Collingwood and his contemporaries*, Kendal: CWAAS Extra Series XXXIV.

Trevelyan, G. M. (1949) *An Autobiography and Other Essays*, Longmans.

Tyler, Ian (1994) *Honister Slate: the history of a Lakeland slate mine*, Caldbeck: Blue Rock Publications.

Wainwright, Alfred (1993) *Memoirs of a Fellwanderer*, Michael Joseph.

Wakelin, Martyn F. (1977) *English Dialects: an introduction*, Athlone Press (revised edition).

Wales, Katie (2006) *Northern English: a social and cultural history*, Cambridge University Press.

Walker, Adam (1792) *Remarks made in a tour from London to the Lakes of Westmoreland and Cumberland in the summer of M.DCC.XCI*.

Waller, Michael (2007) *A Lakeland Climbing Pioneer: John Wilson Robinson of Whinfell Hall*, Carlisle: Bookcase.

West, Thomas (1778) *A Guide to the Lakes … in Cumberland, Westmorland and Lancashire*, Richardson & Urquhart.

Westaway, Jonathan (2013) 'The origins and development of mountaineering and rock climbing tourism in the Lake District, c.1800-1914', in John K. Walton and Jason Wood (eds), *The Making of a Cultural Landscape: the English Lake District as tourist destination, 1750-2010* (Farnham: Ashgate), pp. 155-80.

Whaley, Diana (2006) *A Dictionary of Lake District Place-Names*, Nottingham: English Place-Names Society.

Williams, Chris (2004) 'Smith, Walter Parry Haskett (1859-1946)', *ODNB*.

Wilson, James (ed.) (1915) *The Register of the Priory of St Bees*, Surtees Society 126.

Winchester, Angus J. L. (1979) 'Deserted farmstead sites at Miterdale Head, Eskdale', *CW2*, 79, pp. 150-5.

Winchester, Angus J. L. (1986) 'Medieval Cockermouth', *CW2*, 86, pp. 109-28.

Winchester, Angus J. L. (1987) *Landscape and Society in Medieval Cumbria*, Edinburgh: John Donald.

Winchester, Angus J. L. (1998) 'Wordsworth's "Pure Commonwealth"? Yeoman dynasties in the English Lake District, c.1450-1750', *Armitt Library Journal 1*, pp. 86-113.

Winchester, Angus (2000a), *Discovering Parish Boundaries*, Princes Risborough: Shire Publications (revised edn).

Winchester, Angus J. L. (2000b) *The Harvest of the Hills: rural life in northern England and the Scottish Borders, 1400-1700*, Edinburgh: Edinburgh University Press.

Winchester, Angus J. L. (2003) 'Demesne livestock farming in the Lake District: the vaccary at Gatesgarth, Buttermere, in the later thirteenth century', *CW3*, 3, pp. 109-18.

Winchester, Angus J. L. (2006) 'Village byelaws and the management of a contested common resource: bracken (*Pteridium aquilinum*) in highland Britain, 1500-1800', *Digital Library of the Commons* at www.dlc.dlib.indiana.edu/archive/00001772/

Winchester, Angus J. L. (2011a) 'Personal names and local identities in early modern Cumbria', *CW3*, 11, pp. 29-49.

Winchester, Angus J. L. (2011b) 'Seasonal settlement in northern England: shieling place-names revisited', in S. Turner and R. Silvester (eds), *Life in Medieval Landscapes: people and places in the Middle Ages* (Oxford: Windgather Press), pp. 125-49.

Winchester, Angus J. L. (2016) *Dry Stone Walls: history and heritage*, Stroud: Amberley.

Winchester, Angus J. L. (2017) *Lake District Field-Names: a guide for local historians*, Lancaster: Regional Heritage Centre.

Wordsworth, R. B. (ed.) (2012) *The Cockermouth Congregational*

Church Book (1651-c.1765), Kendal: CWAAS Record Series XXI.

Wordsworth, William (1930) *Complete Poetical Works of William Wordsworth*, Macmillan.

Wordsworth, William (2004) *Guide to the Lakes*, with an introduction by Stephen Gill, Frances Lincoln.

Yalden, Derek (1999) *The History of British Mammals*, Poyser.

ACKNOWLEDGEMENTS

As this book is the fruit of an historical interest dating back over half a century, my debts are great and it is a pleasure to be able to record at least some of them. Many of those who kindled and encouraged my enthusiasm for the local past in my youth have been mentioned already. I should like to record a special debt to Beth Alexander (1895-1985) of Lowpark, Loweswater, who lent me her cottage for the autumn of 1974 and took a real interest in what was by then my doctoral research; and particular thanks to John and Roberta Clark and family, then at Mossergate Farm, who welcomed me into their home each Saturday across one winter; a warmer family it would be hard to find.

When my youthful fascination took a more scholarly turn, I was lucky to be supervised by Brian Roberts at Durham University, whose passion for landscape history was infectious. It is a pleasure to record my thanks to him and to numerous other scholars, both colleagues and students, who have helped to shape my thinking across the years. Among them, Fiona Edmonds of Lancaster University and Diana Whaley of Newcastle University have unstintingly given me the benefit of their expertise on place-names and personal names. I have benefitted greatly from the flowering of local historical research by members of the Lorton & Derwent Fells Local History Society, founded in 1993, and I should like to record my thanks especially to two members of the society, Derek Denman and Sandra Shaw, for their generous and helpful answers to my queries. Others who have gone out of their way to assist me while the book has been in preparation include Kenneth Bell of Hudson Place and Jamie Lund of The National Trust Regional Office.

The late Bill Brooker of Aberdeen; Clara Wigham (1884-1976) of Kirkfell House; Diana Fawcett of Broughton, Hants;

and Peter and Michelle Kerr of Low Stanger Farm have kindly given me access to archives in their possession, and staff in the record offices of Cumbria Archive Service and other record repositories have, as ever, been unfailingly helpful.

Grateful acknowledgement is made to the following: Faber and Faber for permission to quote from Philip Larkin's poem 'Church Going' in Philip Larkin, *The Less Deceived* (Faber and Faber, 1954); Liveright Publishing Corporation, for permission to quote from e. e. Cummings' poem 'i am a little church (no great cathedral)' in e. e. cummings, *Complete Poems* 1904-1962, ed. George J. Firmage (Copyright © 1958,1986,1991, Trustees for the E. E. Cummings Trust); Bucks Music Group Ltd for permission to quote from Ewan Maccoll's 'Joy of Living', published by Harmony Music Ltd. Roundhouse, London NW1 8AW; Cumbria Archive Service for permission to reproduce images of documents in their collections on pages 87, 90 and 114; and Josephine Graham for allowing me to use the photograph reproduced on page 36.

Liz Nuttall of Handstand Press took up the idea for this book with enthusiasm and has been a most congenial, perceptive and supportive editor; it has been a pleasure working with her. I should also like to record my thanks to Russell Holden who designed the book and Sharon Keeley-Holden for proof-reading.

Finally, this has become a joint venture with my wife, Val. She has shared the journey with me since we spent weekends together at Lowpark the autumn before we were married, and our joint memories of the valley now stretch back over more than forty years. Her support has been unfailing and, in reading successive drafts of the book, she has been my fiercest and kindest critic. Her eye for beauty and love of photography have produced most of the images in the book, capturing so well the atmosphere of this special corner of the world.

INDEX

C

G

Gaelic language and names 16, 17, 33, 41, 42, 70, 183
Garnett, F. W. 126
Gasgale Gill (Brackenthwaite) 119, 142-4
Gatesgarth (Buttermere) 126, 174, 175, 209-21, 233-9, 242
geology 159 *see also* mines/mining; quarrying
Gillbrea (Lorton) 85-6
Gille son of Bueth 182-3
Gilpin, William 46, 144, 165, 172
goats 120, 221-2
Godferhead (Loweswater) 72, 169, Plate 7
Graham, Richard B. 243, 259-60
Grasmere 88, 155, 185, 194, 243
Grasmoor 136, 143, 171, 241
grazing rights *see* pasture rights
Great Gable 206, 233, 235, 237
'Green Lussack' *see* Scales (Buttermere Scales)
Green, William 47, 173, 215
Greystoke barony 51, 222

H

Hall, Richard W. (Dick) 62, 228, 235-7, 239, 241, 243
Harbord, Eleanor 97
Hardy, Thomas 3
Harrot (Lorton) 115
Haskett-Smith, Walter 234, 239
Hassness (Buttermere) 54-5, 174, 175, 256
Hatfield, John 174
Hatteringill (Whinfell) 82-3, Plate 9; Head ('Ullscarth') 41, 106
Hawkins, Lil 59
Haystacks 8, 215, 224, 235, 237, 239, 244

N